Beyond Public
Speech and Symbols

Beyond Public Speech and Symbols

Explorations in the Rhetoric of Politicians and the Media

EDITED BY

Christ'l De Landtsheer
AND Ofer Feldman

PRAEGER

Westport, Connecticut
London

Library of Congress Cataloging-in-Publication Data

Beyond public speech and symbols : explorations in the rhetoric of
   politicians and the media / edited by Christ'l De Landtsheer and
   Ofer Feldman.
      p. cm.
   Includes bibliographical references and index.
   ISBN 0–275–96732–8 (alk. paper)
      1. Rhetoric—Political aspects. 2. Discourse analysis—Political
   aspects. 3. Mass media and language. I. Landtsheer, Christ'l de.
   II. Feldman, Ofer, 1954– .
   P301.5.P67B49 2000
   808.5'1'08832—dc21   99–37521

British Library Cataloguing in Publication Data is available.

Library of Congress Catalog Card Number: 99–37521
ISBN: 0–275–96732–8

First published in 2000

Praeger Publishers, 88 Post Road West, Westport, CT 06881
An imprint of Greenwood Publishing Group, Inc.
www.praeger.com

Printed in the United States of America

The paper used in this book complies with the
Permanent Paper Standard issued by the National
Information Standards Organization (Z39.48–1984).

10 9 8 7 6 5 4 3 2 1

Contents

IV. Conclusion

Figures and Tables

FIGURES

TABLES

Preface

In preparing this volume we had several audiences in mind. First, the volume is aimed at communication researchers and graduate students interested in the various aspects of political and public discourse and the role language plays in politics in different cultures. Second, the volume should benefit scholars interested in area studies, such as traditional societies (Japan, China, Venezuela), Western societies (the United Kingdom, the United States, Canada, and the European Union), and societies in transition (Ukraine, Israel). At the same time, the volume is written for the general reader as well as the specialist. We have attempted to avoid technical jargon and statistical discussions so that the book could be read not only by professionals in related fields but also by persons who are interested in current developments in media, culture, technology, and world politics. We sought to present a comprehensive coverage of the state of the arts as well as contemporary research and thinking. We hope this book will provide a firmer and broader source of information.

Editing a volume such as this is never accomplished without help. Many of the authors presented preliminary versions of their chapters at academic meetings such as the Annual Scientific Meeting of the International Society of Political Psychology and the meetings of the National Speech Communication Association, the American Political Science Association, and the International Studies Association. We want to thank the commentators, especially Henk Dekker, for his most useful comments during the ISPP Montreal meeting.

Sincere thanks are due to Dr. James T. Sabin, Director of the Academic Research and Development at Greenwood Publishing Group, who has taken a keen interest in this book and its companion volume, *Politically*

Speaking: A Worldwide Examination of Language Used in the Public Sphere, and has facilitated their publication. We want to also thank the authors for their cooperation in revising their chapters and for their help in preparing the volume.

Christ'l De Landtsheer dedicates this book to all those colleagues and friends with whom over the years she has discussed the issues that are dealt with in this book. Among these are Karel De Clerck, Dean of the Psychology Faculty of the University of Ghent, Belgium; Joan Hemels, Professor of Media History at the University of Amsterdam; James L. Wood, Chair of the Sociology Department at San Diego State University; and Hans IJsenbout, her partner and friend.

Finally, Ofer Feldman would like to thank his sons, Utai and Iri, and his wife, Rie, for their unfailing support throughout the preparation of this volume.

Introduction

OFER FELDMAN

The present volume is a companion to *Politically Speaking: A Worldwide Examination of Language Used in the Public Sphere* (Feldman & De Landtsheer, 1998). Its publication reflects a growing interest, among the general public as well as among scholars, in political discourse, the rhetoric and symbols used by prominent politicians and news media, and the roles that language plays in democratic and non-democratic countries by affecting political behavior and attitudes.

The chapters in this book thus address issues relevant to political discourse in a wide range of societies, with special emphasis on topics that have emerged relatively recently. Because they employ a variety of theoretical, conceptual, and methodological approaches, the chapters—individually and collectively—highlight the need for further research and will, it is hoped, encourage others to follow up with additional methodological tests and theoretical revisions.

The chapters in this volume examine the nature, characteristics, content, and reception of three major areas of discourse: (1) the language of political figures—including the British prime minister, U.S. presidents, Canadian federal party leaders, and a candidate in a Venezuelan presidential election; (2) speech structures used in parliamentary bodies—in the Ukraine, Israel, Japan, and the European Union—and (3) the language of news (and new) media—in the United States, China, and Japan—including the use of editorial cartoons, symbols, and meta-symbols to inform and to affect public opinion. As the chapters are based upon empirical materials gathered in the United Kingdom, the United States, Canada, China, Israel, Japan, Ukraine, Venezuela, and the European Union, they allow comparison among the different structures and contents of speech used in a wide variety of societies from West to East.

Many of the pieces in this volume are follow-ups on topics from *Politically Speaking*. In Chapter 1 of this volume, for example, Peter Bull provides further evidence that televised political interviews played a prominent role in recent general elections in Britain and must continue to be considered one of Britain's most significant means of political communication. In the previous volume, Bull analyzed the nature of political interviews with two former prime ministers—Margaret Thatcher and John Major. In this volume he offers data on the current prime minister—Tony Blair—and argues that it is possible to assess whether a politician's interview performance is skilled or unskilled.

Peter Suedfeld (Chapter 2) further analyzes the language of U.S., Russian, and Canadian political leaders based on *integrative complexity*, the same method he and his colleagues used in the previous anthology to examine how conflicts over environmental issues in Canada affected levels of complexity. Maritza Montero (Chapter 4) provides additional information on the language and icons used by a candidate campaigning in Venezuela's 1998 presidential election; in the previous volume, she and her associate reported on the nature of presidential addresses in Venezuela and several other Latin American countries between 1990 and 1996.

Christ'l De Landtsheer and Lise van Oortmerssen (Chapter 6) offer more data to supplement De Landtsheer's previous chapter on metaphorical discourse within the European Parliament (1981–1993). Shoji Azuma (Chapter 5) provides a detailed account with specific examples of Japanese politicians' discourse to further illustrate the sociocultural framework discussed by Ofer Feldman in the previous volume. Moya Ann Ball (Chapter 3) discusses aspects of U.S. presidents' discourse, adding to data offered in the first anthology by Amos Kiewe and Herbert Barry III on the related issue of the "crisis tool" in rhetoric and slogans used by American presidents. The Israeli and Ukrainian cases discussed in this volume (Chapters 7 and 8) provide information that supplements data on the political languages of Russia, Germany, and France, which were discussed in the first book. And last, chapters in both volumes address the importance of the news media in defining news, deciding how it is interpreted, and framing particular aspects of perceived reality in the United States, Canada, China, and Japan.

Like the previous volume, the present collection includes the work of researchers from a variety of disciplines. In recent years, as interest has grown in political discourse and related issues (including language, speech, rhetoric, propaganda, semantics, metaphors, and political culture), researchers from diverse areas such as communications, political science, sociology, social psychology, psychology, and cultural studies have been showing interest in these themes. But because researchers from different fields typically belong to different professional groups, publish in different professional journals, and attend different scientific meetings, they are often unaware of one's another work. This is especially true in regard to new theoretical approaches.

In recognition of this problem, a major goal of this book is to present the works of individuals from diverse fields of research. Contributors' backgrounds include political science, social psychology, psychology, sociology, mass communications, and linguistics. Their methods include surveys, interviews, experiments, and archival, content, or discourse analysis. Some examine case studies in light of theories and/or hypotheses. For example, Mira Moshe and Sam Lehman-Wilzig (Chapter 7) used Habermas' theory on the "sphere of public discourse" to construct their own model of the Israeli situation. Both Tracey Mitchell (Chapter 12) and Moya Ann Ball (Chapter 3) use the *Symbolic Convergence Theory*, which is based on the assumption that people view reality through a personal set of narratives that represent "the truth" of how the world is for them. Mitchell looks at how various media chose to report the facts and the impact of the bombing of the Murrah Building in Oklahoma City in 1996. Ball uses the theory to suggest that certain elements of communication used among Lyndon Johnson's advisers converged in a way that kept them from seriously considering the option of withdrawing American troops from Vietnam.

Other contributors used multiple research approaches to examine case studies: Nadya Terkildsen and Frauke Schnell, Nadya Terkildsen, and Karen Callagan (Chapter 13) employ theories from both political science and social psychology to interpret results from content analysis of news coverage of the U.S. women's movement and a series of experiments on media use of meta-symbols and the influence these labeling shortcuts exert on citizens' attitudes and participation in a democratic system. Montague Kern, Marion Just, Ann Crigler, and Hong (Iris) Xie (Chapter 11) also use political science and mass communication perspectives to examine the effects of the World Wide Web as a source of U.S. election information in terms of its ability to empower voters. Peter Bull (Chapter 1) bases his analysis on three social psychological theories: *the social skills model, the face model of political interviews,* and *self-categorization theory,* which provide clear criteria by which to evaluate Tony Blair's communicative skills.

Understanding theoretical approaches to the study of political discourse as they are used by researchers from diverse disciplines can lead to a greater appreciation of the rich body of work in this area, as well as to a greater understanding of political language itself. We hope our multifaceted collection will increase political language researchers' knowledge of work being done in various fields, now that literature related to political language can be found not only in most major American political science and communication journals but also in professional journals from other countries, including the United Kingdom, Germany, France, and Japan.

Compared to our first compilation, this volume offers additional research data and further examination of the validity of theories through a wider net of case studies. It was not our intention, however, to accumulate reviews of past work in this volume. Although numerous studies are referenced in these chapters, the emphasis throughout has been on recent and original research and theory. Readers who have an interest in a detailed review of the literature on political discourse are advised to consult De Landtsheer's chapter in *Politically Speaking*.

While all the works in this volume are original and draw on the authors' own research, some of them are ground breaking. For example, Schnell, Terkildsen, and Callagan document media trends in the use of meta-symbols, test how they operate, and present a new perspective of meta-symbols and their role in democratic discourse (Chapter 13). Kern and associates (Chapter 11) use an innovative method aimed at examining what might happen if computers become as widely accessible as telephones or television. And Ball uses primary documents such as meeting transcripts, memoranda, letters, and speeches to analyze how political language choices made by President Lyndon Johnson and his key advisors functioned as rhetorical constraints in the Vietnam decision-making process. Taken together, the chapters point to new directions and methods of inquiry aimed at deeper understanding of the nature and effects of political discourse.

OVERVIEW OF THE VOLUME

As indicated earlier, the goal of this volume is to detail various aspects of political discourse in Western and non-Western societies, with a focus on relatively recent issues. Its 14 chapters provide a broad social-scientific view of political speech from different perspectives (multicultural, multi-disciplinary, multimethodical). The articles demonstrate that many important questions about public discourse are related to political participation versus alienation and that these aspects can be tested empirically through a variety of methodological approaches.

The chapters are divided into three sections: "The Rhetoric of Public Personalities," "Speech Structures in Deliberative Bodies," and "Speech Aimed at Encouraging Citizen Participation."

In Part I, four chapters provide a timely and useful examination of various ways in which candidates and politicians address audiences. In the first chapter, Bull provides a detailed analysis of the rhetoric of Prime Minister Tony Blair, based on five televised interviews with him during Britain's 1997 general election. Blair's use of the "rhetoric of modernization" (a tool for handling awkward questions about the Labour Party's dramatic policy changes between 1983 and 1997) indicates a high level of communicative skill that arguably played a crucial role in the Labour Party's stunning landslide victory in 1997. The chapter demonstrates how Blair succeeded in using that tool to help himself avoid responses that might have been gravely embarrassing to himself and his whole party. This "rhetoric of modernization" goes far beyond enabling Blair to avoid answering difficult questions. Its other significant political advantages include helping to establish an identity for New Labour that attracts people who might never have voted for the old Labour Party while avoiding the alienation of existing supporters.

In Chapter 2, Suedfeld examines domain-related variation in *integrative complexity* by focusing on the rhetoric of Mikhail Gorbachev, Bill Clinton, Newt Gingrich, and various Canadian political leaders. He suggests that people's information processing complexity (*integrative complexity*) is not stable and may change in response to exogenous factors (such as life events, time pressures, and sociopolitical context) and endogenous factors (like age, fatigue, or illness). Higher complexity is noted in domains where the individual is especially interested, committed, or engaged and where higher complexity seems more likely to lead to success. Lower complexity, on the other hand, tends to be experienced during heavy stress or frustration.

A detailed analysis of speeches given by Gorbachev revealed that he consistently exhibited higher complexity when speaking about foreign policy than about domestic issues, perhaps reflecting his greater interest in the former domain. Clinton, unlike most national leaders, showed no overall increase in the complexity of his speeches after he assumed the highest office in his nation's government. This suggests that Clinton's cognitive strategies were not modified by a major change in his political role or by the length of his experience in the presidency. During the 1994 Congressional campaign, Gingrich showed the highest complexity in domains where serious policy differences between the Republican and Democratic parties were most salient: welfare reform and health care. Once he became Speaker of the House, Gingrich's cross-domain differences mostly disappeared, and his overall level of complexity remained roughly uniform.

Suedfeld also noted that the overall complexity of Canadian federal party leaders during the national election in 1997 was particularly low, especially when compared with that of almost any American president. Suedfeld assumes that the low complexity of Canadian campaign speeches compared with those of U.S. presidential candidates was partly due to a cultural factor related to electioneering traditions and was definitely not a function of the Canadian style of political discourse in general. Suedfeld concludes that there is a need to further investigate how different traditions of political and other discourse may affect complexity across cultures.

In a study that combines rhetorical criticism with historical analysis, Ball (Chapter 3) argues that the political language employed by U.S. presidents Kennedy and Johnson and their advisers, in private as well as in public, worked as an internal constraint that rooted them to a combat position, affecting the decision-making process and severely limiting negotiations with North Vietnam. Using primary documents such as letters and memoranda circulated between the presidents and their advisers, meeting agendas, transcripts and notes, as well as interviews with key personnel, Ball examines the way Johnson and some of his advisers seemed constrained in their actions in foreign as well as domestic policy by the phrase "searching for an honorable peace."

The association of peace with the decision-makers' interpretation of honor was perhaps the greatest linguistic constraint in the search for a way out of Vietnam. For Johnson and most of his advisers, honor implied strength and superiority. In this way, "honorable peace" was a symbolic cue that prevented them from considering withdrawal from Vietnam as a viable option. She demonstrates how the linguistic choice of "honorable" peace, with its multiple meanings, became a "screen" that prevented the decision makers from seriously considering the withdrawal of troops until over 860,000 tons of bombs had been dropped and hundreds of thousands of people had been killed.

In Chapter 4, Montero focuses on the 1998 elections in Venezuela, wherein the leading candidates did not belong to any political party and in which one of them, Irene Sáez, was a former Miss Universe with a very short history as a politician. Montero's discourse analysis used both hermeneutical and rhetorical approaches and integrated all of the 20 Sáez press statements and 47 photographs published between November 1997 and April 1998 in two major national newspapers in Venezuela, as well as news articles featured in some Venezuelan and international magazines. The study period begins with the moment when Saez first announced her intention to run for president.

The iconic texts, that is, the numerous pictures accompanying any information or statement from Ms. Sáez, show two versions of the candidate: a glamorous beauty queen contrasting with a drably attired politician. Her scant political verbal texts have neither sufficient depth, rhetorical strategy, metaphors, nor well-founded explanations, while her iconic texts have beauty that is striking, but unrelated to the words. The net effect is that the beauty highlights the triviality of the spoken discourse, while the words cancel the beauty.

Analysis also revealed that Sáez's verbal discourse was characterized by short direct phrases stressing the ideas that she had a mission to unify the country under her rule, that she was independent of established political parties, and that she is religious. The concepts she used most frequently in regard to her governing program were "modernization," "efficiency," "management," "newness," "popular support," "change," and "transformation," but none of these was defined or described in detail.

Part II, which focuses on rhetoric used in parliamentary bodies, opens with a chapter by Azuma (Chapter 5) on discourse styles used by Japanese politicians. Azuma maintains that eloquence has not been considered one of the virtues people value in Japan, as it has been in the European tradition. The speech pattern favored by politicians in this Asian society is indirect and uses ambiguous expressions that allow the speaker to avoid taking responsibility. Members of Japan's national Diet (Parliament) have traditionally used polite speech (formal, indirect, and deferential) and many Sino-Japanese words (which tend to be difficult and abstract), causing them to be psychologically detached from the general public. However, Azuma used data from two years' worth of verbatim stenographic records of Diet committee sessions and from televised Diet sessions to show that a more direct and straightforward mode of communication seems to be emerging among Japanese legislators to replace the traditional, socially prescribed mode.

This emerging style of speech, used conspicuously often by former Prime Minister Ryutaro Hashimoto, can be characterized by a willingness to get involved with the audience on a more personal level, perhaps as a means to win approval from the public. This new style of speech is more direct and less remote, suggests integrity and sincerity, and makes the speaker sound very human. By emphasizing the personal aspects of his ideas, the former prime minister sought to come across as a sincere and trustworthy politician, unlike other politicians who simply read speeches prepared by aides. He tried to show his personal, inner feelings even in the most formal situations, such as Diet sessions, and even when he encountered hostile remarks from members of opposition parties.

In Chapter 6, De Landtsheer and van Oortmerssen examine political discourse in the European Parliament. A sample of debates held between 1980 and 1995 on the topic of the Israeli-Palestinian conflict was analyzed at three rhetorical levels: the European Union's institutions (Parliament, Council, and Commission), the member states (national discourses), and the political factions (ideological discourses). At each level, comparative analysis was performed on the use of both action verbs and stative verbs that had "Europe" as a grammatical subject.

The analysis revealed certain developments over time regarding the positions taken by participants at each level concerning Europe's role in the Middle East peace process from 1980 to 1995. Contrary to the authors' expectation, the differences between member states and between political groups were wider than the differences between the European institutions. The positions of the political groups diverged most. This might indicate that the political integration process of Europe is proceeding rapidly. The Council was quite reserved as far as an active role for the European Union in the peace process was concerned. Instead, both the Commission and the Parliament favored a much more active attitude.

The focus of attention in Chapter 7 is the rhetoric of the Israeli legislative body (*Knesset*) and that of sundry "commissions of inquiry" set up by several Israeli governments, regarding a new communications map of Israel.

Moshe and Lehman-Wilzig present an initial attempt to use empirical tools to determine whether and to what extent the public sphere as defined by Habermans has been weakened. They use Israel—a country that is "consciously planning significant expansion of its electronic media"—as a case study. The authors developed a "Funnel Model," a practical mechanism for exhibiting the actual development of an open and true dialogue in the public arena. They present it as a tool designed to help describe the dynamics of the many public topics that might be discussed. Using the "Funnel Model" involves setting up methods of comparing expected public discourse with actual results. The model examines first ("filling the ideational funnel") the subject areas that legislators wished to see in the expanded media environment and second ("emptying the funnel") the topics that constitute the public sphere's actual post-expansion agenda. Their findings suggest that public discourse did emerge, but not the legislators' "collective," national one. Instead, it was "international"—perhaps more relevant to the sociotechnological reality of the late 20th and early 21st centuries.

Considering the similar ways that media develop in different nations and the omnipresence of the global market, the authors suggest that the "Funnel Model" can be applied to most nations and cultures in which a "communication sphere" has evolved. Moreover, the rapid closing of gaps between lifestyles in different nations, cross-cultural exchange, and growing structural similarities among advanced nations tend to submerge the traditional values and distinctive beliefs that have given each culture its own coloration. This is especially true in countries that have a high level of immigration and those nations that have a persecuted or repressed cultural or religious minority. For such countries, the "Funnel Model" is a useful and efficient tool for analyzing the gap between legitimate expectations from technological advances in communications and the actual success or failure of new media in generating direct and authentic public discourse.

In Chapter 8, Taran examines political metaphors and other semantic figures in political language, as well as mythical and logical types of reasoning used in the Ukrainian Parliament. The theoretical part of the chapter compares the basic assumptions of Aristotelian logic versus those of Mythical reasoning. It describes the origin and nature of modern political discourse and its connection with modern myth creation. The case study includes a sample of debates about budget policy in Ukraine, a country that just declared its independence in 1991. Taran discloses how different political groups used "the political tribune" to strengthen their impact on the public through manipulation involving different types of reasoning. Politicians at the fringes of the political spectrum tended to use more metaphors and elements of Mythical thinking while politicians near the center of the political spectrum preferred logical thinking. Taran notes that politicians can "fix" political discourse at a particular stage not only by using elements of Mythical thinking, but also by using Aristotelian logic. Aristotelian logic seems to be more appropriate for the political center and governing elite, while for the opposition or political extremes, Mythical thinking is more suitable.

Part III consists of five chapters that focus on discourse in mass (and new) media. The authors explore several issues relevant to media content and its effects on citizens' political participation and attitudes. In Chapter 9, Zhang examines Chinese press images and the portrayal of "model intellectuals" (mostly professionals in industry or science, doctors, professors, school teachers, etc.) under economic reform. Following the death of Mao Zedong in 1976, the Chinese Communist Party decided to implement economic reform policies and open to the Western world. By focusing on images of model Chinese intellectuals—a group the Party had always attempted to reform and re-educate—this essay studies reform rhetoric in the People's Daily (the Party newspaper) during the early 1980s.

Zhang focuses on four major model themes: the courage to pursue research, hard work and sacrifice, love of the party, and relationships with others. Zhang argues that the images of model intellectuals presented in those early post-Mao reform years served to promote the Party's new policies regarding intellectuals and to prescribe ideal behavior for Chinese citizens. In other words, the Party raised the social status of intellectuals and encouraged Chinese citizens to actively pursue knowledge and develop science and technology in order to modernize China. Such images reflect changes in values and social culture in China, as well as the Party's efforts to uphold its socialist ideology while pursuing a "middle path" of developing a socialist market economy in China.

In Chapter 10, Feldman details selected aspects of Japanese attitudes toward humor and political humor, focusing in particular on the role of editorial cartoons in two Japanese national dailies as a form of non-oratorical discourse. Editorial cartoons present politicized contexts whose satire, irony, and/or parody can play a significant role in educating the public about the political process. By stimulating thought about issues, questions about ideologies, and laughter at the foibles of political leaders and candidates, cartoons can inspire changes in sensibility and, like other forms of political media, can set political agenda. At the same time, editorial cartoons also portray and reflect political reality in relation to the roles political leaders play and the different styles of political leadership found in a particular country.

Examining Japanese editorial cartoons' tone, content, and way of depicting eight recent prime ministers during their first three months in office, Feldman maintains that the media attached growing importance to the national political leader as a source of political information. In the cartoons, the prime minister appeared as a passive man, relatively indecisive and lacking in leadership ability. To a certain extent, these portraits reflect political reality and the prime minister's weak position within Japanese polity, where, as illustrated in the cartoons, prime ministers do in fact have less power than their counterparts in Western countries. Japan's prime minister does not have the political authority to guide the state, govern the people, or politically dominate the institutions of government. He cannot set national priorities or decide issues that he perceives to be important. In this sense, political cartoons serve as clear reflections of Japanese political culture, political leaders, and their roles.

In Chapter 11, Kern, Just, Crigler, and Xie discuss attitudes toward the use of the Internet in political campaigns. As part of a multiple-method study of the 1996 U.S. presidential election campaign that involved surveys, content analysis, focus groups, and in-depth interviews, they examined interactive "talk-aloud" protocols with novice Internet users during the final phase of the campaign. Participants (including both partisans and independents) in focus groups that met in New Jersey and Los Angeles joined an additional evening of interactive interviews (talk-alouds) and post-experimental interviews through a constructed Web site containing pages created by news media, candidates, parties, and interest groups.

The study differentiated among three types of information users: partisan, issue-oriented, and undecided seekers. The latter tend to browse and are therefore affected by site attractiveness, which suggests that well-funded media and political candidates may have an advantage. Additionally, the study found that novice users who were introduced to a variety of political Web sites appreciated the diversity of information available on the Internet. Kern and colleagues point out some obstacles to widespread use of the Internet as a political tool, including problems related to access, the need for computer education, and Web site design that makes navigation less frustrating and more relevant to users' needs. They also suggest that future investigation should address problems related to the lack of two-way communication on most Web sites and to the likelihood that sites operated by certain news media may draw more users because of name recognition among voters and because big companies have a funding advantage that allows them to create attractive, convenient, and "speedy" sites that are more difficult for minority voices to create.

In Chapter 12, Mitchell examines symbolic convergence in newspaper coverage of the Murrah Building bombing that occurred in Oklahoma City on April 19, 1995. The explosion killed 168 people, wounded 500 others, and caused millions of dollars in damage. Materials were taken from five sources: three national news magazines—*Time, Newsweek*, and *U.S. News & World Report*; one national newspaper, the *New York Times*; and one local paper, the *Daily Oklahoman*. The sample included 126 news articles, photographs, and headlines reporting some aspect of the bombing during the two-week period immediately after the explosion. The content of the coverage was analyzed for recurring images and fantasy themes, which were then combined to reveal the rhetorical visions of the individual sources. Then, the rhetorical vision of the local media was compared with that of the national sources.

Mitchell found that the rhetorical vision of the local newspaper proved to be quite distinct from that shared by the national sources, primarily in its emphasis on positive themes over more negative ones. These differences in emphasis could be tied to differences in the target audiences: the local newspaper's readership had a high degree of proximity to and personal involvement in the disaster, while the national sources' audiences did not. Because the audiences differed in their needs, the media's central messages had to differ as well. Mitchell also offers conclusions about the impact of rhetorical visions on the communities that create them and about the use of narrative, fantasy, and myth in the process of coping with crisis situations.

Chapter 13 deals with how symbolic communication shapes U.S. political debate and influences citizens' attitudes. Terkildsen, Schnell, and Callagan focus on the impact of label-driven media coverage of citizens' attitudes toward social movements, particularly, the U.S. women's movement. Meta-symbols, or group labels that are used to describe or represent an organization and its cause in cursory terms, serve as a shorthand that summarizes a group's beliefs and actions and tend to become detached from the full range of knowledge available about the group. The authors argue that to the extent that media coverage emphasizes meta-symbols for a movement rather than direct, multifaceted discussion about it, information about the group becomes compartmentalized and distorted.

The authors performed content analysis of all articles published about the women's movement and related concerns in the three major U.S. news weeklies—*Time, Newsweek,* and *U.S. News & World Report*—at the height of the U.S. women's movement from 1970 to 1979. Based on those results and evidence from two attitudinal experiments, they reported that (1) most media coverage of the women's movement involved meta-symbols (with the most commonly cited meta-symbols including "feminism," "battle of the sexes," "women's liberation movement," "radicals" and "militants"), (2) the media were at least partly responsible for linking and transmitting negative affect to group emblems associated with the women's movement, (3) symbolized coverage resulted in uniformly negative evaluations of the movement, and (4) a variety of meta-symbols elicited identical attitudinal responses. Terkildsen, Schnell, and Callagan thus found that such labels negatively impacted attitudes toward the women's movement and impaired the processing of additional information about it. The authors concluded that symbolic language has the potential to simplify and distort the democratic process. In other words, effective manipulation of symbols can inhibit or enhance a social movement's ability to make itself heard effectively through the media and to muster public support.

In the concluding chapter, De Landtsheer provides a conceptual overview that ties together and examines the common threads running through the various chapters, especially in terms of their implications for theory, research, and the application of political language.

It is our sincere hope that readers will find this book useful and that it will stimulate further research into political discourse around the world.

PART I

The Rhetoric of Public Personalities

CHAPTER 1

New Labour, New Rhetoric? An Analysis of the Rhetoric of Tony Blair

PETER BULL

In the British General Election of 1983, the Labour Party suffered its greatest electoral defeat since 1918. Labour secured just 209 Member of Parliament (MPs) (the lowest since 1935) from only 27.6 percent of the vote, the smallest share ever won by a principal opposition party; its 8.4 million votes was only just ahead of the 7.8 million cast for the Liberal and Social Democratic Alliance. During the 1980s, Labour was widely seen as "extremist, irresponsible and disunited" (King, 1992). Even following its fourth successive electoral defeat in 1992, the *Sunday Times* editorial (April 12, 1992), entitled "Socialism, RIP," stated bluntly: "The most significant lesson of the General Election of 1992 is that, in its present form, Labour is unelectable." But in 1997, Labour achieved its greatest electoral victory in its entire history, winning 418 seats with 43.2 percent of the vote.

Between 1983 and 1997, the policies of the Labour Party had been transformed. The 1983 Manifesto—memorably dubbed by Gerald Kaufman (a leading member of Labour's Front bench at the time) as "the longest suicide note in history"—called for unilateral nuclear disarmament, withdrawal from the Common Market, massive nationalization and renationalization with much greater planning of the economy, exchange controls and trade barriers. Following the election debacle of 1983, Neil Kinnock replaced Michael Foot as leader, and over the next decade, these proposals were progressively dropped. By 1992, none of these proposals appeared in the Party's Manifesto for the General Election of that year. Neil Kinnock quickly resigned three days after the 1992 election defeat. His successor, John Smith, died of a heart attack in 1994 and was replaced by Tony Blair. By 1997, the Manifesto had an explicit commitment to retaining the Trident nuclear deterrent, to the rapid completion of the European Union single market, to the retention of the Conservative trade union legislation of the 1980s, and a five-year pledge of no increases in income tax—in short, a complete reversal of what the Labour Party stood for in 1983.

Such dramatic changes typically pose a major problem of presentation for political parties. A complete about-turn inevitably reflects badly on what has gone before: There is a clear implication that the previous policies were ill-judged and inappropriate. Presenting the new policies also creates a problem; they may be depicted as cynical, opportunist, and unprincipled, as simply a means of currying support with the electorate. Nowhere is this problem of presentation more pronounced than in the context of a political interview, where interviewers can ask repeated questions, challenge equivocal responses, and draw attention to contradictions in policy. In this chapter, Tony Blair's skill in handling such communicative problems is evaluated, with particular reference to televised interviews that he gave during the 1997 British General Election campaign.

THE CONCEPT OF COMMUNICATION SKILL

The analysis is based on the assumption that communication can be regarded as a skill and consequently that it is possible to assess whether a politician's interview performance is skilled or unskilled. The concept of communication skill stems from a highly influential model of social interaction developed by Argyle and Kendon (1967). In their seminal paper "The Experimental Analysis of Social Performance," they argued that social behavior involves the same kinds of processes as those involved in motor skills such as driving a car or playing tennis. The advantage of this approach, they maintained, is that we know a great deal about motor skill processes; consequently, we can apply our knowledge of motor skills to the study of social interaction. This social skills model (as it has become known) was subsequently elaborated by Argyle in his books on social interaction (Argyle, 1967, 1969, 1972). It has also been extensively criticized; as a consequence, revised versions of the model have been presented, particularly by Hargie and Marshall (1986) and Hargie (1997). But the basic idea—that communication can be regarded as a form of skill—has proved remarkably enduring. It is still highly influential not only within social psychology, where it originated, but also in the wider society as a whole, such that the term "communication skills" has passed into common usage.

One of the revisions proposed by Hargie (1997) is that behavior needs to be understood in terms of what he calls the person-situation context. A major problem of the original Argyle and Kendon model is that it is couched at a very general and abstract level; it does not seek to specify what are the skills appropriate to any particular social context. Thus, in order to evaluate Tony Blair's skill in handling political interviews, it would be necessary to have some criteria specifying what constitutes skilled interview performance. For this reason, further theoretical analysis of the political interview is required.

THE FACE MODEL OF POLITICAL INTERVIEWS

A detailed analysis of political interviews has been proposed by the author and his colleagues, based on the notion of face (Bull et al., 1996). Their starting point was an observation by Jucker (1986: 71) that "It is clear that what is primarily at issue in news interviews is the interviewee's positive face." The term *positive face* was derived from Brown and Levinson's (1978, 1987) theory of politeness and refers to the desire to be approved of by others (whereas the term *negative face* refers to the desire to have autonomy of action). It is maintaining positive face in news interviews that Jucker argued is of particular importance for democratically elected politicians, since their political survival ultimately depends on the approval of a majority of people in their own constituency.

Brown and Levinson's theory was based on the highly influential paper "On Face-Work" by Goffman (1955/1967), according to whom concerns with face are salient in virtually all social encounters. Not only do people defend their own face in social interaction; Goffman points out that there is also an obligation to defend the face of others. In the context of a political interview, politicians might seek to support the face of political colleagues and allies; at the same time, they would not wish to support the face of negatively valued others, such as their political opponents. Goffman further observes that in many relationships, the members come to share a face, so that in the presence of third parties an improper act on the part of one member becomes a source of acute embarrassment to other members. This is especially true of the British party political system, where the party is paramount: Typically, the politician appears on television as the representative of that party to defend and promote its collective face. Consequently, on the basis of Goffman's observations, it was argued that politicians must concern themselves with three faces: their own individual face, the face of significant others, and the face of the party they represent.

On the basis of this theoretical analysis, a study was carried out of the 1992 British General Election, based on 18 televised interviews with the leaders of the three main political parties at that time (John Major, Neil Kinnock, and Paddy Ashdown). A new typology of questions in political interviews was developed, based on their face-threatening properties. Nineteen different types of face-threat are distinguished, divided into the three superordinate categories of face that politicians must defend—their own personal face, the face of the party they represent, and the face of significant others. The 18 interviews were analyzed using the new question typology, and the results showed that almost every question (99%) possessed at least some face-threatening properties.

Further analysis was based on a distinction between two types of question: those for which all the principal possible responses were deemed to be face-threatening and those for which it was considered a response could be produced without damage to face. This distinction was derived from a type of question identified by Bavelas et al. (1988, 1990), which creates what is termed an avoidance-avoidance conflict. In such questions, all the principal possible responses are considered to have potentially negative consequences, but nevertheless a response is still expected. According to Bavelas et al., what people typically do in these circumstances is to equivocate.

Many everyday situations can be seen to create this kind of conflict. Perhaps the most common involves a choice between saying something false but kind and something true but hurtful. For example, a person who is asked to comment on an unsuitable gift from a well-liked friend has two negative choices: saying falsely that he likes the gift or saying hurtfully that he does not. According to the theory, the person will if possible avoid both of these negative alternatives—especially when a hurtful truth serves no purpose. What the person does instead is equivocate; for example, someone might say, "I appreciate your thoughtfulness" with no mention of what he thought of the actual gift.

Bavelas et al.'s theory of equivocation is not restricted to any particular social setting, but they do argue that avoidance-avoidance conflicts are especially prevalent in political interviews. They do not, however, present any underlying theoretical rationale for what it is that politicians are seeking to avoid. Bull et al. (1996), in their analysis of the 1992 British General Election, proposed that it is the danger of losing face that underlies avoidance-avoidance conflicts. That is to say, politicians seek to avoid making certain kinds of responses that may put them in a bad light. This emphasis on losing face was not presented as an alternative to the concept of the avoidance-avoidance conflict, but rather as an explanation of why politicians find particular responses aversive (Bull, 1998a).

In Bull et al.'s analysis, questions for which each of the principal possible responses was considered to present a threat to face were referred to as "Bavelas-type," because these were the questions judged as creating an avoidance-avoidance conflict. Most of the Bavelas-type questions in the Bull et al. data (87%) were couched in a "yes-no" format (Quirk et al., 1985). Given that there are three principal modes of responding to such questions (confirm, deny, equivocate), the probability of an equivocal response occurring by chance is 33%; in fact, the total proportion of equivocal responses to yes-no questions was 66%. The finding that equivocation occurred at twice the rate expected by chance alone supported Bavelas et al.'s proposition that equivocation does occur in response to questions that create avoidance-avoidance conflicts.

However, not all questions posed this kind of dilemma for politicians. There were some questions to which it was considered the politician could respond without necessarily threatening face, in the sense of not incurring any of the 19 face-threats specified in the coding system. Where such a response was considered possible, it was coded as "no necessary threat." Given the postulated importance of face management in political interviews, it was hypothesised that where a "no necessary threat" response was possible, this would be the response the politician would produce. Such questions most typically were couched in a "yes-no" format (66% of "no necessary threat"questions); the total proportion of "no necessary threat" responses to these questions was 87% (proportion expected by chance 33%, as argued earlier).

Subsequently, Elliott and Bull (1996) endeavored to demonstrate how the face-threat typology could be effectively applied to the comparative analysis of questions as a means of analysing interviewer style. They further proposed that the distinction between Bavelas-type and "no necessary threat" questions could be used as a means of evaluating interviewer performance in terms of both toughness and neutrality. Bull and Elliott (1998) went on to conduct such an analysis, based on an evaluation of six leading political interviewers from the 1992 British General Election.

The results of all these studies support the view that face management is of central importance in political interviews. They also support the proposed modification to Bavelas et al.'s theory of equivocation, that it is threats to face that underlie avoidance-avoidance conflicts in this particular social setting. This analysis in terms of face is of direct relevance to the concept of communication skill just outlined here. Given an adversarial political system in which politicians must seek to present the best face, an important criterion for evaluating their interview performance will be how well they succeed in coping with issues of face management. Accordingly, the concept of communication skill and the face model of political interviews form the basis of the analysis of Tony Blair's interview performance presented in this chapter. The data on which this analysis is based comprised five televised interviews from the 1997 British General Election (with David Dimbleby, Jonathan Dimbleby, Sir David Frost, Jeremy Paxman, and Peter Sissons) (Bull, 1998c).

EQUIVOCATION BY TONY BLAIR IN THE 1997 GENERAL ELECTION

In an analysis of these five political interviews by Bull (1998c), it was hypothesized that questions about the dramatic changes in Labour Party policy between 1983 and 1997 would present Blair with a classic Bavelas-type avoidance-avoidance conflict and that his responses would be characterized by equivocation. It was hypothesized that this conflict would occur because of the communicative problems posed by the dramatic changes in Labour Party policy between 1983 and 1997 outlined earlier. In this context, it should be noted that Blair was first elected to Parliament in the General Election of 1983 (to the County Durham constituency of Sedgefield), as a Member for what has come to be known as old Labour. Thus, if he condemned the old Labour Party, he would at the very least be open to the charge of inconsistency; if he were to admit to any lack of belief in the manifesto of 1983, then he would be open to the further charge of hypocrisy. In addition, if he was too critical of old Labour, it might also make his party look bad, and he might well alienate support within his own party. Conversely, as the man preeminently associated with the modernization of the Labour Party, if he failed to acknowledge criticisms of old Labour, then it would naturally invite the question as to why all the changes to New Labour had taken place.

This communicative problem can be aptly illustrated from the attacks of his Conservative political opponents. Soon after Blair's election as Leader of the Labour Party, he was lampooned on the BBC Radio 4 Today program by the then Deputy Prime Minister Michael Heseltine with the question: "Why should you believe a man who has got all the major judgments wrong in the first half of his life, when he tells you he is going to get them all right in the second half of his life?" Blair was similarly mocked by John Major in Major's last speech as Prime Minister to the Conservative Party's annual conference (October 11, 1996): "But it simply won't do for Mr. Blair to say, look I'm not a socialist any more, now can I be Prime Minister please."

In short, the communicative problems posed by the modernisation of the Labour Party provided a particularly apposite context in which to test predictions derived from equivocation theory. In the analysis conducted by Bull (1998c), questions concerning the modernization of the Labour Party were in the first instance identified from the five television interviews with Tony Blair. Each question was content analyzed in terms of potential face-threats (according to the typology devised by Bull et al., 1996). Questions were further categorized according to whether they posed an avoidance-avoidance conflict or whether it was considered possible to produce a response that did not necessarily involve a threat to face.

Preliminary analysis showed that not every interviewer challenged Tony Blair on the issue of modernization. In the interview by Jonathan Dimbleby, there were no questions about modernization; all the questions were addressed to specific policy issues. The other four interviewers all posed at least one question about modernization, giving a total of 17 questions. Most—but not all—the questions about modernization were judged as creating an avoidance-avoidance conflict (71%). Some good examples of this kind of questioning can be found toward the beginning of David Dimbleby's (DD) interview with Tony Blair (TB), as reproduced in the following sequence:

DD: But did you believe in old Labour? (Question 1)

TB: I believed in the values of the Labour Party, yes.

DD: No—did you believe in what they stood for? Did you believe in CND? Did you believe in union power not being curtailed? Did you believe in nationalisation, not privatisation? (Question 2)

TB: There was a whole series of policy positions that I adopted, along with the rest of the Labour Party, but modernisation has been the very process that I have undertaken in the Labour Party.

DD: I know that, but have you abandoned what you said you believed in the eighties? (Question 3)

TB: Look, of course we always believed in the idea of a more just, fair society, and the Labour Party believed for a long period of time that the way to do that was, for example, simply more increased state spending. The whole process of modernisation, David, has been to take the Labour Party away from that to keep true to its principles, but to put those principles properly in a modern setting.

These three questions can all be seen to pose the same kind of Bavelas-type conflict. If Blair affirmed that he did believe in old Labour, he would show himself as inconsistent, since it would invite the question as to why he had made so many changes. If he denied that he believed in old Labour, he could still be seen as inconsistent, as well as laying himself open to the charge of hypocrisy—especially given that he was first elected to Parliament in 1983. An equivocal response would pose the face-threat of being seen as evasive. It should be noted that Blair's response to Question 1 is considered equivocal because his use of the word "values" (which he also stresses vocally) suggests only qualified support for old Labour, that is, there were some aspects of old Labour that he did not support. Dimbleby does not treat this response as a full reply, because in Question 2 he poses it again in a slightly different way; he then interrupts Blair's response, so it is not possible to say whether Blair replies or equivocates. Blair's response to Question 3 is regarded as equivocal because he does not say whether or not he believed in what he said in the 1980s.

There were also five questions to which it was considered possible to produce a response that did not necessarily involve a threat to face. Thus, David Dimbleby asked Blair, "So was Britain right not to vote in a Labour government in 1983 in 1987 and in 1992 in your opinion?" If Blair were to agree with this proposition, he would clearly be making a highly damaging statement about his own party, as well as damaging his own individual face by failing to show party loyalty. Even if he equivocated, thereby failing to explicitly rebut the negative characterization of the Labour Party, he might be taken as implicitly confirming David Dimbleby's proposition, as well as making himself look evasive. But the characterization is so extreme that Blair can reply to Dimbleby's question by rebutting it without incurring a threat to face. To argue for the modernization of the Labour Party is one thing; to advocate that they deserved to lose all three General Elections is quite another.

Questions were then dichotomized into those considered to create an avoidance-avoidance conflict and those to which it was considered possible to produce a response that was not intrinsically face-threatening. Responses were also dichotomized into replies and equivocations. Questions and responses were correlated using a Phi coefficient, which showed a highly significant positive correlation of +.87. This confirmed that Blair typically equivocated in response to questions about modernization judged as creating an avoidance-avoidance conflict and replied to those not judged as creating such a conflict. Thus, the results of this study strongly supported predictions derived from Bavelas et al.'s (1990) theory of equivocation.

The results also strongly supported Bull et al.'s (1996) proposed modification to equivocation theory in terms face management. According to the face model, avoidance-avoidance conflicts in the context of political interviews are created by threats to face, and these could be identified for all the principal potential responses to Bavelas-type questions. To "no necessary threat" questions, it is hypothesized that if a response can be produced that does not necessarily incur a threat to face, this will be the response the politician produces. This also received strong support: In questions judged not to create an avoidance-avoidance conflict, Blair always produced the response considered to be the one that did not necessarily pose a threat to face (in each instance, this also happened to be a reply).

Elsewhere, Bull (1998b) has argued that one means of evaluating the performance of politicians in interviews is in terms of what are called "avoidable face-damaging responses." That is to say, given an adversarial political system in which a politician must seek to present the best possible face, their interview performance may be said to be unskilled to the extent that they produce a face-damaging response where a "no necessary threat" response was possible. In this analysis, it is notable that Blair produced no examples of such "avoidable face-damaging responses" in response to "no necessary threat" questions.

To the other type of question—those judged as creating an avoidance-avoidance conflict—Blair responded in almost every case with equivocation. Of course, equivocation can be face-damaging: Politicians are notoriously evasive, and not replying to questions can be seen as detrimental to the politician by simply confirming this stereotype. But in the context of these interviews, equivocation was arguably far less face-threatening than face-damaging responses that might have reflected badly either on the Labour Party and/or on Blair's own personal competence and integrity.

In fact, there was only one Bavelas-type question to which Blair did not equivocate, when David Frost asked, "But when you said about trades union law that it was scandalous and undemocratic I mean at the moment you said it did you mean it?" This question is regarded as creating an avoidance-avoidance conflict, because whereas Conservative Party trade union law was vigorously opposed by Blair when he was Shadow Employment Secretary (1989–1992), the 1997 Labour Party Manifesto gave an explicit commitment not to reverse that legislation. Thus, if Blair confirmed this proposition, he would have to acknowledge the inconsistency in his position. If he denied it, he would make himself look hypocritical, as well as putting himself in an extremely bad light with both the trade unions and the Labour Party. Failure to reply would not only seem evasive, but might also be understood as meaning that he did not mean what he said at that time but was unwilling to admit this publicly. Hence, in this instance, equivocation might have made Blair seem hypocritical: Anything less than an explicit confirmation that his previous criticisms of trade union law were genuine could be taken as a tacit admission that he had been less than sincere. Given the crucial importance of personal integrity to Blair's electoral stance, this could have been extremely face-damaging. Thus, although he explicitly acknowledges inconsistency by confirming that he meant what he said about trade union law at the time, his reply can still be seen as the least face-threatening way of responding to this question. Hence, even in this apparent exception to the predictions of equivocation theory, Blair can be seen to be presenting the best possible face. Indeed, in his responses to all 17 questions about the modernization of the Labour Party, he can be seen to be highly attentive to presenting the best possible face both for himself and for his party. In terms of face management, his performance can be seen as highly skilled.

THE INTERACTIONAL CONSEQUENCES OF EQUIVOCATION

A further modification of equivocation theory has also been proposed by Bull (1997, 1998a). Whereas Bavelas et al. analyzed the circumstances that give rise to equivocation, Bull argued that consideration should also be given to the interactional consequences of different forms of equivocation. There are many ways of not replying to a question: 30 different forms of non-reply in political interviews were identified by Bull and Mayer (1993). Different forms of equivocation may also vary in their interactional advantages and disadvantages.

The interactional significance of different forms of equivocation was appraised in a study of the celebrated televised interview between Diana, Princess of Wales, and Martin Bashir (Bull, 1997). (The interview was broadcast in November 1995, the year before her divorce from Prince

Charles, just under two years before her tragic death in a car accident). It was noted that Diana made significant use of what were termed "answers by implication," which always took the form of implicit criticisms, especially of Prince Charles and the Royal Family. In Bavelas et al.'s theory, answers by implication would be regarded as a form of equivocation; and Diana's use of such responses, it was proposed, could be understood in the context of equivocation theory. This was because once having agreed to give this interview, Diana had in effect put herself into an avoidance-avoidance conflict. On the one hand, if she was too outspokenly critical, she might alienate public opinion and exacerbate and embitter an already difficult situation with her husband and the Royal family; she might even have been frightened of some form of retaliation. Conversely, if she avoided comment on her husband and the Royal family or even denied there were any problems between them, she would not be able to give her side of the story and would look foolish for having agreed to give the interview in the first place. In this avoidance-avoidance situation, implicative responses would seem to be highly appropriate—a means of putting her side of the story without being too outspokenly critical.

In Bavelas et al.'s theory, no particular distinction is made between not replying to a question and giving an implicit response; they are regarded as simply varying along a continuum of equivocation. But according to the preceding analysis, their interactional significance is not the same and should be regarded as qualitatively distinct. Hence, consideration needs to be given to the interactional significance of different forms of equivocation. For this reason, in Bull's (1998c) analysis of interviews with Tony Blair, it was decided to investigate the ways in which Blair equivocated in response to questions about Labour Party policy changes between 1983 and 1997. The substance of his equivocation can be summarized in a series of propositions, presented here:

1. In responding to questions about changes in Labour Party policy, Blair makes extensive use of the term "modernization." This allows him to emphasize both continuity and change. Thus, with regard to old Labour, he stated, "I believed in the values of the Labour Party," whereas the process of modernisation has been "to keep (the Labour Party) true to its principles but put those principles properly in a modern setting." This allowed Blair not only to explicitly acknowledge the changes that have taken place but also to present them as principled—as representing an adaptation of the traditional values of the Labour Party to the contemporary political situation. In this way, he could claim a positive face for his party—it is both principled but also moving with the times.

2. Blair also points out that the Conservative Party has changed: "John Major stood in the 1970s on a platform of Scottish devolution. Margaret Thatcher was the person that closed more grammar schools than anyone else. She was a member of Ted Heath's government you know." John Major (Conservative Prime Minister, 1990–1997) vigorously campaigned against Scottish devolution in the

1997 General Election; Margaret Thatcher (Conservative Prime Minister, 1979–1990) was Secretary of State for Education in the previous Conservative government of Ted Heath (1970–1974) but vigorously defended grammar schools during her subsequent term as Prime Minister). By drawing attention to these changes in the Conservative Party, Blair seeks to present change as a more general process of political life, not as something peculiar to the Labour Party.

3. In response to an extremely difficult question about a serious trade union dispute in the 1980s (between the media magnate Rupert Murdoch and the print unions), Blair simply declines to reply: "There is no point in going back over the past. There is a different world today. Let us address this world today and let us see how we can make improvements to it. Let us see how we can make Britain a better place."

All these points, Bull (1998c) argued, add up to what might be termed a "rhetoric of modernization": a means of equivocating in response to awkward questions about the dramatic changes in Labour Party policy between 1983 and 1997, whereby Blair can avoid making highly face-damaging remarks both about himself and about the Labour Party as a whole.

THE RHETORIC OF MODERNIZATION

This "rhetoric of modernization" does much more than simply enable Blair to avoid answering difficult questions; it also has other important and significant political advantages (Bull, 1998c). According to Reicher and Hopkins (1996), democratically elected politicians must—in order to maximize their own electoral appeal—seek to define the political context in such a way as to make the ingroup as comprehensive as possible and the outgroup as restricted as possible. Reicher and Hopkins' analysis was based on self-categorization theory (Turner et al., 1987), which has been highly influential in the social psychological analysis of groups and group behavior. According to this theory, individuals form a psychological group insofar as they develop a shared social categorization of themselves in contrast to others that, in a given situation, becomes the basis of their attitudes and behaviors. Which perspective people take toward others depends on the social situation. When people categorize themselves as individuals, they generally strive to attain personal goals, whereas group goals are pursued when people categorize themselves as group members.

In the context of this theory, Reicher and Hopkins (1996) analyzed two political speeches delivered at the time of the British miners' strike (1984–1985), one by Margaret Thatcher, the other by Neil Kinnock. Reicher and Hopkins sought to show how both politicians endeavored to define issues relating to the miners' strike in such a way as to include the greatest possible proportion (and preferably all) of the intended audience within their own group. They also sought to define their own proposals as consistent with that group identity and rival proposals as inconsistent with that group identity. In addition, they sought to define the political context in such a way that they were part of a common group with their intended audience, and hence in a position to influence them.

These are precisely the advantages that can be seen to characterize Tony Blair's "rhetoric of modernization." It seeks to establish an identity for New Labour that will both attract people who might never have voted for the old Labour Party and also avoid the risk of alienating existing supporters:

1. Thus, for those who would never have voted for the old Labour Party, modernization emphasizes that the party has changed.

2. Furthermore, the changes can be presented as principled, a process of applying the traditional values of the Labour Party to the modern world, just as the Conservative Party has also had to change.

3. At the same time, change can be acknowledged without condemning or criticizing the old Labour Party, in order to minimize the risk of alienating traditional Labour support. Although in almost half the questions about modernization Blair is invited to criticize or condemn old Labour, it is notable that he never does so. In this way, Tony Blair seeks to establish an identity for New Labour characterized by a high degree of inclusiveness. This can undoubtedly be seen as a highly skilled form of political communication.

CONCLUSIONS: THE RHETORIC OF MODERNIZATION AS SKILLED COMMUNICATION

The analysis presented in this chapter has been based on three social psychological theories: the social skills model (Argyle & Kendon, 1967), the face model of political interviews (Bull et al., 1996), and self-categorization theory (Turner et al., 1987). These three theories, it has been argued, provide clear criteria on which to evaluate Tony Blair's communicative skill. In the context of political interviews, face management can be seen as of central importance (Bull et al., 1996). Furthermore, democratically elected politicians, in order to maximize their own electoral appeal, must seek to establish the broadest sense of common identity with the electorate (Reicher & Hopkins, 1996). Both the ability to achieve such an identity and the effective protection and enhancement of face in political interviews can be regarded as a crucial communicative skills for any successful democratic politician.

In analysing Blair's interview performance, the term "rhetoric of modernization" was coined to refer to the way in which he handled awkward questions about the dramatic policy changes in the Labour Party between 1983 and 1997. This rhetoric can certainly be seen as a form of equivocation, a means of not replying to questions that create avoidance-

avoidance conflicts, just as equivocation theory would predict. But whereas Bavelas et al.'s theory portrays equivocation as an essentially negative phenomenon, a means of not giving replies to awkward questions, this rhetoric of modernization can also be seen to have distinct political advantages. In a recent special issue of the *Journal of Language and Social Psychology*, equivocation was defined as the "intentional use of imprecise language" (Hamilton & Mineo, 1998). In this context, Blair's strategic use of the imprecise language of modernization can be regarded as a highly skilled form of political communication, a means not only of avoiding the risks of making face-damaging remarks but also of presenting the best possible face for himself and the party that he represents, by striving to create a highly inclusive identity for New Labour.

In fact, the very name "New Labour" can be seen to project this inclusive identity, emphasizing change while still preserving the link with the Labour Party of old. New Labour certainly has a new rhetoric, but it should not be dismissed as "just rhetoric." Blair's use of the "rhetoric of modernization" represents a high level of communicative skill, which arguably played a crucial role in the Labour Party's stunning landslide victory in the British General Election of 1997.

REFERENCES

Argyle, M. (1967; 2nd ed. 1972). *The Psychology of Interpersonal Behaviour*. London: Pelican.

Argyle, M. (1969). *Social Interaction*. London: Methuen.

Argyle, M., & Kendon, A. (1967). The Experimental Analysis of Social Performance. In L. Berkowitz (Ed.), *Advances in Experimental Social Psychology* (vol. 3, pp. 55–97). New York: Academic Press.

Bavelas, J. B., Black, A., Bryson, L., & Mullett, J. (1988). Political Equivocation: A Situational Explanation. *Journal of Language & Social Psychology*, 7, 137–145.

Bavelas, J. B., Black, A., Chovil, N., & Mullett, J. (1990). *Equivocal Communication*. Newbury Park, CA: Sage.

Brown, P., & Levinson, S. C. (1978). Universals in Language Usage: Politeness Phenomena. In E. Goody (Ed.), *Questions and Politeness* (pp. 56–310). Cambridge: Cambridge University Press.

Brown, P., & Levinson, S. C. (1987). *Politeness: Some Universals in Language Use*. Cambridge: Cambridge University Press.

Bull, P. E. (1997). Queen of Hearts or Queen of the Arts of Implication? Implicit Criticisms and Their Implications for Equivocation Theory in the Interview between Martin Bashir and Diana, Princess of Wales. *Social Psychological Review*, 1, 27–36.

Bull, P. E. (1998a). Equivocation Theory and News Interviews. *Journal of Language and Social Psychology*, 17, 36–51.

Bull, P. E. (1998b). Political Interviews: Television Interviews in Great Britain. In

O. Feldman & C. De Landtsheer (Eds.), *Politically Speaking: A Worldwide Examination of Language Used in the Public Sphere.* Westport, CT: Praeger.

Bull, P. E. (1998c). The Rhetoric of Modernisation: An Analysis of Televised Interviews with Tony Blair in the 1997 General Election. Paper presented at the Annual Conference of the Social Psychology Section of the British Psychological Society, September 21.

Bull, P. E., & Elliott, J. (1998). Level of Threat: Means of Assessing Interviewer Toughness and Neutrality. *Journal of Language and Social Psychology*, 17, 220–244.

Bull, P. E., Elliott, J., Palmer, D., & Walker, L. (1996). Why Politicians Are Three-Faced: The Face Model of Political Interviews. *British Journal of Social Psychology*, 35, 267–284.

Bull, P. E., & Mayer, K. (1993). How Not to Answer Questions in Political Interviews. *Political Psychology*, 14, 651–666.

Elliott, J., & Bull, P. E. (1996). A Question of Threat: Face Threats in Questions Posed during Televised Political Interviews. *Journal of Community and Applied Social Psychology*, 6, 49–72.

Goffman, E. (1955). On Face-Work: An Analysis of Ritual Elements in Social Interaction. *Psychiatry*, 18, 213–231. Reprinted in E. Goffman (1967), *Interaction Ritual: Essays on Face-to-Face Behavior* (pp. 5–45). Garden City, NY: Anchor.

Hamilton, M. A., & Mineo, P. J. (1998). A Framework for Understanding Equivocation. *Journal of Language and Social Psychology*, 17, 3–35.

Hargie, O. D. W. (1997). Interpersonal Communication: A Theoretical Framework. In O. D. W. Hargie (Ed.), *The Handbook of Communication Skills*, 2nd ed. (pp. 29–63). London: Routledge.

Hargie, O. D. W., & Marshall, P. (1986). Interpersonal Communication: A Theoretical Framework. In O. D. W. Hargie (Ed.), *The Handbook of Communication Skills* (pp. 22–56). London: Croom Helm.

Jucker, J. (1986). *News Interviews: A Pragmalinguistic Analysis.* Amsterdam: Gieben.

King, A. (1992). *Britain at the Polls, 1992.* Chatham, NJ: Chatham House.

Quirk, R., Greenbaum, S., Leech, G., & Svartvik, J. (1985). *A Comprehensive Grammar of the English Language.* London: Longman.

Reicher, S., & Hopkins, N. (1996). Self-Category Constructions in Political Rhetoric: An Analysis of Thatcher's and Kinnock's Speeches Concerning the British Miners' Strike (1984–5). *European Journal of Social Psychology*, 26, 353–371.

Turner, J. C., Hogg, M. A., Oakes, P. J., Reicher, S. D., & Wetherell, M. S. (1987). *Rediscovering the Social Group: A Self-Categorization Theory.* Oxford: Basil Blackwell.

CHAPTER 2

Domain-Related Variation in Integrative Complexity: A Measure of Political Importance and Responsiveness? Clinton, Gingrich, Gorbachev, and Various Canadian Political Leaders

PETER SUEDFELD

One important distinction in cognitive complexity research is that between the idea of complexity as a state variable and the idea of it as a stable personality trait. This chapter examines one aspect of the "state complexity" emphasis: differences in the level of complexity with which contemporary politicians (Clinton, Gingrich, Gorbachev, and various Canadian political leaders) have addressed different topics or domains (foreign affairs, domestic policy, and human interest).

INFERRING PERSONALITY FROM ARCHIVAL MATERIALS

Profiling or analyzing political leaders "at a distance" (that is, without directly interviewing or testing them) has become a very popular scholarly endeavor in the past few decades. Much of the work in this field proceeds by (a) identifying characteristics that have been measured and studied in the general area of personality, (b) proposing that the particular trait is an important one in political leadership or decision making, (c) devising an assessment procedure appropriate to archival materials, and then (d) testing some hypotheses relating the trait to leader behavior by applying the assessment technique to the leader's utterances.

Some of this work has tended in the direction of qualitative and impressionistic inferences. Perhaps best known is the school of psychohistory or psychobiography. Its adherents apply psychodynamic concepts, adapted from Freud, Erikson, and their colleagues, to political leaders. Psychohistorians infer adult personality and political behavior from what they know or speculate to be the developmental forces in the person's childhood (e.g., Freud & Bullitt, 1966; Iremonger, 1970).

Other holistic approaches concentrate on explicating the relevant personality characteristics of the adult leader. Interesting insights have emerged from such studies. For example, James D. Barber's (1972) taxonomy of political character, based on the orthogonal axes of activity-passivity and positive-negative affect, was a pioneering use of a now standard model of emotions (the pleasure-arousal grid, Russell, Weiss, & Mendelsohn, 1989). Barber argued that the responses of 20th-century American presidents in various political crises were predictable from, and compatible with, the quadrant in which their character placed them. Renshon (1996) also addressed the issue of presidential character, assessing ambition, integrity, and relatedness as they interact with the president's skills, tasks, and environment to determine leadership performance.

A number of researchers have used more tightly focused analyses and more objective, replicable measures. These have included the assessment of the leader's dominant motives (Winter, 1992), level of optimism (Hermann, 1980), and open-mindedness (Ertel, 1972), among other variables. In general, such research implies that the measured quantity of the characteristic is an underlying factor in the leader's ideology, goal selection, decision making, reactions to stress and frustration, and possibly even success or failure.

COGNITIVE COMPLEXITY

With the "cognitive revolution" in psychology, many researchers in different subfields turned their attention to the processes of thinking and remembering. Among them were personality theorists, whose central interest in individual differences was in this context focused upon differences in the intellectual domain. In the 1960s, the concept of "cognitive styles" was widely employed to describe this kind of variable, with cogent theories and solid research showing that there are indeed stable, measurable differences in how people think (Schroder & Suedfeld, 1971). Among cognitive styles relevant to political behavior are dogmatism, rigidity, tolerance of ambiguity, and need for closure.

Although there have been adaptations of several cognitive styles approaches to the assessment of political leaders at a distance (e.g., Ertel, 1972), the major programs of work have concentrated on a variable known as cognitive complexity. The version most used in political psychology is integrative complexity, an offshoot of the conceptual complexity theory of Schroder, Driver, and Streufert (1967). Conceptual and integrative complexity both refer to a disposition or ability to (a) make *differentiations* among stimuli, aspects of stimuli, or the processing of stimuli and (b) perceive possible *integrations* among the components one has perceived in a differentiated way. People low in this ability are prone to compartmentalized, all-or-nothing, black-or-white thinking, while those who are high in

Figure 2.1
Conceptual Schemata for Different Levels of Integrative Complexity

ONE BIPOLAR PERSPECTIVE

UNDIFFERENTIATED,
NO INTEGRATION

UNRELATED DIMENSIONS

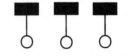

UNRELATED PERSPECTIVES

DIFFERENTIATED,
NO INTEGRATION

DIFFERENTIATED DIMENSIONS

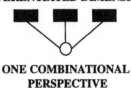

**ONE COMBINATIONAL
PERSPECTIVE**

MODERATE DIFFERENTIATION,
LOW INTEGRATION

DIFFERENTIATED DIMENSIONS

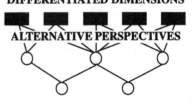

ALTERNATIVE PERSPECTIVES

SUPERORDINATE SCHEMATA

HIGH DIFFERENTIATION,
HIGH INTEGRATION

conceptual complexity tend to see many subtle shadings and to be able to formulate ideas about how these interact or fit together (see Figure 2.1).

Individuals who differ in conceptual complexity also differ on a number of other cognitive styles, because these are related to differentiation and integration. For example, low complexity tends to be associated with high rigidity. Rigid thinkers keep trying to follow a chosen plan even after it is proven inadequate or to defend an opinion even after there are strong reasons to judge it as mistaken.

People low in conceptual complexity also tend to be high in dogmatism: They find it difficult to change their beliefs or attitudes in response to new or contradictory information. They may ignore the information, reinterpret it, refuse to believe it, or explain it away; no matter which strategy they use, it enables them to stick to their previous way of thinking about the issue.

People operating at high levels of conceptual complexity are low in rigidity and dogmatism. They collect and monitor information and can change their plans, beliefs, and attitudes in response to feedback. They are relatively tolerant of ambiguity and lack of closure; that is, they are not unduly upset when situations, problems, or solutions are unclear, there is a high degree of uncertainty, a decision cannot be made immediately, or one must wait a while to learn how events turn out.

The relevance of this construct to political leadership is quite obvious. In politics, uncertainty, doubt, delay, and confusion are not uncommon; programs and plans are sometimes unsuccessful; and alternative positions or choices may have small but important differences or may be open to synthesis if the leader perceives that possibility. One may not be able to obtain clear information, advice, and solutions or avoid uncertainty, doubt, and contradictory pressures. Sometimes, conclusions may have to be deferred and plans modified; problems may not have solutions that are obviously either right or wrong, good or bad, but only alternatives with some good and some bad aspects.

A couple of aspects of this theory are open to misinterpretation. One is that it is limited to cognitive tendencies, a point that has escaped some critics. For example, Stone (1993) has described complexity theory as "an extreme simplification of authoritarian personality theory" (p. 168). It is not, of course; although low conceptual complexity may be a cognitive characteristic of authoritarian personalities, complexity theory does not claim to say anything about the many other dimensions of authoritarianism—developmental origins, interpersonal and intergroup attitudes, emotional tendencies, orientations toward social hierarchies, responses to moral issues, and so on.

Another point that is sometimes overlooked is that complexity theory does not ascribe superiority, either morally or pragmatically, to any level of complexity over any other level. Without belaboring the point, we may just point out that in mid-19th-century American politics, fervent supporters of slavery *and* of the immediate abolition of slavery were both lower in complexity than advocates of the slow, negotiated, gradual emancipation of slaves. Had the last of these groups had its way, the United States might have avoided the Civil War; but the moral high ground seems to belong to the abolitionists (Tetlock, Armor, & Peterson, 1994).

Neville Chamberlain's complexity at Munich was markedly higher than Hitler's. In this case, higher complexity led to an unquestionably inferior strategy. Its moral standing is doubtful. I, for one, would be willing to argue that complexity can be misplaced when one is confronting an evil adversary in a situation that really is "black or white" (Suedfeld & Tetlock, 1992). Some other occasions where low complexity may be pragmatically preferable include when a decision has to be made quickly, when much of the available information is trivial or irrelevant, and when other, perhaps more serious problems are awaiting the leader's attention.

MOVING FROM PERSONALITY TO BEHAVIOR

Although the original conceptual complexity theorists explored the situational factors that could affect information processing behavior, it was the underlying stable dimension of ability that primarily governed problem solving and decision making. Conceptual complexity was assessed through a number of measures, mostly paper-and-pencil, the most commonly used being the Paragraph Completion Test (PCT). The PCT asked respondents to complete and extend sentence stems tapping such general domains as relations to authority, social rejection, and uncertainty about a proper course of action (Schroder et al., 1967).

About 15 years after the original publication of conceptual complexity theory, I and some of my students started to take a somewhat different tack. We accepted the idea that each person may have a stable ceiling level of complexity, as is the case for intellectual capacity and muscular strength. But we were interested in *state* complexity. We proposed that people's information processing complexity is not stable and that its variability is interesting. Changes might occur in response to both exogenous and endogenous factors. The former would include life events, time pressure, information overload, and sociopolitical context; the latter, age, fatigue, illness, and approaching death. We named this reactive aspect of information processing *integrative complexity*, to mark its difference from conceptual complexity. We also worked out a way to score differentiation and integration within archival, or in fact any, connected verbal material. Integrative complexity scoring of such materials uses the same principles and the same 1–7 scoring system as does the PCT (Suedfeld & Rank, 1976) (See Table 2.1).

The state complexity view underlies the cognitive manager model (Suedfeld, 1992). This model advances the following propositions:

1. The more complex a solution or decision strategy is, the more resources it uses up. These resources include time, attentional focus, energy, intellectual effort, and sometimes material resources for information search, data processing, and the like.

2. Therefore, problems tend to be approached with the lowest level of complexity that appears adequate for solving them.

Table 2.1
Scoring Integrative Complexity

Score	Characteristics
1	Undifferentiated, no integration
2	Transitional
3	Differentiated, no integration
4	Transitional
5	Differentiated, low-level integration (e.g., interaction)
6	Transitional
7	Differentiated, high-level integration (e.g., superordinate schemata)

Note: In the following tables, numerical complexity scores refer to scores along this 1–7 scale.

3. The cognitive and other resources committed to solving a problem will depend on how important and how difficult the problem is perceived to be in the context of all decisions that have to be made within the same general time period and the degree to which resources are available to be devoted to a solution.

4. *Disruptive stress* leads to a drop in complexity if the decision maker's resources are depleted because the problem proves to be intractable. Complexity may also decrease if resources must be diverted to other, more important or more urgent problems.

Thus, we would expect higher complexity in domains where the individual is especially interested, committed, or engaged and where higher complexity seems more likely to lead to success. We expect reduced complexity under high stress or frustration.

As mentioned earlier, other variables also affect complexity level; but differences across domains should generally show the pattern just described. Interdomain differences, of course, imply that state factors outweigh the trait dimension in establishing the operating complexity level.

ASSESSING LEADERS' COMPLEXITY AT A DISTANCE

Mikhail Sergeyevitch Gorbachev

The first study focusing on this issue was published by Tetlock (1988), who reported that different Soviet leaders showed quite different levels of complexity when addressing domestic policy or international relations. In a detailed analysis of the speeches of Mikhail Gorbachev (Table 2.2a) my research group (Wallace, Suedfeld, & Thachuk, 1996) found that he exhibited consistently higher complexity in speaking about foreign policy than about domestic issues. This pattern possibly reflects Gorbachev's greater

Table 2.2a
Mean Complexity by Domain: Gorbachev, 1985–1991

Year	Foreign Affairs	Domestic Policy
1985	1.57	1.48
1986	1.51	1.32
1987	1.80	1.72
1988	1.64	1.59
1989	2.41	2.01*
1990	2.09	1.83*
1991	2.07	1.65*

*p ≤ .01.

interest in the former domain. It is also the case that his complex approach to international diplomacy led to considerably more success and acclamation than his domestic policies.

Table 2.2b shows some of the salient events in each domain for the last few years of Gorbachev's leadership. It should be noted that there was an overall increase in complexity in both domains until 1989; thereafter, complexity in both domains decreased. Such a curvilinear pattern may reflect first, the commitment of increasing resources to solving problems in complex ways, and then a decline when those resources are exhausted or the problems are recognized as unsolvable. During his worst times at home (1989–1991), his complexity changes were compatible with the disruptive stress hypothesis (Wallace et al., 1996).

William Jefferson Clinton

We have taken another look at this issue in data on contemporary North American politicians. Our first example is President Clinton, whose complexity we scored during his 1992 election campaign and his first year in office (Suedfeld, 1994). Table 2.3 shows his level of complexity during the campaign and during his first month in office. Tetlock (1981 and personal communication, 1998) has tabulated the complexity scores of other 20th-century presidents who reached that office through election (i.e., not succeeding to the presidency because of the death or resignation of their predecessor). As Table 2.3 shows, Clinton's speeches during his first month in office were among the least complex of all the presidents' speeches. Only Presidents Reagan and Bush scored lower than he did. Furthermore, Clinton showed the second lowest complexity increase from before to after the elections that put him into office.

Table 2.2b
Chronology of Important Events: Gorbachev, 1989–1991

Foreign Affairs	Domestic Affairs
1989	
End of war in Afghanistan	CP loses in parliamentary elections
Brezhnev doctrine renounced	Slumping productivity
Visits to China and Western Europe; meeting with President Bush	Nationalist violence
1990	
Well-received Western tours	CPSU formally separated from government
U.S. most-favored-nation status	President's power reduced
Mediation role in Gulf Crisis	SSRs declare sovereignty
Nobel Prize for Peace	First food rationing since 1940s
Arms control, aid, and trade treaties	
1991	
Western tours	Baltic crisis
High popularity abroad	Negotiations with SSRs
	Coal strike
	Political splits widening
	Coup attempt; Yeltsin rises
	USSR dissolved; Gorbachev resigns

Table 2.3 is derived from an expanded database, which analyzed Clinton's complexity levels across different topics during the campaign and through his first *year* in office (Suedfeld & Wallace, 1995). Although Tetlock (1981) found very little change in the complexity of U.S. presidents' speeches when comparing the first month in office with all subsequent time periods, we thought that perhaps Clinton took longer to emerge from the low-complexity campaign mode and might show the candidate-to-president increase a little later after taking office than his predecessors. This hypothesis was not confirmed.

These findings were essentially replicated in a study by Panos (1998). According to his data, Clinton's complexity averaged 1.5 in the 1992 candidate debates and 1.9 in the 1996 debates. The mean score of his presidential speeches, calculated year by year between 1993 and 1997, ranged from 1.8 to 2.6. These data are quite compatible with our own.

Unlike most democratic and even non-democratic national leaders (Suedfeld & Rank, 1976; Tetlock, 1981), Clinton showed no overall increase in

Table 2.3
Mean Change in Integrative Complexity: U.S. Presidents[a]

President	Pre-Election	1st Month	% Change
Eisenhower*	1.9	3.4	+79
Kennedy	2.1	3.6	+71
F.D. Roosevelt*	2.2	3.5	+59
McKinley*	2.1	3.1	+48
Taft	2.4	3.5	+46
Wilson*	3.2	3.9	+29
Nixon*	2.5	2.9	+16
Reagan, 1st Term	1.3	1.5	+15
Reagan, 2nd Term	1.2	1.4	+17
Carter	2.7	3.1	+15
Harding	2.2	2.5	+14
Bush	1.8	2.0	+11
Clinton, 1st Term	2.3	2.2	–4
Clinton, 2nd Term**	2.1	2.3	+10
Hoover	3.8	2.8	–26

[a]Data for all presidents except Clinton from Tetlock (1981 and personal communication, 1998).
*First term only.
**Inaugural address only.

complexity between his speeches before and after taking the highest office in government. Furthermore, there was no overall change in his complexity over time, such as was seen in the case of Gorbachev. These stable patterns indicate that neither a major change in Clinton's political role nor increasing experience in the presidency was associated with modifications in his cognitive strategies.

Clinton showed relatively little variation across topics. During the electoral campaign, he did exhibit somewhat higher complexity in speeches on economic policy than on other issues, and as president his speeches on health care and the environment were slightly more complex than the rest. These differences presumably identify areas that are of special concern to him but are not seen as daunting or unsolvable problems. However, even in these areas the level of complexity was not really high.

Serious trouble seems to have some effect on the president's complexity. Panos (1998) reported that during the first two months after the Lewinsky scandal broke, Clinton's speeches (including the State of the Union address) scored at a mean of 2.0. A recent addition to our own data was a comparison of President Clinton's two televised addresses to the nation in August 1998, both in response to major crises. One was perhaps his personal nadir up to that point, his first speech concerning the Monica Lewinsky imbroglio (August 17, M complexity = 1.93); the other, only a few days later, dealt with a national tragedy and the president's response: the American retaliation against the terrorists responsible for the bombing of the U.S. embassies in Nairobi and Dar-es-Salaam (August 22, M complexity = 1.83). Again, there was no meaningful difference between topics. In both cases, Clinton's complexity was unusually low even for him, barely reaching the level of implicit differentiation. If this is not a trait characteristic, it indicates a high level of stress (which would not be surprising, under the circumstances).

My own interpretation of the entire Clinton data array is that it demonstrates a stable attribute: low conceptual (i.e., trait) complexity, which does not change much in response to environmental influences. This is quite surprising, in view of journalistic descriptions of this president that seem to be consistent with *high* complexity: information seeking, flexibility in changing decisions and plans, listening to contradictory advice, and so on (Suedfeld & Wallace, 1995).

Although further research is indicated, it seems upon closer reading that this is an unusual case, in which the apparently high level of complexity is paradoxical, accompanied by low measured complexity. This is possible because impressionistic accounts of cognitive behavior do not necessarily translate into equivalent objective scores. That the person listens to and seeks information does not mean that the cognitive strategy is either differentiated or integrated, because such behavior does not directly determine how the received information is processed; and sequentially abandoning one plan and moving to the next represents a series of simple decisions, not a complex one.

Newt Gingrich

Another American politician, Newt Gingrich, showed an interesting pattern during the 1994 congressional campaign and the first three months after he became Speaker of the House (Suedfeld, 1995; Table 2.4). Gingrich is the first politician whose complexity we have scored while he campaigned to become leader of the opposition, not of the national government. We would expect a somewhat different pattern of complexity in such a case: those whose task is to criticize policy almost always show lower complexity than those who propose or defend it.

During the campaign, Gingrich showed the highest complexity in domains where serious policy differences between the two political parties were most salient: welfare reform and health care. Once he was in office,

Table 2.4
Mean Complexity by Domain: Gingrich, 1994–1995

Topic	Campaign	In Office
Crime	1.5	1.5
Economy		1.7
Education	1.6	
Government	1.8	1.9
Health Care	2.1	1.8
Religion	1.8	
Welfare	2.4	1.6
Overall	1.9	1.7

cross-domain differences mostly disappeared, and the overall level of complexity remained about the same. A more detailed analysis—e.g., looking at topics as particular policy proposals were debated and approached a vote—might be informative as to how opposition leaders process relevant information.

Canadian Federal Election, 1997

Our most recent analyses deal with Canadian federal party leaders during the most recent national election, in June 1997. At the time of the election, the contenders were, in order of strongest to weakest, as follows:

The Liberal Party is a slightly left-of-center, pragmatic party, that is, it is not strongly ideological and both operates and attracts support on the basis of specific policies. In the previous election, it commanded major support in Ontario, the most populous province, and strong support in Quebec with scattered seats in other parts of the country. The Liberal Party had a parliamentary majority going into the election, and its leader, Jean Chretien, was therefore Prime Minister. The Liberal Party is sometimes described (not entirely facetiously) as the natural governing party of the country, having controlled Parliament for most of this century.

The official Opposition was the Bloc Quebecois, dedicated to the separation of Quebec from Canada. This is the party's major platform; secondarily, it tries to ensure that power and economic benefits go to Quebec as much as possible. Its leader at the time of the 1997 campaign was Gilles Duceppe, who had recently replaced the highly effective and respected Lucien Bouchard when Bouchard became Premier of Quebec. The Bloc had no Members from outside Quebec.

The Reform Party, led by Preston Manning with a power base in Western

Canada, was a hair's breadth from taking over the official Opposition slot. Reform is a populist party whose policies on such issues as immigration, social welfare programs, the economy, and multiculturalism lean more toward the conservative end of the political spectrum than those of its competitors.

The New Democratic Party (NDP) is a social democratic party, with strong ties to organized labour and other left-leaning groups. Its policies are consistent with that affiliation. The party leader was Alexa McDonough. NDP support was scattered, with some parliamentary seats in the West and some in the Eastern part of the country.

The traditional Opposition (i.e., historically the second strongest and occasionally the strongest party) was the Progressive Conservatives or PC, led by Jean Charest. The PC party is, like the Liberals, a pragmatic middle-of-the-road conglomeration of varied interests. Its stand is slightly to the right of center on many issues; the distance between it and the Liberals is not great, and both policies and individuals have been known to move easily from one to the other (in fact, the 1997 national PC leader became, in 1998, the leader of the Liberal Party in Quebec). The party normally had seats from across the country, but it had been devastated in the previous election and held only two seats in 1997.

All forecasts were that the Liberals would be returned with a majority of seats, the opposition being scattered among four other parties; the major questions were: how large a majority, who would be the official Opposition, and would the PC Party stage a comeback?

Table 2.5 shows the complexity levels of the party leaders in speeches prior to the election. The overall level of complexity in most cases reached only the category of low differentiation. This compares unfavorably with almost all American presidents (even Clinton), most of whom had scores in the 2–3 range during election campaigns (Tetlock, 1981). It was, however, well within the range of all but two Canadian party leaders in 10 elections between 1945 and 1974. The two exceptions were Lester Pearson in 1958 and Pierre Trudeau in 1972, both of whom scored around 2.3 (Suedfeld, Bluck, Ballard, & Baker-Brown, 1990). The overall differences among the 1997 leaders were not striking, but the pattern across leaders and domains is informative.

Two topics, federal-provincial relations (labeled "Intergov't" in the table) and the economy, elicited higher complexity from most leaders than did other domains. The exception was McDonough's low score in the former area, one that was not highly emphasized in the NDP's platform. However, McDonough's complexity was fairly low overall, perhaps a trait factor but similar to young NDP supporters assessed in an earlier study (Suedfeld, Bluck, Loewen, & Elkins, 1994). We had expected her to show high complexity when discussing her party's health and social programs and job programs, two areas of great concern to the NDP and its left-wing and

Table 2.5
Complexity Level of Canadian Campaign Speeches: June 1997 Federal Election

			Leader (Party)		
TOPIC	Chretien (LIB)	Duceppe (BLOC)	Manning (REFORM)	McDonough (NDP)	Charest (PC)
Health/Social	1.7	1.8	1.1	1.4	1.5
National Unity	1.8	1.4	1.6	1.5	1.5
Criticism	1.3	1.0	1.4	1.1	1.2
Jobs	1.9	1.4	1.5	1.2	1.7
Intergovernmental	1.9	2.4	2.1	1.1	1.8
Campaign	1.3	1.0	1.8	1.4	1.3
Own Party					1.9
Economy	2.4		2.6	1.6	2.6
All	1.7	1.4	1.7	1.4	1.6

organized labor supporters, but this was not apparent in her scores. On the other hand, we were not surprised at the low level of complexity with which she criticized the other parties, a predicted characteristic for an ideologically committed leader.

Gilles Duceppe also leads an ideologically based party. He, however, showed high complexity when dealing with the relations between the federal and provincial governments, a perennially crucial issue in Quebec and the focus of constant negotiation and debate. It is interesting to see that Duceppe did not show either very high or very low complexity in the area of national unity, a matter that is the raison d'être of his party.

The Prime Minister, primarily concerned with defending his administration's record, showed fairly high overall complexity. He is known as an outstanding defuser of political landmines, able to deflect criticism and put a positive spin on almost any mistake. Given that his party had been making the decisions in all domains, it is not surprising that he was able to articulate relatively complex policies in particularly important areas such as health and social programs, national unity, intergovernmental relations, and the economic situation.

Preston Manning was a surprise to members of my research group. Because he is a conservative populist with "politically incorrect" views on many topics, my liberal (although not necessarily Liberal) academic apprentices expected him to score at the bottom of the complexity scale. Instead, he functioned at the same level as the Prime Minister, the two of them leading the group overall. Manning showed particularly high complexity in dealing with the economy and intergovernmental relations, in

Table 2.6
Complexity Scores for Topics in the 1997 Speech from the Throne

Topic	M Complexity
A new century for Canadian achievement	3.5
Creating opportunity for young Canadians	3.4
Knowledge and creativity	3.2
Investing in our children	3.0
Looking outward	2.8
Health and health care	2.2
All topics	2.9

both of which areas the Reform Party has a highly articulated platform that differs radically from the mainstream: enthusiastic about private enterprise on the one hand and about decentralization on the other. It just goes to show that, as I have always said, any policy or decision can be developed through any level of structural complexity.

Jean Charest is generally considered a thoughtful and moderate leader, but among the general topics only economic policy seemed to engage his complex thinking. Throughout the campaign, he was deeply concerned with rebuilding a moribund party whose decline had been unprecedented in Canadian history. On the topic of his own party, which no other leader addressed at length, he was indeed complex.

The Liberals, by the way, did win the election, with a commanding parliamentary majority. The Reform Party took over second place as the official Opposition, the Bloc Quebecois kept the majority of seats from that province, and both the NDP and the Progressive Conservatives increased their representation, but not by very much.

The Throne Speech, 1997

The next major political utterance was the Speech from the Throne, which is delivered by the Governor General of Canada (the representative of the monarch) at the opening session of each new Parliament. The speech is written by representatives of the government—that is, the party that has a majority in the Parliament, in this case the Liberals—and reflects the concerns and thinking of that party's leaders.

We scored the Throne Speech given immediately after the 1997 election. As seen in Table 2.6, the speech showed substantially higher complexity overall than did the campaign speeches, including those of the leader of the Liberals, Prime Minister Jean Chretien.

On most of the topics mentioned, with the striking exception of health care—where the government had been strongly criticized and problems were pressing—the Throne Speech was well differentiated. On several, particularly those dealing with the 21st century and the next generation, it approached integration. It may be that, with the stresses of the election over and the government again safely in their hands, the Liberals could turn their attention from immediate economic and social problems and consider, in a relatively complex way, how to deal with the more distant but rapidly approaching future.

CONCLUSION

Based on these diverse data sets, I think it is safe to conclude that complexity does vary across domains to some extent. How much? It's too early to tell. The data presented here generally support both the cognitive manager and the disruptive stress models, although not uniformly; for example, the Canadian election results showed that complexity did not always peak with the topics that were presumably most salient in the political thinking of the various party leaders.

It is clear that there are complexity patterns that do not change much from situation to situation. President Clinton's flat curve is one example and may be a function of trait complexity. Incidentally, a previous study (Wallace & Suedfeld, 1988) found similarly stable, but high, complexity among several statesmen who successfully continued to occupy high governmental positions throughout a succession of difficult crises.

No one has yet looked systematically at how different traditions of political and other discourse may affect complexity across cultures. Earlier research had not shown significant differences in materials emanating from different countries or even different centuries. One possible exception was that speeches of the U.N. delegates of the United States and Israel during the period 1947 to 1976 were generally higher than those of the U.S.S.R. and the United Arab Republic; however, these differences could also be explained by situational pressures that varied among those nations (Suedfeld, Tetlock, & Ramirez, 1977).

Perhaps the low complexity of Canadian campaign speeches compared with those of U.S. presidential candidates is due to a cultural factor related to traditions in electioneering, although other hypotheses are tenable. It is clearly not a function of the style of political discourse in general, given the high level of complexity in the Throne Speech (a change that is consistent with the usual pre- to post-election increase among victorious leaders).

It appears that the interactive variables determining the level of complexity in various situations are complicated. To remove confounded effects and clarify how each factor influences the outcome may require systematic manipulation rather than merely inferences or correlational patterns.

Therefore, future researchers may need to expand their use of experimental, as opposed to only archival, research methods.

I believe that when disruptive stress sets in, interdomain differences will collapse; but we need studies that follow information processing from the first response to a problem until its resolution or resource depletion, preferably correlated with an actual measure of how important the problem solver judges the problem to be and his or her expectations of success. Optimally, both of these variables would be followed over time.

In some situations, it might prove interesting to correlate complexity differences with measures of expertise across topics. It has been suggested that people who are experts in a field would perceive fine distinctions and subtle relationships that would be opaque to the novice. In other research, comparing complexity in areas of varying importance with a measure of trait complexity like the Paragraph Completion Test would assess both the degree to which the trait factor establishes a general baseline and the degree to which situational factors induce variability around that baseline.

Another concern arises from the problems confronting President Clinton at the time of this writing, in September 1998. It would be useful to be able to predict how a decision maker might address different issues arising simultaneously, such as a national leader trying to establish important public policy while at the same time dealing with a serious personal problem. The question of how the unfolding of one situation would affect strategy in the other domain is of both theoretical and practical importance. This, and other intriguing questions, must wait upon further research.

NOTE

Portions of this chapter were included in a presentation, "Domain specificity in the integrative complexity of political leaders," to the International Congress of Applied Psychology, San Francisco, CA, August 1998. I am grateful to the Social Sciences and Humanities Research Council of Canada for the financial support that has made my research on integrative complexity possible, and to Erin Soriano for her assistance in conducting the research.

REFERENCES

Barber, J. D. (1972). *Presidential Character: Predicting Performance in the White House.* Englewood Cliffs, N.J.: Prentice-Hall.

Ertel, S. (1972). Erkenntnis und Dogmatismus. *Psychologische Rundschau, 23,* 241–269.

Freud, S., & Bullitt, W. (1966). *Thomas Woodrow Wilson: A Psychological Study.* New York: Avon.

Hermann, M. (1980). Assessing the Personalities of Soviet Politburo Members. *Personality and Social Psychology Bulletin, 6,* 332–352.

Immelman, A. (1993). The Assessment of Political Personality: A Psychodiagnostically Relevant Conceptualization and Methodology. *Political Psychology*, 14, 725–741.

Iremonger, L. (1970). *The Fiery Chariot: A Study of the British Prime Ministers and the Search for Love*. London: Secker & Warburg.

Panos, P. (1998). *A Test of Integrative Complexity in Political Rhetoric*. Unpublished master's thesis, North Carolina State University.

Renshon, S. A. (1996). *The Psychological Assessment of Presidential Candidates*. New York: New York University Press.

Russell, J. A., Weiss, A., & Mendelsohn, G. A. (1989). Affect Grid: A Single-Item Scale of Pleasure and Arousal. *Journal of Personality and Social Psychology*, 57, 493–502.

Schroder, H. M., Driver, M. J., & Streufert, S. (1967). *Human Information Processing*. New York: Holt, Rinehart & Winston.

Schroder, H. M., & Suedfeld, P. (Eds.) (1971). *Personality Theory and Information Processing*. New York: Ronald.

Stone, W. F. (1993). Psychodynamics, Cognitive Functioning, or Group Orientation: Research and Theory in the 1980s. In W. F. Stone, G. Lederer, & R. Christie (Eds.), *Strength and Weakness: The Authoritarian Personality Today* (pp. 159–181). New York: Springer-Verlag.

Suedfeld, P. (1992). Cognitive Managers and Their Critics. *Political Psychology*, 13, 435–453.

Suedfeld, P. (1994). President Clinton's Policy Dilemmas: A Cognitive Analysis. *Political Psychology*, 15, 337–349.

Suedfeld, P. (July 1995). The Integrative Complexity of Newt Gingrich. Paper presented at the meeting of the International Society of Political Psychology, Washington, DC.

Suedfeld, P., Bluck, S., Ballard, E. J., & Baker-Brown, G. (1990). Canadian Federal Elections: Motive Profiles and Integrative Complexity in Political Speeches and Popular Media. *Canadian Journal of Behavioural Science*, 22, 26–36.

Suedfeld, P., Bluck, S., Loewen, L., & Elkins, D. J. (1994). Sociopolitical Values and Integrative Complexity of Members of Student Political Groups. *Canadian Journal of Behavioural Science*, 26, 121–141.

Suedfeld, P., & Rank, D. A. (1976). Revolutionary Leaders: Long-Term Success as a Function of Changes in Conceptual Complexity. *Journal of Personality and Social Psychology*, 34, 169–178.

Suedfeld, P., & Tetlock, P. E. (1992). Psychological Advice about Foreign Policy Decision Making: Heuristics, Biases, and Cognitive Defects. In P. Suedfeld & P. E. Tetlock (Eds.), *Psychology and Social Policy* (pp. 51–70). New York: Hemisphere.

Suedfeld, P., Tetlock, P. E., & Ramirez, C. (1977). War, Peace, and Integrative Complexity: UN Speeches on the Middle East Problem, 1947–1976. *Journal of Conflict Resolution*, 21, 427–442.

Suedfeld, P., & Wallace, M. D. (1995). President Clinton as a Cognitive Manager. In S. A. Renshon (Ed.), *The Clinton Presidency: Campaigning, Governing, and the Psychology of Leadership* (pp. 215–233). Boulder, CO: Westview.

Tetlock, P. E. (1981). Pre- to Post-Election Shifts in Presidential Rhetoric: Impression Management or Cognitive Adjustment? *Journal of Personality and Social Psychology*, 41, 207–212.

Tetlock, P. E. (1985). Integrative Complexity of American and Soviet Foreign Policy Rhetoric: A Time-series Analysis. *Journal of Personality and Social Psychology*, 49, 1565–1585.

Tetlock, P. E. (1988). Monitoring the Integrative Complexity of American and Soviet Policy Rhetoric: What Can be Learned? *Journal of Social Issues*, 44, 101–132.

Tetlock, P. E. (August 1991). An Integratively Complex Look at Integrative Complexity. Paper presented at the annual meeting of the American Psychological Association, San Francisco.

Tetlock, P. E., Armor, D., & Peterson, R. (1994). The Slavery Debate in Antebellum America: Cognitive Style, Value Conflict, and the Limits of Compromise. *Journal of Personality and Social Psychology*, 66, 115–126.

Wallace, M. D., & Suedfeld, P. (1988). Leadership Performance in Crisis: The Longevity-Complexity Link. *International Studies Quarterly*, 32, 439–451.

Wallace, M. D., Suedfeld, P., & Thachuk, K. A. (1996). Failed Leader or Successful Peacemaker? Crisis, Behavior, and the Cognitive Processes of Mikhail Sergeyevitch Gorbachev. *Political Psychology*, 17, 453–472.

Winter, D. G. (1992). Content Analysis of Archival Data, Personal Documents, and Everyday Verbal Productions. In C. P. Smith (Ed.), *Motivation and Personality: Handbook of Thematic Content Analysis* (pp. 110–125). New York: Cambridge University Press.

CHAPTER 3

Political Language and the Search for an Honorable Peace: Presidents Kennedy and Johnson, Their Advisers, and Vietnam Decision Making

MOYA ANN BALL

In 1961, President John F. Kennedy made the public statement, "We are Americans, determined to defend the frontiers of freedom by an honorable peace if possible, and by armies if arms are used against us" (undated folder, 9/30/67). While researching the speech-writing practices of the Lyndon B. Johnson administration, I found numerous references to this 1961 Kennedy quote filed away in the speech files at the Johnson Presidential Library in Austin, Texas. I was not particularly surprised by this discovery, for I have argued elsewhere that, after the tragic assassination of John F. Kennedy, President Johnson seemed haunted at every turn by the Kennedy specter (Ball, 1994). It is not my purpose here to recount all the ways in which Johnson was haunted by the Kennedy persona except to point out that, during his years in presidential office, Lyndon Johnson continued a course in Vietnam policy making that had been largely forged in the Kennedy administration.

A few weeks before Kennedy's death, the prime minister of South Vietnam, Diem, and his brother, Nhu, were killed during a coup. President Kennedy and his advisers had probed the possibility of such a coup for over two years eventually encouraging it. In previous research, I have suggested that the deliberations surrounding the proposed coup had many of the characteristics of a non-decision (Ball, 1990). That is, the communication was characterized by confusion and vacillation, with a decision emerging haphazardly, propelled by specific language used by the decision makers. Repeatedly expressing a need to act before it was too late and the war was lost, Kennedy and his advisers were rooted to increased American involvement in Vietnam. Thus, there was an inertia to the coup deliberations, which, having been set in motion, kept going even though the situation in Vietnam presented a prime opportunity for American withdrawal.

Ironically, Johnson, who had argued against the Diem Coup, inherited its chaotic consequences. Forty-eight hours after taking the oath of the presidency, he, like Kennedy before him, had defined the Vietnam problem as "critical" (Wicker, 1968). From then until he announced his decision not to seek re-election in 1968, Johnson and his advisers continued to employ political language that kept them in a combat position and that prevented them from withdrawing from Vietnam. Ignoring opportunities for withdrawal had tragic ramifications. By the end of 1966, 860,000 tons of bombs had been dropped on North Vietnam (Spector, 1993). By 1968, the Vietnam War had grown so much that it was taking American lives at a rate of 25,000 a year and American resources at $30 billion a year (McPherson, March 18, 1968), to say nothing of the devastation in North and South Vietnam.

Considering this information, the question remains, "Why didn't President Johnson and his advisers seize opportunities for withdrawal when the war was taking such tragic tolls in lives and resources?" The purpose of this chapter is to try to answer that question. I wish to argue that the political language employed by presidents Kennedy and Johnson and their advisers, in private as well as in public settings, was an internal constraint that rooted them to a combat position, severely limiting the negotiation process. Specifically, I want to make these claims: (1) that the Kennedy phrase "an honorable peace" and its variations chained out through the Johnson Administration and into the public arena so much so that it affected the negotiation process in different ways; (2) that the negotiation process was hampered by a persistent linguistic theme that war was a game; (3) that the language surrounding the negotiation process was embedded with labels indicating that, at least for some of the Johnson group, negotiation was viewed as weakness; and (4) that these communication characteristics converged in such a way that the withrawal of American troops was not a viable option for Lyndon B. Johnson and his advisers.

Before moving on to theoretical assumptions of this study and then my analysis, it should be pointed out that an enormous body of research has been carried out on the Vietnam War and that to summarize it would, at minimum, result in a lengthy monograph. Some key works dealing with the Vietnam War, though, include Irving Janis's germinal work *Victims of Groupthink* (1972), Larry Berman's *Planning a Tragedy* (1982), and *Lyndon Johnson's War* (1989), in which he maintains that Johnson manipulated his advisers in order to legitimize the war to the public. Other authors have traced the development of the Vietnam War over a period of years, suggesting that the war was a culmination of Harry Truman's containment policy (Herring, 1986) or that it was a complex reaction to strategies used by Hanoi (Smith, 1985). Perhaps the most richly documented works are the volumes written by Gibbons (1986), who traces the war meticulously in exceptional volumes.

More recently, Barrett (1993) and McMaster (1997) have approached some of my own work, in that Barrett has examined the role of Johnson's advisers in the Vietnam War and McMaster has looked at the relationship between Johnson, McNamara, and the Joint Chiefs of Staff. As all these authors, however, are either historians, political scientists, or social scientists, and so they have not approached their analyses from specialized communication perspectives. Some of them, too, have relied on secondary accounts because their work was carried out without access to more recently declassified documents.

As far as the communication discipline is concerned, few scholars have studied the Vietnam decision-making process of presidents Kennedy and Johnson and their advisers. Turner (1985) and Zarefsky (1986) have carried out in-depth studies of the Johnson Administration, although neither has examined the private communication of Johnson and his advisers. Bostdorff (1994) has carried out an in-depth analysis of the crisis rhetoric of several presidents, including Lyndon Johnson; and Olson (1995) has produced a major work on the role of Senator Mike Mansfield and the Vietnam War. In short, there is much room left for analyses of the political language employed by these presidents and their advisers in private as well as in public contexts.

THEORETICAL ASSUMPTION

Before substantiating my former claims with an analysis of the communication of presidents Kennedy and Johnson and their advisers, it is necessary to explain this study's theoretical assumptions as well as its method. As a communication scholar I agree with Kenneth Burke (1966), a rhetorical critic, when he writes that "we use words, words use us." In fact, Burke's idea is ancient, having its roots in Homer's "violent thoughts lead to violent words lead to violent deeds" (Enos, 1993), attesting to the same intimate relationship between speaking and acting. Isocrates, too, implies that speaking can help train a moral consciousness, and that the arguments we use to persuade others are the same employed on our own thoughts (1988). In other words, when we persuade others, we persuade ourselves, a phenomenon that has been confirmed by social scientists in the 20th century (Hart, 1987). Even the feminist author Susan Faludi has written about the transforming effect of speaking in public. According to Faludi, "until you translate personal words on a page into public connections with people, you aren't really part of a public movement . . . women need to be heard not just to change the world, but to change themselves" (1992). If words have a self-persuasive, self-modifying effect, they also serve to frame and define our experiences of the world. Kenneth Burke (1989) would call this linguistic effect a "terministic screen," in that reality is screened, reflected, deflected, and even distorted by the terminologies we use. In other words, the terms we use affect the nature of our observations of the world. Such effects are amplified when people use language over a period of time and, when that language is repeated by others, chaining out in such a way that the result is called "symbolic convergence" (see Bormann, 1982). In effect, symbolic convergence occurs when groups of people share a common language, a language embellished with similar themes, metaphors, and other figures of speech. Eventually, they begin to share a common view of reality, a social reality in which are embedded common values, attitudes, and beliefs that then become an impetus for decision and action. It is my argument here that the political language of presidents Kennedy and Johnson and their advisers converged in such a way that the option of withdrawing troops was constantly undermined.

METHOD

In order to answer my basic research question, the bulk of this chapter is based on primary sources collected from the Lyndon Baines Johnson Presidential Library in Austin, Texas, and the John F. Kennedy Presidential Library in Boston, Massachusetts. During visits to these libraries over the last 15 years, I have gathered several thousand pages of photocopied documents. These documents include letters and memoranda circulated among presidents Johnson and Kennedy and their advisers; transcripts of group meetings; meeting agenda and notes; cables sent between Washington, D.C., and Saigon; official department histories regarding the Vietnam War; public speeches; and oral history interviews of key personnel. In examining this rich data, I looked for specific patterns of communication and symbolization. I have attempted to fill in any gaps in the information provided by these primary sources by referring to well-documented secondary accounts. Essentially, then, this study is a combination of rhetorical criticism and historical analysis. A rhetorical perspective brings back the human focus in historical research, and the historical record places rhetorical discourse in its context. A rhetorical perspective ultimately prods us to ask what persuasive discourse means in its historical context. As we begin to consider that meaning, we are playing the role of critic.

ANALYSIS: AN HONORABLE PEACE AND ITS
VARIATIONS

After President Johnson and his advisers had decided to greatly increase American involvement in Vietnam and had announced this decision in July 1965, a meeting was held to discuss information problems. At that meeting, Greenfield made the prophetic comment, "we are involved in too many cliches . . . for example, we should look again at 'our country's honor is at stake'; one day we may be sorry that we are tied too closely to this stand" (memorandum, dinner meeting, August 4, 1965). Greenfield, however, was not at the center of the decision-making circle, and so his comment seemed to fall on deaf ears. In fact, the president and his key advisors had been tied to this cliche since their days in the Kennedy administration. President Kennedy and his "new frontiersmen" had seen themselves on a mission to restore the United States' reputation, power, and prestige. Accordingly, a powerful symbolic theme portrayed their need to prove that the United States was not a "paper tiger." For instance, Walt Rostow, a member of the State Department, wrote that Vietnam was the place where "in the Attorney General's [Robert Kennedy] phrase—we must prove that we are not a paper tiger" (letter, April 21, 1961). Actually, the phrase had originated with the Chinese who, Senator Dodd told then Vice-President Lyndon Johnson, had put forward the "propaganda line" after the Bay of Pigs incident, saying, "America is a paper tiger, America will sell you short" (telegram, May 13, 1961). Another version of this linguistic theme went, "Our troubles with the British and French in SEATO have permitted us a bit of the luxury of the drunk at the bar who cries 'let me at 'em' while making sure he is firmly held by his pals" (Rostow, August 17, 1961). In the next few years, the Kennedy and Johnson decision makers would wrestle with ways to prove they were not paper tigers to the point that restoring the United States' prestige and power became both a personal and a political test.

South Vietnam became a test case of the Johnson administration's competency as well as the United States' ability to confront communism. Essentially, South Vietnam became the prize in a much greater struggle between two dominant ideologies: communism and capitalism. As the Johnson group prepared to send thousands of troops to South Vietnam, Department of Defense member John McNaughton observed that of the United States' aims in Vietnam, 70 percent was directed to "preserving its national honor" (unsigned document, July 13, 1965). President Johnson gave yet another version, "the negotiators, the pause, all other approaches—have been explored. It makes us look weak—with cup in hand" (meeting notes, July 21, 1965). This "paper tiger" echo was heard also when McGeorge Bundy (National Security Adviser) said to the president that if the United States gave up bombing, "they will reach the conclusion that we are weak and ready to quit" (January 24, 1966). Secretary of Defense Robert McNamara said that the option of withdrawal would be under "conditions humbling to the United States and very damaging to our future effectiveness on the world scene" (July 20, 1965). At the same time, and in response to Under-Secretary of State George Ball's opposition to any escalation of the war, Johnson remarked, "Wouldn't all these countries say Uncle Sam is a paper tiger—wouldn't we lose credibility breaking the word of these presidents" (meeting notes, July 21, 1965). Here, of course, Johnson was referring to President Kennedy and others who had vowed to support South Vietnam. Another adviser, James Thomson, also outside the power circle of decision makers, perceptively wrote that "American national honor" only stood or fell "as a direct result of their own rhetoric and actions" (July 1965).

Systematically, therefore, an honorable peace became associated with such characteristics as not being a paper tiger, not going to the bargaining table in a weak position, not eroding the country's prestige, not humiliating themselves, and, consequently, not withdrawing. To withdraw was to admit one's weakness. For instance, in December 1965, General Taylor, then U.S. Ambassador to Saigon, wrote to the president quoting the long-deceased Sir Francis Drake, who, persevering against the Spanish Armada, said, "There must be a beginning of every matter but it is continuing to the end that yields the true glory" (December 27, 1965).

Effectively, then, such language became a terministic screen through which their decisions and actions were filtered. This filtering affected the negotiation process in several ways. When negotiation was discussed, it was often in the context of attaining an honorable peace. Ambassador to South Vietnam Ellsworth Bunker wanted a "just, durable, and honorable peace" (cable, January 16, 1969). According to Special Assistant Jack Valenti, the United States could "never achieve a settlement that [was] honorable" until "they had demonstrated to the VC [Viet Cong] and Hanoi that they can't win" (memorandum, January 25, 1966). In this way, an "honorable peace" was endowed with a sacredness that effectively prevented them from just withdrawing without having further damaged or punished North Vietnam.

During 1967, the war had noticeably turned sour. By the end of that year there were about 485,000 U.S. troops in South Vietnam, riots had rocked American cities, and angry antiwar protesters had marched on the White House and the Pentagon. Press Secretary George Reedy had left for the Struthers Corporation, Special Assistant Horace Busby had left to practice Law, Special Assistant Jack Valenti was heading up the Motion Picture Association, Press Secretary Bill Moyers was working for *Newsday*, and National Security Adviser McGeorge Bundy had gone to the Ford Foundation. Even Robert McNamara had started to wobble from his hawk-like position, announcing his intention to head up the World Bank. At this time, a meeting was held with a group that was dubbed "the wise men"—a group of outside advisers who were known for their experience in foreign policy and war issues. At this meeting, General Omar Bradley advised the president to "talk less about negotiation" because "Hanoi would see it as a sign of weakness" (memorandum, November 3, 1967). At the same meeting, McGeorge Bundy, still an influential adviser even though he no longer worked in the White House, stated unequivocally that the United States should not "pull out" of Vietnam (memorandum, November 10, 1967). In the next three months, though, the United States faced one of its greatest setbacks in the Vietnam War.

On January 30, 1968, the North Vietnamese launched the Tet Offensive, Tet being the Vietnamese New Year, a time for family reunions and celebrations. During February, American casualties reached an all-time high, and in one week 543 were killed and 2,542 wounded (NSC History of March 31 Speech). Even so, the North Vietnamese secured a psychological rather than a military victory, for records indicate that at least 58,000 of them were killed during this time (C. Clifford, 1991). The American public's confidence was shattered. The North Vietnamese had demonstrated that they were greater in number, more daring, and more resolute than anyone had imagined. As a military response to this realization, General Wheeler submitted a bleak report at the end of February, as well as General Westmoreland's request for 205,179 additional troops (February 27, 1968).

On March 19, 1968, James Rowe, another valued outside adviser, wrote a memorandum with the title, "Peace with Honor in Vietnam" (March 19, 1968). He urged the president to "do something exciting and dramatic to recapture the peace issue," noting that after Tet "everyone has turned into a dove" and that, consequently, Johnson should become the "peace with honor candidate" in the 1968 presidential election. The preceding examples demonstrate how, from 1961 to 1968, the phrase "peace with honor" or an "honorable peace" and variations permeated the communication of the two presidents and their advisers. For them, a peace that was honorable could never be unconditional. Honor was associated with strength and superiority and so peace would be negotiated on U.S., not Vietnamese terms. On March 21, 1968, the Postmaster General wrote to Johnson, "I do not believe we can or should withdraw" (O'Brien, March 21, 1968). For Johnson and most of his advisers, withdrawal was an admission of weakness. Thus, the overtly simple addition of the word "honorable" in the search for peace was a linguistic constraint that had tragic ramifications.

WAR AS A GAME

Not only was the negotiation process hampered by the Johnson Administration's search for an "honorable" peace, it was also affected greatly by the constant portrayal of war as a game. To speak of war as a game is an ancient custom. Huizinga (1950), who has studied the "play" elements of various cultures, asserts that "ever since words existed for fighting . . . men have been wont to call war a game." The majority of Greek contests were fought out in deadly earnest, yet they exhibited all of the formal and most of the functional features of a game. Huizinga goes on to suggest that a "blend of adolescence and barbarity has been rampant in the 20th century." This blending of an adolescent game mentality and a deadly earnestness was especially apparent in the Kennedy Administration's language use. John F. Kennedy had come from a family that valued physical fitness. Team games were drilled into the Kennedy brothers at an early age. Robert Kennedy once told a group of college sports coaches, "except for war, there is nothing in American life—nothing—which trains a boy better for life than football" (Clinch, 1973). This emphasis on sports resonated throughout the communication of President Kennedy and his advisers.

Foreign policy became a "gamble." Prior to Kennedy's inauguration, Khrushchev was perceived as "trying to play a pair of deuces like a royal flush" (undated paper, Foreign Policy General File), language that surely diminished the status of the enemy, the Soviet Union. Gambling allusions also were used to diminish South Vietnamese Prime Minister Diem, who was characterized as a "losing horse" (memorandum, April 6, 1962). In both the Kennedy and Johnson administrations, war as a game was enacted in a series of simulated war games played out in secret by select members (R. Gilpatric, February 1962; Sigma I-64). Critiques of these war games actually predicted failure of increased U.S. intervention but failed to make any impact on the decisionmakers. Such failure did not fit into their shared social reality, did not fit into their "honorable peace" terministic screen.

In the Johnson administration, war was a gamble, a basketball game, and a boxing match. At a cabinet meeting in 1964, the recorder noted that "the President did not wish to enter the patient in a 10-round bout when he was in no shape to hold out for one round" (memorandum, September 14, 1964). Johnson, of course, was referring here to the weakened state of the South Vietnamese Army. Later, he repeated the same theme with a slight twist when he said, "Not want to send widow woman to slap Jack Dempsey. DRV[Democratic Republic of Vietnam] will bomb Saigon once then we're off to the races . . . we could have kept Diem" (handwritten notes, December 1, 1964). Disregarding the maze of mixed metaphors, it should be noted that when war was talked about as a game, the decision makers tended to see themselves in a win or lose situation. Subsequently, the option of negotiation was negated because, at least in the United States, games are played out until there is a clear winner or loser.

There is another danger, though, to the image of war as a game: it may create a detachment from the realities of war. If war is merely a game, those involved may be playing at war, and its more realistic horrors may be submerged beneath less threatening language. The game analogy is somewhat paradoxical, though: on the one hand, it may detach the communicators from the horrors of war; on the other hand, it attaches them to a win, making it more difficult to consider an option such as withdrawal. In games, athletes withdraw only after they have been badly injured. Winning is connected to play, for it involves showing some superiority. As Huizinga points out, "honor and esteem belong to the victor" and the fruits of victory are "honor, esteem, and prestige."

Given this linguistic context in the Johnson administration, it is not too difficult now to understand how the depiction of war as a game made negotiation an unpopular option in the Vietnam deliberations and withdrawal an impossibility. In fact, the prospect of negotiation was dramatically portrayed as a high-stakes card game, particularly when it involved stopping all bombing of North Vietnam. According to Maxwell Taylor, "such a tabulation of negotiating blue chips and their purchasing power emphasizes the folly of giving up any one in advance as a precondition for negotiation. Thus, if we give up bombing in order to start discussions, we would not have the coins necessary to pay for all the concessions" (memorandum, April 27, 1966). An unsigned letter to McNamara also talks about war as a card game, indicating a need for "playing our bombing card" (December 4, 1967). In 1968, after the Tet Offensive and Lyndon Johnson's speech saying that he would not seek re-election, Ambassador Bunker wrote, "Hanoi will hold strong cards at the negotiating table and we must assume they will play them with skill . . . but, we have very strong cards, too . . . we should not hesitate to play them" (memorandum, April 8, 1968).

Interestingly (at least for any student of language), by March 1968 speeches had become part of the War Game arsenal. In a handwritten meeting record, McGeorge Bundy said that a forthcoming presidential address needed "a left hook" (handwritten record, March 20, 1968). As demonstrated previously, boxing was a favorite Lyndon Johnson metaphor. Sometimes Johnson portrayed himself as being in the boxing ring with Ho Chi Minh; at other times, he saw himself as a coach who "needed to get results" (record of meeting, February 17, 1967). At all times, at least for Lyndon Johnson, war as a game was personalized as a kind of endurance match between the leaders of the opposing sides. Once again, language served to lock the decision makers into a combat position, making it extremely difficult to consider what to them was the "humiliating" option of withdrawal.

THE NAMING OF OPERATIONS AND PEACE INITIATIVES

Problems associated with naming bombing programs and peace initiatives were evident throughout the Johnson administration and, to some extent, in the Kennedy administration, too. For example, apart from a bombing program named "Rolling Thunder," operation names were usually innocuous. In the Kennedy administration, the decision makers were anxious to maintain the impression that Prime Minister Diem was in control of any action in the Vietnam War, but this was not an easy task and it was not honest. In April 1962, the State Department was concerned that the press had implied that the United States was directing rather than supporting and training the South Vietnamese Army. In a cable to Ambassador

Nolting, Assistant Secretary of State Averill Harriman conceded that innocuous operation names such as "sunrise" and "farmgate" certainly suggested U.S. rather than Vietnamese planning (cable, April 4, 1962). Indeed, Sunrise and Farmgate were covert operations in which U.S. pilots flew American planes on bombing missions (Hilsman, March 19, 1962).

The naming of these operations gave an Orwellian twist to the making and prosecuting of war because it was another example of the way the decision makers protected themselves from the harsh realities of their actions. In a similar fashion, they talked and wrote about "reconnaissance flights," which in reality meant that "you took a plane up in the air and then shot at anything that moved" (Thomson, October 22, 1986). In a memorandum to the president, Senator Mike Mansfield criticized the use of phrases such as "targets of convenience," and Johnson replied:

I think the implied criticism of "targets of convenience" in your third paragraph is somewhat unfair. This military phrase is not a perfect one, but all that it means is that along certain carefully defined communication routes, pilots are authorized to attack whatever military targets they encounter. (April 12, 1965)

Such phrasing and the naming of operations became a form of double-speak, distorting some of the realities of the Vietnam situation. In 1964, the "peace-keeping" theme President Johnson used against Barry Goldwater's more robust stand in the presidential campaign began to disturb McGeorge Bundy. In May, Bundy had told Johnson that "the peace-keeping theme will have been at the center of the whole enterprise from the beginning" (May 25, 1964). Late that year, however, he seemed to recognize the theme's inherent deception when he wrote to the president, "we do not want the record to suggest even remotely that we campaigned on peace in order to start a war" (October 1, 1964).

Incidentally, the peace-keeping theme may have been another continuation of the Kennedy era. President Kennedy had sent Peace Corps volunteers to fight disease and famine in third-world countries at the same time he was sending Green Beret soldiers to fight in the jungles of Vietnam. Both of these endeavors were a part of the overall war against communism.

Another term that harmonized with Johnson's peace-keeping theme was "pacification." As Frederick Nolting pointed out in an oral history interview, though, it could easily be translated into war, and such a translation was an "enormous psychological error" affecting the United States as well as Vietnam (November 11, 1982). During the war, a cable sent to Johnson by Tayor alluded to the problem associated with the operation's name, informing him that the term "rural reconstruction" had been substituted for "pacification" because "it had fallen into disrepute as being negative and ill-descriptive of the liberation of the country from the Viet Cong" (April 28, 1965). The term "rural reconstruction," though, was simply another benign phrase that actually represented an attempt to camouflage an operation that removed villagers from their ancestral homes, uprooting them from the safety of familiar surroundings and from their life's work.

Such terminology encouraged a certain amount of self-delusion, to the extent that the decisionmakers became prisoners of their own rhetoric. But there were other effects, too. Operations were coded to provide some measure of secrecy; for instance, some were "top secret" and others "secret." Both the Kennedy and Johnson administrations subscribed to a normative behavior of secrecy that, ultimately, served to separate the "insiders" from the "outsiders" in the decision-making process. When certain documents and pet projects were coded as secret or top secret, they were seen as especially important; thus, even the term "secret" was used as a power tool. According to McGeorge Bundy, "It is very easy to become the prisoner of a document whose importance is asserted primarily because it has a cover sheet and a series of code words on it—a document that is somehow claiming to be important because nobody else has seen it" (February 26, 1964). The implication, therefore, is that such coding became a rhetorical device in order to gain attention and compliance. Also, insiders—those at the center of the decision-making circle—were privy to the coded documents; those on the periphery of the group were not.

Perhaps nowhere is the coding of projects more intriguing than in the series of peace initiatives undertaken in the years 1965–1968. Such initiatives were usually combined with a publicly announced bombing pause. In this way, bombing was suspended for five days in May 1965 (Cooper, 1966). In December 1965, a 37-day pause began with a Christmas truce and lasted until January 31, 1966. There is some evidence here that the pause was used as a rhetorical ploy to attain congressional support for a massive increase in defense spending. On November 17, McGeorge Bundy had been against a bombing pause, suggesting that it would signal that bombing was the cause of all the "trouble" (memorandum), but by November 27 he had seen the proposed budget and had changed his mind about the pause, implying that if it failed it would send a stronger signal to the American public, presumably a signal that the sharp increase in the budget was justified (memorandum). Interestingly, Ho Chi Minh viewed this particular pause as a "sham," saying that he would never talk until the United States agreed to accept North Vietnam's four-point stand (letter, January 29, 1966). Such bombing pauses were a part of an ineffective carrot-and-stick policy designed to bring the North Vietnamese to the negotiating table. The coding of them, however, raises intriguing questions.

According to George Herring, the first peace initiative, in the form of a bombing pause, was coded with the name "Mayflower" (1994). Following that initiative, others were coded in a similar fashion so that a Polish negotiating connection was named "Marigold," an Indian negotiating connection, "Gladiola," and another peace initiative, "Sunflower." In 1967,

Rostow referred to yet another program as "buttercup" (memorandum, November 2, 1967). Even before the overt escalation of the Vietnam War, Chester Cooper had associated a flower metaphor with the development of bombing pauses, commenting to McGeorge Bundy, "they [peace initiatives] should be permitted to blossom—if indeed Hanoi intends them to blossom" (Cooper, 1965).

Such coding is intriguing because, from the beginning of the Johnson administration, the president and some of his advisers had associated such peace initiatives and the option of negotiation as a sign of weakness and a "sell-out." Even in the Kennedy administration, there is some indication that negotiation was a "devil term." For President Kennedy and his advisers, talk was seen as passive and weak when compared to action (memorandum, November 14, 1961). At times, negotiation was referred to as "a shibboleth" (Forrestal, November 7, 1963). These negative connotations associated with negotiation continued under Johnson, being most apparent prior to the overt decision to escalate the war in 1965. In February, James Thomson wrote that negotiation involved a win-win situation, but it had been "equated with sell-out (and ultimately, treason)" (February 19, 1965). Peace settlements and negotiation, therefore, were equated with weakness, and even with betrayal. The coding of peace initiatives with flower names may be another indication of the "weakness" connotation. Flowers are often associated with femininity and fragility. Flowers bloom for a short time and then they wilt and die. Flowers are used for decoration usually, rather than for subtantive purposes. They are rarely permanent. There is another negative association with the "flower" name, or at least it would have been negative for the president and his advisers: In the 1960s, many of the young people who were peace-lovers were also referred to as "flower children," who had as their motto, "Make love, not war." Once again, the word "flower" alluded to something that was antagonistic to the Johnson group's culture.

Certainly, the code names may have been used initially to thoroughly obscure the nature of the operations; however, they reflect also what were probably persistent negative associations with negotiation and an unconditional peace. In the Johnson Administration, "peace-lover" was used in a derogatory fashion and associated with what was feminine (telegram, January 14, 1969). This feminine association was extended in an inflammatory speech Johnson made in which he referred to his critics as "nervous Nellies" (Johnson, 1987).

The preceding discussion demonstrates the interconnections between decision makers' words and their ultimate actions. With all the negative associations attached to the option of negotiation and bombing pauses, it is no wonder that America's longest war was in Vietnam.

CONCLUSION

This study has demonstrated how President Johnson and his advisers, inheriting a chaotic situation in South Vietnam after the Diem Coup in 1963, became entangled in symbolic webs that had been spun first in the Kennedy administration. Perhaps the greatest linguistic constraint in the search for a way out of Vietnam, however, was the association of peace with the decision makers' interpretation of honor. For Johnson and most of his advisers, honor implied strength and superiority. In this way, an "honorable peace" was a linguistic constraint, a symbolic cue that prevented them from considering withdrawal from Vietnam as a viable option.

Another constraint was the depiction of war as a a game, further reducing the likelihood of withdrawal. Indeed, it was an impetus for action, for continuing to fight until there was a loser and a winner. As this kind of figurative language wove its way into negotiation discussions, it converged with other linguistic choices and amplified other negative associations with peace initiatives, talks with the enemy, and bombing pauses. All of these negative associations converged to form a social reality of the Vietnam situation from which there seemed no "honorable" escape. Entangled in symbolic webs of significance they themselves had spun, both the Kennedy and Johnson administrations missed key opportunities for withdrawal in 1963, 1964, and 1965. Each opportunity was followed by a slow and deadly increase in the widening of the war.

In 1968, the Tet Offensive was the straw that broke Johnson's back. It and the response of the American people shocked the president and his advisers. On March 31, Johnson gave a major public speech in which he put forward some peace overtures to Hanoi and then made the surprising announcement that he would not seek re-election. Thus, Lyndon B. Johnson rather than withdrawing from Vietnam, withdrew himself. During the remainder of his presidency, the war dragged on; in 1968, 182,740 enemies were killed as well as 23,884 South Vietnamese military and 14,491 American soldiers, to say nothing of injuries and deaths sustained by the civilian population. Perhaps Johnson retired so that he could retreat with honor, but surely there was little honor in the shedding of so much blood.

REFERENCES

Ball, M. A. (1990). A Case Study of the Kennedy Administration's Decision-Making Concerning the Diem Coup of November 1963. *Western Journal of Speech Communication,* 54:4, 557–574.

Ball, M. A. (1994). The Phantom of the Oval Office: The John F. Kennedy Assassination's Symbolic Impact on Lyndon B. Johnson, His Key Advisers, and the Vietnam Decision-Making Process. *Presidential Studies Quarterly,* 24:1, 105–119.

Barrett, D. (1993). *Uncertain Warriors*. Lawrence: University of Kansas Press.

Berman, L. (1982). *Planning a Tragedy*. New York: W. W. Norton and Company.

Berman, L. (1989). *Lyndon Johnson's War*. New York: W. W. Norton and Company.

Bormann, E. G. (1982). Fantasy and Rhetorical Vision: Ten Years Later. *Quarterly Journal of Speech*, 68, 288–305.

Bostdorff, D. M. (1994). *The Presidency and the Rhetoric of Foreign Crisis*. Columbia: University of South Carolina Press.

Bundy, M. (February 26, 1964). Talk to Overseas Writers. Box 1. Aides File—Bundy. National Security File. Lyndon Baines Johnson Library, Austin, TX.

Bundy, M. (May 25, 1964). Memorandum to President. Box 19. Aides File. NSF. Lyndon Baines Johnson Library, Austin, TX.

Bundy, M. (October 1, 1964). Memorandum to President. Box 2. Bundy Memos. NSF. Lyndon Baines Johnson Library, Austin, TX.

Bundy, M. (November 17, 1965). Memorandum to President. Box 5. Aides File—Bundy. NSF. Lyndon Baines Johnson Library, Austin, TX.

Bundy, M. (November 27, 1965). Memorandum to President. Box 5. Lyndon Baines Johnson Library, Austin, TX.

Bundy, M. (January 24, 1966). Memorandum to President. Box 92–94. Countries—Vietnam. National Security File. Lyndon Baines Johnson Library, Austin, TX.

Bundy, M. (November 10, 1967). Memorandum to President. Box 1. Reference File—Vietnam. Lyndon Baines Johnson Library, Austin, TX.

Bunker, E. (April 8, 1968). Box 95–96. Countries—Vietnam. NSF. Lyndon Baines Johnson Library, Austin, TX.

Bunker. E. (January 16, 1969). Cable to President. Box 259–260. Countries—Vietnam. NSF. Lyndon Baines Johnson Library, Austin, TX.

Burke, K. (1966). *Language as Symbolic Action*. Berkeley: University of California Press.

Burke, K. (1989). Language as Action: Terministic Screens. In J. R. Gusfield (Ed.), *On Symbols and Society*. Chicago: University of Chicago Press.

Clifford, C. (1991). *Counsel to the President*. New York: Random House.

Clinch, N. G. (1973). *The Kennedy Neurosis*. New York: Grosset and Dunlap.

Cooper, C. (January 22, 1965). Memorandum to M. Bundy. Box 27. Countries—Vietnam. NSF. Lyndon Baines Johnson Library, Austin, TX.

Cooper, C. (January 28, 1966). Memorandum to M. Bundy. Box 27. Countries—Vietnam. NSF. Lyndon Baines Johnson Library, Austin, TX.

Dodd, T. (May 13, 1961). Telegram to Lyndon B. Johnson. Box 10. Vice Presidential Security Files, Lyndon Baines Johnson Library, Austin, TX.

Enos, R. (1993). *Greek Rhetoric before Aristotle*. Prospect Heights, IL: Waveland Press.

Faludi, S. (January 1992). Speak for Yourself. *New York Times Magazine*, p. 29.

Forrestal, M. (November 7, 1963). Memorandum to M. Bundy. Box 202–203. Countries—Vietnam. National Security File. John F. Kennedy Library, Boston.

Gibbons, W. C. (1986). *The U.S. Government and the Vietnam War, Parts I and II*. Princeton, NJ: Princeton University Press.

Gilpatric, R. (February 7, 1962). Memorandum to M. Bundy. Box 231 A. Regional Security. NSF. John F. Kennedy Library, Boston.

Handwritten Notes of Executive Committee Meeting. (December 1, 1964). Notes File. Papers of Lyndon B. Johnson. Lyndon Baines Johnson Library, Austin, TX.

Handwritten Record of Meeting. (March 20, 1968). Box 271. LBJ Statements. Lyndon Baines Johnson Library, Austin, TX.

Harriman, A. (April 4, 1962). Cable to Ambassador Nolting. Box 196. Countries—Vietnam. NSF. Lyndon Baines Johnson Library, Austin, TX.

Hart, R. P. (1987). *The Sound of Leadership*. Chicago: University of Chicago Press.

Herring, G. C. (1986). *America's Longest War: The U.S. and Vietnam 1950–1975*, 2nd ed. New York: Alfred A. Knopf.

Herring, G. C. (1994). *LBJ and Vietnam*. Austin: University of Texas Press.

Hilsman, R. (March 19, 1962). Memorandum for Record. Box 3. Hilsman Papers. John F. Kennedy Library, Boston.

Huizinga, J. (1950). *Homo Ludens: A Study of the Play Element in Culture*. Boston: Beacon Press.

Isocrates. (1988). *Against the Sophists and Antodosis*. In Benson T. and M. H. Prosser (Eds.), *Readings in Classical Rhetoric* (pp. 47–52). Davis, CA: Hermagoras Press.

Janis, I. (1972). *Victims of Groupthink*. Boston: Houghton-Mifflin Company.

Johnson, L. B. (April 12, 1965). Letter to Senator M. Mansfield. Papers of LBJ. Lyndon Baines Johnson Library, Austin, TX.

Johnson, L. B. (1987). Remarks at Democratic Party Dinner, May 17, 1966. In T. Windt, *Presidential Rhetoric*. Dubuque, IA: Kendall/Hunt Publishing Company.

Kennedy, J. F. (November 14, 1961). Memorandum to D. Rusk and R. McNamara. Box 128. President's Office Files. John F. Kennedy Library, Boston.

McMaster, H. R. (1997). *Dereliction of Duty*. New York: HarperCollins Publishers.

McNamara, R. (July 20, 1965). Memorandum to President. Box 4. Aides File. NSF. Lyndon Baines Johnson Library, Austin, TX.

McPherson, H. (March 18, 1968). Memorandum to President. Box 53. Office Files of H. McPherson. Lyndon Baines Johnson Library, Austin, TX.

Meeting Notes. (July 21, 1965). By J. Valenti. 10:00 A.M. Box 2. DSDUF. Lyndon Baines Johnson Library, Austin, TX.

Memorandum for Record of Meeting. (September 14, 1964). Box 2. Aides File. NSF. Library. Lyndon Baines Johnson Library, Austin, TX.

Memorandum for the Record. (August 4, 1965). Dinner Meeting. Box 196, 197. Countries—Vietnam. National Security File. Lyndon Baines Johnson Library, Austin, TX.

Memorandum of Conversation. (April 6, 1962). President, A. Harriman, M. V. Forrestal. Box 320–321. Meetings and Memoranda. NSF. John F. Kennedy Library, Boston.

Minh, H. C. (January 29, 1966). Letter. *New York Times*. Box 27. Countries—Vietnam. NSF. Lyndon Baines Johnson Library, Austin, TX.

National Security Council History of March 31 Speech. Box 47. NSF. Lyndon Baines Johnson Library, Austin, TX.

Nolting, F. (November 11, 1982). Oral History Interview by Ted Gittinger. Lyndon Baines Johnson Library, Austin, TX.

O'Brien, L. (March 21, 1968). Memorandum to President. Box 5. File of W. Rostow. NSF. Lyndon Baines Johnson Library, Austin, TX.

Olson, G. A. (1995). *Mansfield and Vietnam*. East Lansing: Michigan State University Press.

Record of Meeting with President. (February 17, 1967). Box 7. Files of W. Rostow. NSF. Lyndon Baines Johnson Library, Austin, TX.

Rostow, W. R. (April 21, 1961). Memorandum to the President. Box 64A. Staff Memoranda, President's Office Files. John F. Kennedy Library, Boston.

Rostow, W. R. (August 17, 1961). Memo to President. Staff Memoranda. POF. John F. Kennedy Library, Boston.

Rostow, W. R. (November 2, 1967). Memorandum to President. Box 127. Countries—Vietnam. NSF. Lyndon Baines Johnson Library, Austin, TX.

Rostow, W. R. (November 3, 1967). Memorandum re: Meeting to President. Box 25. Memos to President. NSF. Lyndon Baines Johnson Library, Austin, TX.

Rowe, J. (March 19, 1968). Memorandum to President. Box 30. Files of M. Watson. Lyndon Baines Johnson Library, Austin, TX.

Sigma I-64 Critique. (April 6–9, 1964). Box 30–33. Agency File. Joint Chiefs of Staff. NSF. Lyndon Baines Johnson Library, Austin, TX.

Smith, R. B. (1985). *An International History of the Vietnam War*. New York: St. Martin's Press.

Spector, R. A. (1993). *After Tet*. New York: Vintage Books.

Taylor, M. (April 28, 1965). Cable to President. Box 3. Bundy Memos. NSF. Lyndon Baines Johnson Library, Austin, TX.

Taylor, M. (December 27, 1965). Memorandum to President. Box 259–260. Countries—Vietnam. NSF. Lyndon Baines Johnson Library, Austin, TX.

Taylor, M. (April 27, 1966). Memorandum to President. Box 259–260. Countries—Vietnam. NSF. Lyndon Baines Johnson Library, Austin, TX.

Telegram. (January 14, 1969). Saigon Embassy to Secretary of State. Box 259–260. Countries—Vietnam. NSF. Lyndon Baines Johnson Library, Austin, TX.

Thomson, J. C. (February 19, 1965). Memorandum to M. Bundy. Box 40. NSC History. NSF. Lyndon Baines Johnson Library, Austin, TX.

Thomson. J. C. (July 1965). Incomplete Draft. Box 26. Papers of J. C. Thomson. John F. Kennedy Library, Boston.

Thomson, J. C. (October 22, 1986). Conversation with M. Ball. Boston.

Turner, K. J. (1985). *Lyndon Johnson's Dual War: Vietnam and the Press*. Chicago: University of Chicago Press.

Undated Notes, Folder "9/30/97," Box 247, Statements of Lyndon B. Johnson. Lyndon Baines Johnson Library, Austin, TX.

Undated Paper. Foreign Policy General File. Box 540. Papers of Pre-Presidency. John F. Kennedy Library, Boston.

Unsigned Document. (July 13, 1965). Analysis and Options for South Vietnam. McNaughton Files. Papers of Paul Warnke. Lyndon Baines Johnson Library, Austin, TX.

Unsigned Letter. (December 4, 1967). Box 3. Files of W. Rostow. NSF. Lyndon Baines Johnson Library, Austin, TX.

Valenti, J. (January 25, 1966). Memorandum to President. Box 27. Countries—Vietnam. NSF. Lyndon Baines Johnson Library, Austin, TX.

Wheeler, B. (February 27, 1968). Memorandum to President. Box 47. NSC History. NSF. Lyndon Baines Johnson Library, Austin, TX.

Wicker, T. (1968). *JFK and LBJ: The Influence of Personality upon Politics.* New York: William Morrow and Company.

Zarefsky, D. (1986). *President Johnson's War on Poverty.* Tuscaloosa: University of Alabama Press.

CHAPTER 4

The Eyesore of the Beholder: Beauty as Political Discourse in the 1998 Venezuelan Presidential Elections

MARITZA MONTERO

The 1998 election in Venezuela, contrary to previous occasions, had a batch of candidates surprisingly different with respect to traditional leaders running for that office in the past. The three leading competitors did not emerge or develop within established political parties, while some natural party leaders, due to their loss of credibility, had to step aside to give way to these new candidates, whose distinctive characteristic was to present themselves as having nothing to do with that type of organization. It is these "new" leaders, insistently "independent" and alienated from party organizations, who filled the first places in the polls, and later one of them, Hugo Chávez Frías, won the election by an ample 56 percent of the vote. The better part of their efforts and public communications went to demonstrate that they were not contaminated by the status parties, while paradoxically at least two of them, Irene Sáez and Enrique Salas Romer, tried to attract the support of those same parties from which they wished to appear so distant. Chávez Frías (age 44), ex-participant in a coup d'état, willing to interrupt the democratic continuity in 1992, in 1998 sought the presidency of the Republic as leader of the group that then supported him and that had transformed into an electoral movement. Claudio Fermín (46), in a move which was electorally fatal for him, confronted Acción Democrática, the party of which he had been a prominent member, thus acquiring a certain not-too-convincing independence. Salas Romer (61), an independent who formerly had Social Christian inclinations, likewise appeared as free from any party ties. And Sáez (36), the former Miss Venezuela (1980), Miss South America (1980), and Miss Universe (1981), whose political discourse is the subject of this analysis, declared herself to be apolitical and independent, thus performing a political action: while pointing out her absence of ties with the parties that courted her due to her popularity during 1997, when she was the only one overtly declaring her presidential aspirations, she did not refuse their organization, votes, and support. All of this had a rather astute appearance if one took into account that her support group, I.R.E.N.E. (the spanish acronym for Integration, Renovation, New Hope), lacked the experience, machinery, and trained supporters of the traditional parties.

WHY A DISCOURSE ANALYSIS?

Discourse analysis is a method of giving systematic access, not only to the explicit contents of communications, but also to the messages and intentions hidden between the lines. In the case of political discourses, it has particular interest inasmuch as such discourses constitute affirmation systems which construct (and sometimes destroy) political actors, government programs, and power structures and relationships, besides affecting the development of civil life because they are aimed at the public field and happen within the public space. Therefore, a discourse analysis pays attention not only to the explicit contents of the text, but also to the spatial and temporal environment within which it is presented; and to the differences contained in the text, comparing them within the same version and with versions of other texts by the same author. It pays attention as well to the details, regardless of how small they may seem; it seeks the rhetorical organization, that is, the arguments constructed to convince, dissuade, or attract those persons to whom the text is addressed. Likewise, it attempts to demonstrate the responsibility for the statements, suggestions, accusations, interpretations, and in general the information presented in the discourse (Edwards & Potter, 1992; Montero & Rodríguez, 1998). Within the discourse analysis a deconstruction process takes place consisting of the decomposition of the structures supporting the conceptual construction of the argument system used in the text. This is carried out in order to know about its relationship with other concepts or descriptions, its mode of configuration, and its sense within the text. The analysis tries to present the hidden face of the discourse, the underground currents which flow through it with more or less turbulence, bringing to the surface the non-manifest but intense and basic interests of the discourse's author. A discourse goes beyond what is spoken or written; it is not limited to verbal language but comprises as well actions accompanying the text.

It is in this sense that the discourse of Irene Sáez will be analyzed. If something characterized Sáez's discourse, that was expressing herself more in actions and physical presence than verbally. At the same time, her candidature represented a deviation from tradition that could not be ignored. She is a woman, young and beautiful; she does not militate in an established political party; her political performance is of recent date (twice mayor of a Caracas district during the 1990s); and she has been and, regardless of her efforts to the contrary, continues to be connected to a social sphere characterized by frivolity, although as I have mentioned elsewhere (Montero, 1998), not at all exempt from organization and success: the Venezuelan beauty pageants.

THE CORPUS ANALYZED

The corpus of this analysis comprised 20 press satements of Irene Sáez published in the newspapers *El Universal* and *El Nacional,* with national coverage, between November 1997 and April 1998, and 47 photographs appearing in the magazines *Variedades, Bohemia, Feriado* (Venezuelan), *Hola* (Spanish with Latin American coverage), *Vanidades* (Latin American), *Madame Figaro,* and *Paris Match* (French), published during the same period. The period covers the moment when Sáez explicitly manifested that she was running for president, and the moment when she officially registered as a competitor for the presidency. A characteristic of this corpus is that, contrary to what usually occurs with the presidential candidates, Irene Sáez did not disdain to appear in what in Spain has been termed as "the press of the heart" (pulp romance and jet-set stories). In fact, magazines of this type were not only the first to publish the most extensive and detailed reports on the political rise of Irene Sáez, but besides that, frequently include brief notes about her trips or attendance to international social events, illustrated by color photographs of her.

THE METHOD

The analysis was based on the hermeneutics perspective (Gadamer, 1976), combined with a rhetorical deconstructionist approach. It started from an anticipatory project already described in the preceding paragraphs: to know the meaning of the political discourse of Irene Sáez, deciphering what is generally designated as "political thought," considering the public verbal expression referring to her political activity and the image presented along with that activity in her photographs. In order to do this I had to repeatedly read the verbal texts and examine the photographic texts, taking into account and analyzing the different possible projects which might derive from the knowledge so acquired. And then I contrasted the verbal text with the iconic texts, the word with the physical image, presented by both the Venezuelan newspapers and the above-mentioned magazines.

In this manner, categories for the analysis were developed, and discarded, merging, dividing, increasing, or decreasing, according to each new reading and its interpretation. These continuous readings followed the pattern hereunder shown:

- General understanding of the texts.

- Distinction between textual quotations and summaries made by the journalists responsible for the edition of such texts in each publication, discarding the latter.

- Separation and classification of the contents by subject (a sort of content analysis).

- Re-structurations of the system for classification of topics.

- Initial description of Irene Sáez's discourse style (first level of analysis).

- Search for the main ideas or ideas-theme, or related, subordinate, and isolated ideas.

- Identification of expressions more frequently used in each discourse and in the corpus (second level of discourse).

- Identification of argumentative strategies and grammatical figures (third level of discourse).

THE ANALYSIS

First Level of Description

An initial approach shows that often Sáez's discourse is punctuated by silences and accompanied by her photographic image (photos more than double verbal texts). Her verbal discourse is plain, brief, characterized by short phrases, in which deixis (the assumption of responsibilities for the contents of the phrase; or accountability) abound: "I believe," "I am conscious," "I am," "I join," "I do not have fear . . .". With this Irene Sáez, like many a politician, and in general like those persons used to attracting attention are inclined to do, places herself at the center of the discourse as its main actor. This is particularly evident inasmuch as a great part of her discourse is devoted to defining herself, talking about herself, explaining to the public who is Irene Sáez. Some examples of that discourse say:

It is said that I am not qualified, many things are being said and even worse things will be said (*Univ.*, p. 1-12, 1/31/98). I am practicing my profession, my vocation (*Univ.*, p. 1-12, 1/31/98). . . . I have begun to assume responsibilities, to profoundly reflect, to prepare myself, and I am doing this with the greatest responsibility, with a proposal, and at the right moment, respecting the law. (*Univ.*, p. 1-12, 2/25/98)

The use of the expression "I have begun to assume" when referring to responsibilities and reflection indicates an admission of her lack of experience, of her being an amateur in political hazards. But she claims to possess "an instinct that develops with greater fullness from day to day" and which gives her "much serenity" (*Univ.*, p. 1-12, 2/25/98), but which she does not define. She also states that she has been a woman who has given firm demonstrations and is clear "about her position and commitments with the collective" (*Univ.*, p. 1-12, 2/25/98). And finally, she considers that such a stock of qualities make of her an "atomic bomb."

Mentions about state institutions, defense, and compliance with the law, which are repeated in various texts, besides reflecting what may be a personal conviction, might equally be interpreted as a criticism of Hugo Chávez Frías, her most important contender and a true threat to the triumph that the polls at the end of 1997 foresaw for her. They could be a form of emphasizing the difference between her candidature and that of someone who attempted to disrupt the democratic continuity. This is the only theoretical strategy found in Sáez's discourse, although not a very elaborated one. Surprisingly, no argumentative figures, the convincing tool most often used by politicians, are applied by Irene Sáez. In this sense, hers is a very simple discourse.

Irene Sáez states that she is an admirer of the Pope, Gandhi, Mother Theresa, and Margaret Thatcher, and during a trip to Spain, profusely publicized in the illustrated magazines, she expressed how in a three-day visit, during which she met several politicians, she already had "several political idols" among them.

Her discourse abounds with phrases of self-definition that are summarized in the following qualities which seem to constitute the nucleus of her political personality:

- A young woman.
- Energetic and brave.
- Defender of the status represented by democratic institutions and the observance of the law.
- Hard-working.
- Conscious (this is an expression that she frequently uses, applying it to a variety of subjects).
- Defensive regarding her political qualifications, which she needs to affirm due to the criticism she receives.
- Possessor of an undefined but developing instinct that gives her assurance. She said she had always been protected by "a star" (TV channel 21, 5/26/98), and that she is a "natural" leader.
- Clear about her status and commitment with the collective, which she does not explain.
- Respectful of other persons' opinions and ideologies.
- Not mean, and free of hatred. A very religious person.
- Considering that any criticism received is part of a "dirty campaign."

This is complemented by her claim to be the recipient of popular support:

The important thing is that here is a solid trust that the people place in my hands, which will be defeated by no one because it is real and has deep roots. And it is not of today, it has been so for years (*Univ.*, p. 1-12, 2/25/98). What will be important is the faith that the people have [in her] (*Univ.*, p. 1-12, 12/14/97) . . . in a spontaneous manner the whole country is giving me confidence (*Nac.*, 11/23/97). 9000 workers of SIDOR gave me a vote of confidence and deposited a hope in my hands, so that I may protect, not negotiate, them. (*Univ.* 2/25/98, p. 1-12)

At least one aspect is interesting in the construction of these sentences: Irene Sáez places herself in a position of superiority: she receives in her hands, she protects (obviously those whose weakness so demands), but as the politicians from which she wishes to be differentiated, the support that she receives from those "weaklings" is what is important ("What is important is the support that I am receiving") (*Nac.*, D-8, 3/22/98).

This self-definition comes along with abundant iconic texts: photographs of Sáez sitting in front of her PC, with smiling face; Sáez surrounded by some people in the streets of Caracas ("pressing flesh": a classic in electoral propaganda), or posing in a more elaborate way, like when she seems to be praying, admiring some work of art, or visiting some politicians. In those pictures she looks at the camera with the ease and know-how of those accustomed to the lens, her beauty displayed.

Second Level of Analysis: The Ideas-Theme in Irene Sáez's Discourse

Apart from using the discourse to define herself as a political actor, the public statements of Sáez have a marked thematic emphasis on the following ideas: the definition of her political action as a *mission and struggle of unification or consensus*, her being a person *independent from established political parties*, her *conception of political parties*, and her *religiousness*. Although not receiving special attention within Sáez's discourse, I looked for her *proposals for a governing program*, including that topic in this section.

The Unifying Mission and Struggle

Irene Sáez places great emphasis in saying that she does not seek "to destroy what until now has been done in the country," since "there are also positive things" (*Univ.*, p. 1-12, 2/25/98): At the same time she assumes the political process as a struggle, which she underlines as hard (*Univ.*, p. 1-12, 2/14/98), and of which she considers herself a product:

I am the offspring of that struggle that you (the Causa R party) undertook to demonstrate that there do exist natural leaderships (*Nac.*, D-4, 1/31/98). (Irene Sáez) joins the cause of the struggle for Venezuela (*Nac.*, D-4, 1/31/98). (Irene Sáez) will undertake and confront with great struggle and tenacity what is to come (*Univ.*, 1/2/98).

She was then struggling, but respectful to other people, and without hatred, without destruction. This again seems to be aimed at Chávez Frías, who during the coup d'état of February 4, 1992 attacked with armored cars the presidential offices in Caracas. Embedded in the idea of struggle is the idea of unification, which had the major weight in Sáez's discourse and was also its leitmotiv (it came up in all her declarations to the press). Although she never developed the forms that that union would take, the manner of expressing it permits us to point out the following aspects:

- It refers to *unifying a country*; unifying *Venezuela*; re-unifying *the Christian social family*; unifying *everybody; drawing together the* [people's] will; joining *all the forces*; joining *all political organizations*.
- This unification is a process of struggle (*Univ.*, p. 1-2, 1/31/98).
- It constitutes a mission (*Univ.*, p. 1-12, 1/31/98).
- It will be done *by the people, with the people and for the people* (*Univ.*, p. 1-2, 1/14/98), by means of a government program open to *all political organizations and other sectors in order that we do it together. . . . That program is open, it does not belong to Irene Sáez* (*Univ.*, p. 1-12, 2/25/98).
- This is why she calls to *a national consensus, with no distinction of party or religion* (*Univ.*, p. 1-12, 12/14/97; *Nac.*, 11/23/97) and declares that she is *concerting, calling all factions* (*Univ.*, p. 1-12, 1/31/98; p. 1-12, 2/25/98).
- The aim of this unification is the progress of our people, a people that belongs to us (*Univ.*, p. 1-12, 1/31/98); to make a *proposal to the country* (*Univ.*, p. 1-12, 2/25/98); to put into effect a *policy of fighting poverty* (*Univ.*, p. 1-12, 2/25/98).

Besides the clichés of every political campaign (progress, combating poverty, "by the people with the people, for the people") and the indication that the unification is aimed at a proposal (not defined) for the country, what the discourse outlines is that Irene Sáez considers that the country is divided and that it is necessary to unite it ("Our country has been torn to pieces") (*Univ.*, p. 1-12, 12/14/97). And such a task will be her "mission."

Even though vague and imprecise, the idea does not fail to be messianic and at the same time politically naive. This unification upon which Sáez so much insists also seems to be a simplification of the Punto Fijo Pact, through which in the early 1960s a democratic alternative was taken after ten years of General Pérez Jiménez's dictatorship, but in a superficial and schematic version, which makes it pass unnoticed among the well-worn phrases of an ambiguous discourse.

Sáez's Conception of Political Parties

The discourse of Irene Sáez shows what seems to be a love–hate relationship with the political parties. On the one hand, her affirmation of independence needed not only to be differentiated, but to explicitly be declared; on the other hand, her evident need of their support introduced contradictions which made clear her position with regard to a relationship with the different traditional parties (she accepted both the support of the Causa R, a former leftist movement now placed toward the center, and of COPEI, a traditional Social Christian party. The second forced her to separate from the former, and later, fifteen days before election day, dropped her to give support to Salas Romer.

On the one hand, she expressed that in a democratic system political organizations are important and fundamental "to the aim of serving the country, the people in need" (*Univ.*, p. 1-12, 1/14/98) because they are "fundamental in a democracy" (*Univ.*, p. 1-12, 2/25/98; p. 1-12, 1/14/98; *Nac.*, D-4, 11/21/97), since "they have a fundamental role within the State," and one has to look into them for "new generations with a clear picture of the country and willing to give and not to receive" (*Nac.*, D-4, 11/21/97). She also indicated that she respects them (*Nac.*, D-2, 1/10/98; D-8, 8/2/98) by adding: "We might coincide with government programs prepared by the political organizations" (*Univ.*, p. 1-12, 2/25/98), and she appealed to "that mystique which exists in political parties" (*Univ.*, p. 1–2, 2/25/98), besides including them in "her mission of unification."

However, at the same time she denounces how useless they have been, and took very good care of verbally disaffecting herself from them, indicating that she had not made any concession or pact in which her unsullied character of independent candidate could be compromised, emphatically expressing that she had never been a member of "any political party" (*Univ.*, p. 1-12, 1/14/98; p. 1-12, 2/25/98; *Nac.*, 1/10/98) and rejecting the mentality of "party commitment or concentration of power" (*Univ.*, p. 1-12, 2/25/98). Furthermore, she indicated that it is necessary (implying that there is an absence, a lack of quality) that political parties "assume the challenge of understanding the national reality and of changing" (*Nac.*, D-4, 11/25/97), and that they "promote the efficiency and participation of the communities by them represented, whereby the need of a change is posed to them" (*Univ.*, p. 1-12, 3/15/98), adding: "we wish to have better parties and better politicians, since although they are fundamental for the State, they are not the State" (*Nac.*, D-4, 11/25/97).

Sáez's discourse says that she is not contaminated by the ills suffered by the political parties, and as an independent she presents herself as representative of that majority which are not members of them and that have "chosen to take other way" (*Univ.*, p. 1-12, 3/25/98), seemingly, that of claiming the right to speak and participate with "different, more dignified manners of doing politics . . . than the present ones" (*Univ.*, p. 1-12, 3/25/98). However, her concept of the parties notwithstanding, which was adjusted to the definition that the same parties have traditionally maintained every time that their existence had to be justified, she admitted their right to continue doing what they have been doing until now, if and when they limit themselves to contend for governorships and mayoralties (*Univ.*, p. 1-12, 2/25/98), tacitly expressing that the presidency would be hers. Moreover, she accepts them as sources of positive political actors ("generous new generations with a clear picture of the country"), and wishes their participation in the unification which she aspires to achieve and rule, but with no strings attached: "All the political organizations that wish to accompany me may do so, that being their decision, but they must be conscious that to do it will mean an adherence with no conditions whatsoever attached because, I repeat, I am independent" (*Univ.*, p. 1-12, 3/15/98).

When asked about alliances, her movement was busily negotiating (with Causa R and with COPEI), she would repeat those phrases, or keep silent (*Nac.*, D-8, 3/22/98). Nevertheless, with the expression "that being their decision," Sáez made it explicit that she had nothing to do with it, although the process of her negotiation with COPEI and Causa R was being covered from the start by the national press (she was designated presidential candidate of both parties in early May, but as said before, ended with only the support of her own movement, I.R.E.N.E.).

And in both cases, when the pacts were signed, her picture holding hands, smiling, being embraced, and celebrating with the leaders of both parties (looking admiringly at her) appeared in newspapers and magazines, showing the unification obtained.

About Religiousness

Another aspect, no less important than the above-mentioned, cuts across the political discourse of Irene Sáez: her professed faith in God, her apparent close contact with Him and His representatives on Earth. This aspect seems to be related to a prudish morality expressed by measures as hilarious as the prohibition of kissing in the parks of the municipality that she administered, and afterwards retracting it with the explanation that it did not refer to kisses but to scenes with "a high emotional degree" (*Univ.*, p. 4-2, 10/29/97), explaining later that "some persons had been doing the sexual act in the parks" (*Univ.*, p. 4-2, 10/29/97). This episode shows how she tried to cover the reference to coitus, ending by confusing sex with emotion and kisses.

That religiousness is also expressed in a manner typical of Venezuelan popular expressions: in the photographs published with the interview granted to *Paris Match* (*Nac.*, D-2, 1/10/98), numerous religious images of saints, together with one of Bolívar on horseback can be seen placed behind her desk—something that the interviewer notes, as he also registered the denomination of "advisors" which Sáez gives to these images. In that sense, that is not too different from the altars erected to several cults. This can be seen too in an interview published by the magazine *Variedades* (No.° 1362, November 1997), where she is photographed in front of her PC, and Salas Romer (near 38%), seems to indicate that although "beauty is in the eye of the beholder," it does more than fill that eye. Contradictory discourses coming simultaneously from the same source cancel out each other. A verbal discourse lacking depth, accompanied by an iconic discourse based in only one type of content, beauty, can have a detrimental effect. It is as if putting them together invests them with contrary signs. What is positive in one becomes negative for the other, in such a way that the negative character of words contaminates or overcomes the positive character of beauty. Verbal texts can become the eyesore of the beholders, and then beauty ends, silencing itself.

REFERENCES

Edwards, D., & Potter, J. (1992). *Discursive Psychology*. London: Sage.

Gadamer, H. G. (1976). *Verité et Méthode*. Paris: Editions du Seuil.

Montero, M. (1998). Identidad, belleza y cultura popular [Identity, beauty and popular culture]. In C. E. Aleman & M. M. Suárez (Eds.), *Venezuela: Tradición en la modernidad* [Venezuela: Tradition within modernity] (pp. 109–125). Caracas, Venezuela: Equinoccio-Fundación Bigott.

Montero, M., & Rodríguez, I. (1998). Discourse as a Stage for Political Actors: An Analysis of Presidential Addresses in Three Latin American Countries. In O. Feldman & C. De Landtsheer (Eds.), *Politically Speaking: A Worldwide Examination of Language Used in the Public Sphere* (pp. 91–106). Westport, CT: Praeger.

PART II

Speech Structures in Deliberative Bodies

CHAPTER 5

Linguistic Strategy of Involvement: An Emergence of New Political Speech in Japan

SHOJI AZUMA

A sociohistorical event or a sequence of such events can change the way people speak and also the way people perceive speech style (e.g., Azuma, 1997a, 1997b; Wasburn, 1997). In politics, controlling various speech styles is a vital asset to a politician who seeks to gain social and psychological approval from his audience. This study investigates the speech styles of politicians in Japan, which has been facing a series of domestic as well as international challenges in recent years. The primary data for this study come from two years of the Diet Record (October 24, 1995–November 18, 1997), which is a verbatim stenographic record of Diet committee sessions, and also from televised sessions by the NHK [Nippon Hoso Kyokai]–Japanese Broadcasting Cooperation TV station.

Although the traditional Japanese speech style of being indirect and obscure is still amply observed among politicians and high-ranking government officials, a more direct and Western style of speech is also emerging as a way to obtain approval from the audience and the general public. This style of speech can be characterized as an involvement strategy in which a speaker tries to get involved with the listeners on a more personal level.

involvement that encourages through humor.

HONORIFICS IN JAPANESE

Before beginning a discussion of speech style and its effects, a brief discussion of the Japanese honorific system is in order. Unlike languages such as English, Japanese is a language that requires a speaker to choose an appropriate linguistic form to mark the social relation of the speaker to the addressee/referent. For example, English speakers can use the same linguistic form *Today is Saturday* to anyone, whether a professor, a friend, or even a dog. In Japanese there is no neutral form as such. A Japanese speaker always has to choose an appropriate verb form with respect to politeness/ formality depending on whom is being addressed (Matsumoto, 1989).

For the sake of the analysis of honorifics, I will adopt the two-axis analysis of polite forms (e.g., Jorden, 1962; Martin, 1964; Wetzel, 1994). That is, there is a distinction between honorific and humble forms (i.e., *sonkeigo*, "respectful words," and *kenzyoogo*, "humble words") as one axis, and there is another axis of "formality" or "style" (i.e., informal and formal). For example, a Japanese verb, iu (say), can be represented in a two-axis dimension as shown in item (1).[1]

(1)

	Honorific	*ossharu*	*osshai-masu*
Polite			
	Humble	*mooshi-ageru*	*mooshi-age-masu*
Plain		*iu*	*ii-masu*
		Informal	Formal

The verbal axis of polite forms encodes deference for some referent, whereas the horizontal axis encodes formality, which is generally determined by the relationship between the speaker and addressee (e.g., how well the speaker knows the addressee). It is not common for honorific forms to be used in talking about the speaker or a member of the speaker in-group (e.g., colleagues, family members). This is because the speaker or a member is not supposed to show respect for the self or for his or her in-group members. On the other hand, the humble forms are commonly used in talking about the speaker or a member of the speaker's in-group.

In what follows, I will discuss traditional political discourse and identify several characteristics that make speech detached from the audience and less involved with it. Then, I will discuss the emerging speech style, particularly that of former Prime Minister Ryuutaroo Hashimoto, which is more direct and involved with the audience.

TRADITIONAL STYLE: DETACHMENT FROM THE AUDIENCE

Formal Form

Politicians try to be formal when they speak in the Diet. Formality may provide politicians the authority that they need most at the cost of being remote and detached from the audience. In Japanese, the level of formality is expressed, among other ways, in sentence-final predicates, as discussed in (1). For example, politicians end their utterances with the formal *-desu/-masu* verb form instead of the plain *-da* form. Interestingly, in some cases, they overshoot this effort to be formal and use *-desu/-masu* verb forms even in subordinate clauses, although it is enough to make the final verb in the main clause formal. Observe the following utterance.[2]

(2) Akarui 21 seeki wo *tsukuriage-masu* tameni, chie no
     bright   century ACC build   in order to knowledge GEN
     kagiri wo   *tsukushi-mashite . . . ari-masu.*
     limit   ACC   complete   are
     "In order to build the bright 21st century, (we) are expected to use the maximum of our knowledge."

(Diet Record, October 14, 1997)

The verbs in the subordinate clauses, *tsukuriage-masu* and *tsukushi-mashite*, are in the formal *-masu* form, although the plain *tsukuriageru* is sufficient because in Japanese the level of formality is expressed by the final verb *-masu* in the main clause. Observe the following example, which again exhibits the formal form being used in the subordinate clause.

(3) Kokutetsu   ga   unchin shuunyuu wo   uwamawaru
     national railway NOM   fare income   ACC   above
     riharai ni *nari-masita* toki   hasan   ni   *nari-masita.*
     return   to became   when bankruptcy to   became
     "When the National Railway paid (stockholders) more than it generated from, selling tickets, it went bankrupt."

(Diet Record, October 14, 1997)

The first occurrence of *nari-masita* in the subordinate clause is in the formal form instead of its plain equivalent, *natta*. The formal form in the subordinate clause is not necessary because the final verb in the main clause (i.e., the second occurrence of *nari-masita*) has sufficiently showed the level of formality. Politicians often use the formal form more than is required by grammar rules.

Humble Form

Distancing strategy is also accomplished by employing humble forms. By using this form, which lowers the position of the speaker and in turn elevates that of the addressee, the speaker can gain distance from the addressee and successfully establish psychological distance between the two. This strategy is commonly observed in politicians' speech. The following examples are taken from former minister of finance Mitsuzuka's utterances.

(4)   Baburu taiji wo   *yara-sasete*   *itadaki-mashita.*
        bubble attack ACC   do-permitted   received-HUM
        "I humbly damage-controlled the 'bubble economy.' "

                                                (Diet Record, October 14, 1997)

The morpheme *-saseru*, "let," conveys the speaker's feeling that he was given permission from someone higher than him in social status. The final verb *itadaki-mashita*, "received," again reinforces the speaker's atittude that he received the favor (permission) from a superior person. All together, the complex verb *yara-sasete itadaki-mashita* functions to humble the speaker, thus distancing him from the addressee. Politicians' speech often makes ample use of these humbling expressions. Some of the most frequently used forms are *gozai-masu*, "be"; *itashi-masu*, "do"; and *ori-masu*, "be." Observe the following utterances, which include these forms.

(5)   Mondai   ga   dete-kuru wake   de *gozai-masu.*
        problem NOM   come out   reason at be-HUM
        "(I humbly say) that a problem will emerge."

                                                (Diet Record, October 14, 1997)

(6)   Koo   shoochi   wo   *itashite*   *ori-masu.*
        this understanding ACC   do-HUM   be-HUM
        "(I) humbly understand this."

                                                (Diet Record, October 14, 1997)

The following utterance includes a humble form of the verbal noun *choo-dai*, "receiving." Again, the form functions to elevate the addressee and to downgrade the speaker.

(7)   Kisha kaiken   de dooyoo no   o-tazune   wo
        press conference at same GEN   HON-question ACC
        choodai   *itashimasita.*
        receiving-HUM did-HUM
        "(I) humbly received the same question at the press conference."

                                                (Diet Record, October 14, 1997)

Both *choodai* and *itashi-masita* indicate the speaker's humbling himself to the addressee. The tone resembles that of a servant speaking to his master.

Honorifics

The honorific form or *sonkei*-go ("respect language") is a process to elevate the subject of the sentence. Because this functions to create an uneven relationship between the speaker and the subject (addressee), it can be viewed as another distancing strategy. Observe the following examples.

(8) Sono baai no   sekinin wa doo to-*rare*-masu ka.

that situation GEN responsibility TOP how take-HON   Q

"How would you fix this problem?"

(Diet Record, April 10, 1996)

This is a sentence addressed to one of the cabinet members by an interpellator (i.e., questioner). The verb is suffixed by the subject honorific morpheme -*rare* to show deference to the subject (addressee) of the sentence. Observe another example:

(9) Giin   wa   go-giron   wo   tenkai   shite o-rare-masu.

senator TOP HON-argumentation ACC develop   do   be-HON

"The senator is developing your argument."

(Diet Record, May 13, 1997)

In addition to the honorific morpheme -*rare*, the addressee also uses the prefix *go-* to show deference to the act of *giron* ("argumentation"). These honorifcs are used to elevate the position of the subject (addressee).

Kango (Sino-Japanese Words)

Another characteristic of politicians' speech style is a heavy reliance upon Sino-Japanese words (*kango*, "Chinese words"), which refer to loan words of Chinese origin, instead of native Japanese vocabulary (*wago*, "Japanese words" or *Yamato-kotoba*, "Yamato words"). Although there are many synonyms among Sino-Japanese words and native Japanese words, different shades of meaning and stylistic values accompany them. Native Japanese words belong to the colloquial language, while their Sino-Japanese counterparts are used in the literary language and in academia. Observe the following sets of synonymous vocabulary.

(10) | Gloss | "think" | "stiff" | "show" |
|---------------|-----------|-----------|---------|
| Native | *kangaeru* | *katai* | *miseru* |
| Sino-Japanese | *kentoo* | *koochoku* | *hiroo* |

Sino-Japanese words convey a more formal and abstract impression than their counterparts in native Japanese. Shibatani (1990) points out that the difference is similar to that of Germanic words and their Latinate counterparts in English, such as *hide* and *conceal*.

Politicians' heavy use of Sino-Japanese words, which are formal and abstract, functions as another way to distance themselves from the audience. Some examples are given in items 11–13.

(11) Sono *katei* de *kentoo* shite mairi-tai to   omotte ori-masu.
      that stage   at examine do   go-
      want COMP think   be
      "(I) am thinking of examining the problem."
                                                (Diet Record, November 9, 1996)

(12) *Koochoku-see* no mondai ga   dete-kuru wake de gozai-masu.
      stiffness   GEN problem NOM come out reason at be
      "A problem of inflexibility will emerge."
                                                (Diet Record, October 14, 1997)

(13) Moo   o-wakari   no   koto deshoo kara
      already know-HON GEN   thing will   because
      koko   de   *go-hiroo*   wa   mooshiage-masen.
      this place at   HUM-exhibition TOP   say-HUM-not
      "Because you already know, (I) will not speak about (it) again."
                                                (Diet Record, October 14, 1997)

For each *kango* word, there are synonymous *yamato kotoba* available, but the speakers deliberately chose the *kango*. All of these *kango* give the impression that the utterances are formal, academic, abstract, and lack clarity. Use of such vocabulary distances speakers from the audience.

Indirect Style

Westerners sometimes consider Japanese discourse indirect, obscure, and difficult to understand (e.g., Yamada, 1997). In his study of contrastive analysis of rhetoric, Kaplan (1966) characterizes Oriental discourse (including Japanese) as non-linear sequential, unlike English, which is linear sequential. Japanese has many ambiguous expressions and does not go straight to the point, while in English the flow of argumentation is straight and to the point. Hall (1976) and Hall and Hall (1987) point out that Japanese discourse style falls into what they call "high context," in which the amount of shared information among interlocutors is very high, as opposed to "low context," in which the shared information is low. In a high-context society (e.g., Japan), since interlocutors have considerable knowledge and experience in common, they do not have to state their message explicitly. Instead, they rely on non-verbal means to communicate, which may be seen as "indirect."

This discourse style is most vividly observed in politicians' speech. For example, the speech of one former prime minister, Noboru Takeshita, is said to be *gengo meiryoo imi fumeiryoo*, which means "clear in language but meaningless" (Maynard, 1994). This adherence to obscurity is not limited to Takeshita, but it is observed by most politicians. Especially when matters become sensitive, politicians tend to choose an indirect and obscure style so that they can avoid any commitment to the content of their utterances (e.g., Shibatani, 1990).

The following utterances made by interpellators in Diet sessions show that cabinet members and high-ranking government officials are indeed indirect and do not answer questions in a straightforward way.

(14)   Kichinto   tooben   shite   kudasai.
         orderly ․ answer   do   give me
         "Please answer clearly."

                                        (Diet Record, May 29, 1997)

(15)   Chanto   sutoreeto   ni   kotaete   kudasai.
         clearly straight   in   answer   give me
         "Please give a straight answer."

                                        (Diet Record, April 10, 1996)

(16)   Shitsumon   ni   *kotaete-nai.*   Iinchoo,   shitsumon   ni
         question   to answer-not   Chairman   question   to
         chanto   kotae-sasete   kudasai.
         clearly answer-make   give me
         "(You) do not give me a straight answer. Chairman, please make him give a straight answer to my question."

                                        (Diet Record, May 29, 1997)

It is not difficult to find similar expressions in the Diet Record. Specifically, the blunt response in (16) illustrates how frustrated the interpellator was with the obscure answer he was given. The plain abrupt ending of the first utterance (*kotaete nai*, "do not answer") sounds like something a teacher would say to a misbehaving student. There is not even a hint of respect for the addressee. The second utterance with the causative verb *saseru*, "make," shows the interpellater's belief that a straight answer has to be demanded. The following utterance also shows that a straight answer was not given.

(17)   Ima   soo-iu   koto   w   kiite-iru-no-jya-nai. . . .
         now that   thing   ACC   ask-be-NEG
         gomakashi-cha   dame   desu   yo.
         evade   bad   be   TAG
         "I am not asking that. You cannot evade my question."

                                                      (Diet Record, May 29, 1997)

The interpellator is overtly claiming that the answerer evaded a question and the evasion cannot be tolerated.

The linguistic forms discussed so far show that politicians are in general employing a linguistic strategy of detachment, psychologically distancing themselves from the audience. In Japanese society, using the linguistic strategy of detachment is actually expected as a social norm in formal situations such as Diet sessions. Ide (1989) calls such conventions *wakimae* or "discernment."

However, we also note that a new type of discourse, which seeks more involvement with the audience, is emerging. In what follows, we will briefly summarize the political scene over the last decade, and then we will examine this new type of linguistic style in Japanese politics.

THE EMERGENCE OF A NEW POLITICAL DISCOURSE: *"UCHI"* SPEECH AND INVOLVEMENT

Historical-Contextual Information

Officially organized in 1955, the Liberal Democratic Party (hereafter LDP) was for decades the dominant and largest political party. Producing many prime ministers, the LDP did not face any viable competition until recently. Reviewing the Japanese postwar period up to 1986, Curtis (1988) noted that "there is little the political opposition can do to win political power. The question is whether the LDP will do something to lose it. Surely one way to lose it would be to let the public's confidence in the LDP's competence be shaken" (p. 239). Indeed, what Curtis (1988) addressed has happened to the LDP. The public began losing confidence in it in the late 1980s when a series of political corruptions emerged. For example, in the Lockheed scandal, former prime minister Kakuei Tanaka was indicted on bribery charges and later pronounced guilty. The Recruit scandal, which involved insider stock deals, claimed as its victims top LDP leaders, including finance and justice ministers as well as Prime Minister Takeshita. Prime Minister Uno succeeded Takeshita, but Uno was blamed for paying a geisha for sexual favors and later resigned. In the *Sagawa kyuubin* scandal, the parcel delivery company had made illegal contributions of 500 million yen to Takeshita faction leader Kanemaru, who in turn distributed it to members of the faction.

Generally, Japanese people are said to be indulgent in allowing political corruption, summing up their feelings in the expression *tokage no shippo kiri*, "cutting the tail of the lizard" (Hayes, 1995). By breaking off its tail, the lizard can always escape the predator's attack, and the lost tail will soon be regenerated. Eventually, the lizard will fully recover as if nothing had happened to its body. However, this time the LDP began to lose its grip on the Japanese political system. In addition to the scandals, the problems brought on by the collapse of the "bubble economy" and an inability to enact political reforms have increased the public's dissatisfaction with the LDP. For the first time, the LDP was forced to form a coalition party with other parties in 1993, and Hosokawa from the *Sakigake* party became the prime minister. After Hosokawa, Hata became the prime minister, but this government lasted only two months. Then, another coalition government was formed, which was headed by Prime Minister Murayama, leader of the Socialist Party. After this, another coalition government was inaugurated on January 11, 1996. It was a coalition of the LDP, the Socialist Party, and *Sakigake*. The prime minister for this government was Ryuutaroo Hashimoto, a member of the LDP.[3]

As the last hope of the troubled LDP, Hashimoto was expected to play a critical role in regaining the trust of the public. The issue of public confidence is a serious concern for the LDP. Political scandals as well as mounting domestic and international problems, such as staggering economy and an unpopular 3 percent sales tax, focused public attention on politicians to a greater extent than at any time since the war (e.g., Kan, 1998). Politicians are expected to be sincere and to make their plans and ideas more transparent than ever. One of the strategies to gain approval from the public is to show integrity and sincerity by using a less remote speech style with the audience.

In what follows, we will examine the speech style of former prime minister Hashimoto, which can be characterized as a strategy of involvement.

Overt Use of the Pronoun "I"

As the primary organizing principle for Japanese communication, the dichotomy of *uchi* ("in, inside, private, hidden") versus *soto* ("out, outside, public, exposed") has been proposed (e.g., Bachnik & Quinn, 1994; Maynard 1997). Makino (1995) points out that this *uchi* versus *soto* difference is captured by the degree of speaker involvement with addressee. According to him, *uchi* is a locus for engagement, privacy, and informality, and *soto* is a locus for detachment, publicness, and formality. The key factor of *uchi* and *soto* is [+/− involvement]. For example, when a speaker uses a formal and authoritative speech style, not revealing his or her inner feelings, it is *soto* speech and there is less involvement with the audience (−involvement). On the other hand, when a speaker shows his inner personal feelings and is less formal, this is *uchi* speech, which allows for more speaker involvement with the audience (+involvement).

Traditionally, in Japanese political discourse, *soto* speech, through which one suppresses and demotes oneself as the speaker, has been considered a desirable way to communicate. A linguistic manifestation of this speech style is subject-less syntax, which is perfectly grammatical in Japanese. A speaker does not overtly present himself or herself as the speaker; rather he or she makes statements as if they were somebody else's. However, the present study shows that overtly presenting "self" in speech is emerging as a new strategy to maintain positive face in speech. For example, former prime minister Hashimoto frequently frames utterances with an overt subject, as the following examples show.

(18)   *Watashi* wa soo   omou-no-desu.
        I   TOP so   think
    "I think so."

                                   (Diet Record, October 7, 1997)

(19)   Kokoro kara   *watashi* wa soo   omotte   ori-masu.
        heart   from   I   TOP so   think   be
    "I think so from the bottom of my heart."

                                   (Diet Record, October 7, 1997)

When the prime minister uttered these sentences, he placed strong emphasis on *watashi*, making them sound very personal. By emphasizing the personal aspect of his statements, the former prime minister seeks to come across as a sincere and trustworthy politician, unlike some others who simply read speeches prepared by aides.

This strategy of overtly presenting oneself as the speaker is a new means of creating and maintaining a positive self-image of oneself. This strategy of promoting (instead of demoting) self is also viewed as a way to build camaraderie with addressees by diminishing the psychological distance between oneself and them. In Table 5.1 a comparison is made between the relative frequency of the use of the first-person pronoun among three LDP leading politicians; Mitsuzuka (former finance minister), Obuchi (former foreign minister), and Hashimoto (former prime minister). The numbers

Table 5.1
Frequency of Overt First-Person Pronoun Use

Mitsuzuka	Obuchi	Hashimoto
7	5	24

were obtained by analyzing speech samples from the Diet Record (October 7 and 14, 1997). Former Prime Minister Hashimoto used the overt first-person pronoun far more frequently than the other two politicians did. More examples follow.

(20)   Soo-iu mmono de wa nai to *watashi* wa omoi-masu
       that   thing be TOP NEG COM I   TOP think
       "I don't think it is what you described."

(Diet Record, October 14, 1997)

(21)   Kono ten wa *watashi* wa aratamente mooshi-age-masu
       this point TOP   I   TOP   again   say-HUM
       "I will say this point again."

(Diet Record, October 7, 1997)

(22)   Kore mo heekoo   shite susumete
       this too parallel do   promote
       ikanakereba-naranai *watashi* wa soo omoun-desu.
       must   I   TOP so   think
       "I think that this has to be promoted in parallel (with others)."

(Diet Record, October 14, 1997)

Note that, in all of the examples, the first-person pronoun could be deleted grammatically without altering the sentence's meaning. Still the former prime minister retains the pronoun in his utterance in order to stress that the statement is his own, not someone else's. Stressing his role as speaker makes his utterance sounds more personal. Revealing inner thoughts and feelings contributes to making the utterance an *uchi* statement. Through the linguistic strategy of overt pronoun use, the speaker seeks to emphasize his sincerity and willingness to get involved with interpellators and other audience members.

Adverbs of Sincerity

Another strategy of involvement is to use words and phrases that explicitly express the sincerity of the speaker. These are often adverbs and include *kokoro yori*, "from the bottom of my heart"; *shoojiki ni*, "honestly"; *socchoku ni*, and "frankly speaking." By using such expressions of sincerity, the speaker points out his inner true feelings, or *uchi*, and publicly commits himself to the content of his statement. This is another means speakers use to show the serious nature of utterance. Observe the following examples, which include adverbs of sincerity.

(23)   Watashi wa gyoosei   kaikaku o   matome-ageru
       I   TOP administration reform ACC   complete
       hoo ni kyooryoku wo   itadaki-tai *kokoro yori* negai-masu
       side to cooperation ACC receive-want heart from   request
       "I want to request from the bottom of my heart your cooperation to complete government reform."

                                          (Diet Record, October 14, 1997)

(24)   Zehi   go-rikai   wo   tamawari-tai
       by all means HON-understanding   ACC   receive-want
       watashi wa *kokoro kara* soo negatte ori-masu
       I   TOP heart   from   so hope   be
       "I truly hope from the bottom of my heart to receive your understanding."
                                          (Diet Record, October 14, 1997)

(25)   Dekiru kagiri no   doryoku wo   tsumi-kasanete
       can   limit GEN   effort   ACC add
       iki-tai   *sottyoku ni* watashi wa   soo   omott-ori-masu.
       go-want   frankly to   I   TOP so   think-be
       "I frankly think that I want to continue my effort to its limit."
                                          (Diet Record, April 10, 1996)

(26)   Watashi wa *shoojiki ni* . . . mooshi-age-mashita.
       I   TOP   honest   in   said-HUM
       "I said (this) honestly."
                                          (Diet Record, October 14, 1997)

Juxtaposition of Plain and Formal Forms

Another aspect of Hashimoto's speech is the framing of more intimate *uchi*-style messages within the rigid and formal *soto* style. Even using the formal, more remote *soto* speech style, he can embed a feeling of involvement with the audience. This is accomplished by juxtaposing a plain linguistic form (*uchi* form) and a formal linguistic form (*soto* form). Observe the following examples.

(27) Kokumin keizai   ga   hatan *shite shimau.* Kore wa moo
      public   economy NOM fail   do complete   this TOP already
      sakete tooru koto ga   deki-nai koto ni naru   to   omoi-masu.
      avoid go   COM NOM cannot COM to become COM think
      "The public economy will end up failing. I think this will be inevitable."

                                        (Diet Record, October 14, 1997)

The first sentence ends with the informal form *shimau*, which is embedded in the formal sentence with the *-masu* form of *omoimasu*. By using the informal *uchi* style in the first sentence, the prime minister reveals his personal thoughts while maintaining his formal *soto* style, which is the norm for Diet sessions. In other words, he shows his personal thoughts with the first informal *uchi* sentence, while maintaining his integrity as the prime minister through the second formal *soto* sentence. He succeeds in retaining both involvement and integrity by juxtaposing the two sentences. Consider another example in item 28.

(28) Giin   no   go-shiteki   no yoona jyookyoo wo   fumae-nagara
      senator GEN HON-suggestion GEN like   situation ACC consider-ing
      taioo *shite ika-nakereba-naranai* sono yooni omotte ori-masu.
      deal do   go   must   that like   think   be
      "I have to deal with the issue keeping in mind the point you raised. That's what I think."

                                        (Diet Record, November 18, 1997)

The former prime minister frames his intentions in very informal uchi speech, which ends with the plain form *naranai*. Then, he reverts back to *soto* speech, emphasizing his formal role as the prime minister, and ends the utterance with the formal form *ori-masu*. By juxtaposing the two types of sentences, the former Prime Minister exudes both involvement (*uchi*) and integrity (*soto*).

HOW LONG WILL THE PRIME MINISTER ADHERE TO THIS STRATEGY OF INVOLVEMENT?

The preceding discussion of linguistic strategies showed that former prime minister Hashimoto sometimes chooses a speech style of involvement with an audience, unlike some of his predecessors and colleagues in the Diet. By using *uchi* speech, the former prime minister seeks to show his personal inner feelings even in the most formal situations, the Diet sessions. Does the prime minister maintain his style of involvement even when he encounters hostile or rude speech from interpellators from an opposition party? Interestingly, it seems that Hashimoto strives to keep his strategy of involvement even in such situations.

The following is a dialogue between the prime minister and Ueda, a member of the Japanese communist party in the Diet. An interpellator from the opposition party, Ueda asks if there was a secret agreement between the Japanese government and the U.S. government in the past regarding military operations in Korea. Ueda claims that the agreement was to let U.S. warplanes fly to Korea from Japan without prior approval from the Japanese government. Ueda insists that he obtained secret documents that prove the existence of such an agreement and that then Secretary of State Rogers as well as Kissinger allegedly signed the documents. Note the harsh tone of the statement Ueda made to the prime minister.

(29)
Ueda: Makoto ni kanashii desune. hoodoo dake ja nain-desuyo. Bee seifu no koo-kai monjo desu yo. Rojaazu kokumu chookan, henrii kissinjaa, kore henrii kissinjaa no sain desu yo. sooiu mono wo hoodoo ja-nai, genbutsu dakara, bei seifu no. Sore wo hoodoo ni arukoto wa nai nannte, yoku-mo maa sooiu kotoo heeki de ii-masu ne. Kooiu kookyuu-kanryoo wa gyoosei-kaikaku no taishoo ni senakya-naranu to sae watasi wa omoun-desu-ga soori doo-desu ka?
Hashimoto: Nani ga?
Ueda: *Anata nee. Anata shushoo nanda yo?* . . .
Hashimoto: Sakihodo-rai taihen gekietsu na chooshi de iroiro go-shiteki itadaita koto wo watashi wa *shinken ni haichoo itashite ori-mashita* keredomo . . .
Ueda: I am terribly sad. It's not just a report. There are public documents issued by the U.S. government, you know. Rogers, who was the Secretary of State; Henry Kissinger, this is the signature of Henry Kissinger, you know. All of these are not just reports. They are actual documents of the United States government. The fact is that these documents exist. How in the world can you say there is nothing like what was reported? I even think that those high-ranking government officials who take this attitude should be the targets of administration reform. What do you think of this, Prime Minister?
Hashimoto: What?
Ueda: You! You are the Prime Minister, right? . . .

Hahsimoto: I was humbly listening to what you pointed out in a rather harsh manner, however . . .

(Diet Record, November 18, 1997)

Ueda, who was apparently frustrated by the response from the prime minister, made an unmistakably informal and rude statement, *Anata nee. Anata shushoo nanda yo* ("Hey you! You are the Prime Minister, do you know that?"). This remark is impolite in several respects. First, the second-person pronoun *anata*, "you" is used to address the prime minister. In Japanese, it is generally considered rude to address a person with an overt pronoun. Instead of the pronoun, a culturally appropriate means of address is to use the rank or title of the person. In this case, the speaker should have used *shushoo* or *soori* ("prime minister") instead of *anata* ("you"). The verb *nanda* also adds to the rude tone because it is the informal -*da* form, not the formal -*masu* form. The morpheme -*nda*, which is a casual form of -*noda*, also contributes to the rude tone of the utterance. The morpheme -*noda* is usually used to refer to the assumed-to-be common knowledge between the speaker and the addressee.

In this sentence, the common knowledge is that Hashimoto is prime minister. Because this fact is obviously familiar to both speaker and addressee, the statement sounds sarcastic. In addition, very informal hedges such as *nee* and *yo* ("right") further lower the tone and show that Ueda has very little respect for the prime minister.

It is interesting to note that even with the harsh rude tone of the remark by Ueda, the former prime minister maintains his tone of being humble and sincere to his colleague. Hashimoto's response was *shinken ni haichoo itashite ori-mashita* ("I was humbly and carefully listening"). With this polite remark, Hashimoto continues his answer in a professional way to Ueda's rather unprofessional remark. Hashimoto continues to use involvement tactics even in a most unfriendly situation.

CONCLUSION

A linguistic analysis of the speech of politicians from Japanese Diet sessions has shown that a strategy of involvement is surfacing as a way to gain the audience approval. This strategy appears to be especially useful for politicians, particularly those in the LDP, who are losing credibility with the public because of a series of scandals. Politicians are expected to be sincere and to make their ideas more transparent than ever. A strategy of involvement, such as the overt use of a first-person pronoun, is a way to present a speaker (politician) as a responsible person who is willing to take responsibility for his opinions and to involve himself in clear direct discourse with the audience.

Unlike the European tradition of rhetoric, eloquence has not been considered one of the virtues people are encouraged to learn in Japan. The favored speech pattern is to be indirect, and the tactic of "beating around the bush" is a desired mode of communication. Traditional among politicians have been hedges and a preference for other ambiguous expressions that allow one to avoid taking responsibility, as one must do when making a clear, direct statement. The present study has shown, however, that a more direct and straightforward mode of communication is emerging, in spite of the socially prescribed means of communication. Interestingly, this new speech style originated with the most unexpected speaker, the former prime minister Ryuutaroo Hashimoto, who was expected to be a speaker with all of the traditional Japanese values of communication.

NOTES

1. While this chapter was being written, Hashimoto resigned as prime minister and assumed responsibility for the LDP's losing seats in the general election. He served for two terms as prime minister, which is considered substantial. Some of his predecessors held the office for very short periods of time in the last decade: Uno, two months; Hosokawa, nine months; Hata, two months. Following the convention used in English, "Mr." was not used to refer to the prime minister or any other politicians.

2. For presentation of Japanese data, the following abbreviations were used. ACC (accusative), GEN (genitive), NOM (nominative), HUM (humble), HON (honorific), TOP (topic), Q (question marker), NEG (negative), TAG (tag), COMP (complimentizer).

3. In Japanese, vowels can be either short or long. In this chapter, I adopt the convention of using a single letter for a short vowel and two consecutive identical letters for a long vowel. Thus, for example, "o" is used for a short vowel and "oo" is used for a long vowel.

REFERENCES

Azuma, S. (1997a). *Shakai gengogaku nyuumon.* Tokyo: Kenkyuu-sha Publishers.
Azuma, S. (1997b). Speech Accommodation and Japanese Emperor Hirohito. *Discourse and Society,* 8:2, 189–202.
Bachnik, J. M., & Quinn, C. J. (1994). *Situated Meaning: Inside and Outside in Japanese Self, Society, and Language.* Princeton, NJ: Princeton University Press.
Curtis, G. (1988). *The Japanese Way of Politics.* New York: Columbia University Press.
Hall, E. T. (1976). *Beyond culture.* New York: Doubleday Anchor Books.
Hall, E. T., & Hall, M. R. (1987). *Hidden Differences: Doing Business with the Japanese.* New York: Doubleday Anchor Books.
Hayes, L. D. (1995). *Introduction to Japanese Politics.* New York: Marlow and Company.

Ide, S. (1989). Formal Forms and Discernment: Two Neglected Aspects of Universals in Linguistic Politeness. *Multilinu*, 8:2, 223–248.

Jorden, E. (1962). *Beginning Japanese*. New Haven, CT: Yale University Press.

Kan, N. (1998). *Daijin* [Ministers]. Tokyo: Iwanami Shoten.

Kaplan, B. R. (1966). Cultural thought patterns in inter-cultural education. *Language Learning*, 16, 1–20.

Makino, S. (1995). Review of Bachnik and Quinn (1994). *Journal of Japanese Studies*, 21:1, 207–211.

Martin, S. (1964). Speech levels in Japan and Korea. In D. Hymes (Ed.), *Language in Culture and Society* (pp. 407–415). New York: Harper and Row.

Matsumoto, Y. (1989). Politeness and Conversational Universals: Observations from Japanese. *Multilingua*, 8, 207–221.

Maynard, S. K. (1994). Images of Involvement and Integrity: Rhetorical Style of a Japanese Politician. *Discourse and Society*, 5:2, 233–261.

Maynard, S. K. (1997). Nominalization in Japanese Television News. *Language in Society*, 26:3, 381–399.

Shibatani, M. (1990). *The Languages of Japan*. Cambridge: Cambridge University Press.

Wasburn, P. C. (1997). The Symbolic Construction of Rival Nations: Radio Japan's Coverage of U.S.-Japanese Trade Disputes. *Political Communication*, 14, 191–206.

Wetzel, P. (1994). Contemporary Japanese Attitudes toward Honorifics (keigo). *Language Variation and Change*, 6, 113–147.

Yamada, H. (1997). *Different Games, Different Rules*. New York: Oxford University Press.

CHAPTER 6

A Psycholinguistic Analysis of the European Union's Political Discourse Regarding the Israeli-Palestinian Conflict (1980–1995)

CHRIST'L DE LANDTSHEER AND LISE VAN OORTMERSSEN

The European Union's (EU) political integration has raised expectations regarding a constructive role of the Union in international conflict negotiations. It is often argued that the EU—unlike the United States, which has vested interests in one side and is deeply distrusted by the other (Grahl & Teague, 1990: 285), is particularly able to further the Middle East peace process. The EU's geopolitical situation, its links with the parties concerned and its experience of regional cooperation and integration support such a theory. So does the fact that the situation in the Middle East has obviously been a concern of the member states of the EU, ever since the unification process. This concern gave rise to the first joint declaration of the member states since the establishment of the European Political Cooperation (EPC) in 1970. More recently the EU became the most important economic donor to the Occupied Territories–Palestine (Cogen & François, 1995).

The Israeli-Palestinian conflict goes back to 1948, with the creation of the state of Israel. Since then, the region has been involved in a deep conflict characterized by war and violent bloodshed. There have been many national and international attempts to solve the conflict. The most recent attempt started in 1991 after the Gulf crisis, when the United States and Europe decided to settle the Israeli-Palestinian conflict under their aegis. They applied their pressure on Israel to agree to the peace discussions that led to the Madrid talks. However, these talks collapsed in June 1993 without any solution to the conflict. In August, it was announced that secret negotiations between the PLO and Israel on the first step toward autonomy for Gaza and Jericho had taken place in Oslo. The terms of the Declaration of Principles (DoP) subsequently were signed in the White House on September 13 of the same year. By now, the peace process is on the brink of collapse, because Israel and the Palestinian Authority failed to reach an agreement according to the timetable. Despite its decisive economic role in the peace process, the EU seems to be unable to come up with firm international initiatives (McDowall, 1998).

The aim of this study is to explore differences of opinion within the EU about it's role in the peace process. The EU is characterized by many cultural divergences; as a Greek representative in the European Parliament, Nikolaou, stated, "Account has to be taken, on the one hand, of the political groups, and on the other, of the nationalities" (Debate of July 5, 1983).

In order to understand Europe's role in the Israeli-Palestinian conflict, several considerations need to be taken into account, such as the need for international involvement, and the danger of doing nothing and leaving the peace process in a stalemate; one also needs to take a close look at the internal process of decision making in the European Union. There is a great risk in leaving the peace process in its current fragile situation (Corbin, 1994; McDowall, 1998). With such a phase of no-war, no-peace, the future promises more bloodshed than ever in both societies, the Palestinian and the Israeli. International involvement seems indispensable to bring about any progress in the negotiations. The decision-making process in the EU is based on three institutions with divergent positions and powers, namely, the Council of Ministers, the European Commission (EC), and the European Parliament (EP). The EP, directly elected since 1979, is the EU's only democratic institution. Since the signing of the Maastricht Treaty (1991), it has in some domains the right to co-decide, together with the council. With the Treaty of Amsterdam (1997), its powers have increased somewhat again. The EP is not a major player, but it has become more important over time. The council is the most important legislative body of the EU. It sets out the main policy goals and is authorized to commit the governments of the Member States. It is the commissioners and their cabinets, who are appointed by agreement among the Member States, who actually design the policy lines of the EU, which are eventually approved by the Council of Ministers. Informal bargaining and exchange of resources are additional important elements of EU decision making (European Parliament Secretariat, 1972: 24; Bellier, 1996; Crawford, 1996; Bomberg & Peterson, 1998).

As we choose to focus on Europe's dispositions in the Israeli-Palestinian conflict, we will perform a psycholinguistic analysis of the European Union's political discourse. For a profound analysis of the method and theoretical background of such a psycholinguistic political discourse analysis, we refer the reader to another volume edited by Feldman and De Landtsheer (1998), *Politically Speaking*, and more especially to Chapters 1 ("Introduction to the Study of Political Discourse") and 11 ("The Political

Rhetoric of a Unified Europe"), written by De Landtsheer. We content ourselves here in saying that this psycholinguistic analysis should be seen as part of a wider project to develop a rhetorical, or discursive, psychology which points to the role of language in constituting psychological states (Billig, 1998: 199–200). Our discursive approach, which follows the philosophy of Wittgenstein, assumes that the ideas of ancient rhetoric offer a crucial psychological insight into the nature of human thinking and that dialogue, especially argumentative dialogue, includes phenomena that constitute many of the traditional topics of psychology (Billig, 1998: 200, 203). Performing such a discourse analysis of political discourse is not merely using a method like content analysis; this analysis brings us within a cross-discipline in its own right (political discourse analysis), a discipline in which also political science is involved (van Dijk, 1997: 37). As the following paragraph describes, we will perform such a psycholinguistic analysis by means of an investigation of the use of action verbs and stative verbs when mentioning the Middle East in the Europarliamentary rhetoric. By focusing on debates held in the European Parliament between 1980 and 1995, this study will be examining to what extent the different institutions, countries, and political factions advocate a more or less active role for the EU in (resolving) the Israeli-Palestinian conflict. We assume action verbs to coincide with points of view that favor action and stative verbs to coincide with reserved positions. Conclusions may point at particular power-levels that might—more than other levels—advance initiatives to be taken by the EU toward a more constructive role in the Middle East peace process.

A PSYCHOLINGUISTIC ANALYSIS

Action verbs (e.g., "to negotiate") and stative verbs (e.g., "to believe") are the main verb categories listed in Semin and Fiedler's Linguistic Category Model (1991). Experiments show that action verbs express action and drive the attention of message receivers toward concrete actions. Stative verbs refer to mental states and appeal to emotion. Questions containing action verbs lead to answers describing concrete events, whereas questions containing stative verbs evoke abstract answers. Both verb types transfer similar lexical information, even though (pragmatically) the meanings of these verb types differ (de Poot, 1996). The subjective choice aspect, which directs the use of action verbs or stative verbs, informs us about the speaker's preferences. In order to distinguish verbs that denote a state from those verbs that denote an action or process, the following questions are useful: What is happening? What happened? If one cannot answer these questions, because nothing is happening at all, the verb is describing a *state*. If the questions can be answered, the central verb belongs to the category *action* (Chafe, 1970: 98–100). The following examples include action verbs (among them process verbs) and stative verbs.

In this respect the Community will *play* the most important role (action).

We *met* all the official representatives (process).

The Twelve *have the opinion* that any settlement should comply with the resolutions 242 and 338 of the UN Security Council (state).

PROCEDURE

Our research design is based upon the design of a metaphor study of European Parliamentary rhetoric (De Landtsheer, 1998b). Metaphorical power was calculated according to political groups, nationality, language, and gender. Political style was found to correspond rather more with ideology and to a lesser degree with gender and nationality than with the language used. This study differentiates among three rhetorical power levels. The first level (the institutional level) represents the rhetoric of politicians in the three different institutions (Parliament, Council, and Commission). The second and third levels deal with, respectively, the discourses of representatives of the member states (national discourses) and the discourses of representatives of political groups (ideological discourses). At each level, comparative analysis was performed on the use of both action verbs and stative verbs, where "Europe" was the grammatical subject. We assume that the discourses at each level will reveal certain developments over time with regard to the positions taken by the participants at each level (institutions, political groups, and nations) concerning the role of Europe in the Israeli-Palestinian conflict. Each of the three rhetorical levels thus expresses, by the use of its language, a degree of "activeness" with regard to the EU's policy (See Tables 6.1 and 6.2).

We used the Dutch versions of the proceedings of the European Parliament debates (published in the *Official Journal of the European Union*). Literature would appear to justify the use of translations of the debates. Although we acknowledge the importance of the linguistic variable, previous results show that stylistic differences of speeches within European parliamentary rhetoric are negligible at the linguistic level (De Landtsheer, 1998b). We focus on formal characteristics by investigating verbs. While we are dealing with the content of stylistic elements, this semantic content is universal. The nature of a verb remains the same if translated accurately. The Dutch language contains about 100 stative verbs and about 1,000 action verbs (de Poot, 1996: 45). Ratios (A/B:1) will be calculated for action verbs (A) and stative verbs (B) in all the subject categories at all three levels. We assume the ratio (A/B:1) to express the disposition toward action in a corpus of speeches. When applied to the central verb in the sentence

Table 6.1

Discursive Levels of Analysis in EP Debates (1980–1995)

---

1. Institutional level: Council (R), Commission (C), Parliament (P).

2. Member state/national level: Austria (Os), Belgium (Be), Denmark (Da), Finland (Su), France (Fr), Germany (De), Greece (Gr), Ireland (Ir), Italy (It), Luxembourg (Lu), The Netherlands (Ne), Portugal (Po), Spain (Es), Sweden (Sv), United Kingdom (En).

3. Political group/ ideological level (the groups have changed over time): ARC (Rainbow), COM (Communist group), DEP (European Progressive Democrats), DR (European Right), ED (European Democrats), L (Liberal group), LDR (Liberal Democratic and Reformist group), PPE (European People's Party), S (Socialist group), V (Greens), CG (Left Coalition), GUE (European United Left), RDE (United European Democrats), ARE (European Radical Alliance), EDN (Europe of Nations), ELDR (European Liberal Democratic and Reformist party), FE (Forza Europe), GUE/NGL (European United Left/Nordic Green Left), PSE (Party of European Socialists), UPE (Union for Europe), NI (Independent).

---

or clause, used in combination with the subject "Europe" (or an equivalent), the ratio A/B:1 indicates whether one sees a more active or passive role for the EU in a certain sphere (the topic of the debate). Our assumption refers to sentences and clauses that have (parts of) the European Union as the grammatical subject. Only these are included in the analysis. Where sentences contain more than one verb, we consider the infinitive to be the central verb. If they include a past participle, this participle constitutes the central verb, provided it is not a nominal part of the predicate. In the latter case, the finite form is considered to be the central verb.

Ratios were calculated for a 1980–1995 sample of European parliamentary debates regarding the Middle East (Israel, the Palestinians, or both parties). This sample is based on two indexes: the annual registers of the European Union *Bulletin* for the period 1980–1985 and the *European Parliament On-line Query System* (Epoque) for debates after 1985. It consists of about 90 pages of text (80,221 words). For each year, we analyzed on average five pages from one or more debates. We preferred to use a debate containing both an address by a member of the Council and one by a member of the Commission. If such a debate was not available, we selected two debates, one involving a speech by a representative of the Council at all, and the other a speech by a commissioner. If the debates did not include text from the Council, we selected one debate in which the Commission was represented. If both were absent, we selected another debate concerning the Middle East. If there was more than one debate that met these criteria, title and length were taken into consideration. Preference was given to debates of approximately five pages and with a title referring to the Israeli/Palestinian conflict in general. If the subject was mentioned during a debate but not by more than one speaker in succession, for example, in

Table 6.2

Symbols for Grammatical Subjects Referring to Actors at Three Levels of Analysis

---

eu: Europe, the European Economic Community, the (European) Community, and the EU

li: the member states, the Twelve/Fifteen (or, before, a lower number), the states of Europe, the governments

ra: the (members of the) Council, the ministers (of foreign affairs)

co: the (members of the) (European) Commission

pa: the (members of the) (European) Parliament

we: we

---

a working program led by the acting chairman of the Council of Ministers, the debate was not considered for analysis. If a debate was longer than five pages, we analyzed only part of it. It always consisted of one continuous piece of text either at the beginning or the end of the debate, depending on where the address by the Council or Commission was situated. Text contributed by the chair was not analyzed because its content is purely procedural. Quotations (from declarations, for example) were also omitted because they were not the speaker's own words and originate from a different context involving a different style. Only states and groups whose total amount of text exceeded 400 lines were considered. The amount of text was converted from lines into words. Since the layout of the debates varied over time, the average amount of words per line varied: between 1980 and 1996 four different layouts were used.

HYPOTHESES

Suggestion of the European and international studies (e.g., Cogen & Francois, 1995) provide us with the suggestion of the following hypotheses for the sample period 1980–1995 regarding the central issue of this chapter.

At *level 1*, the contents of the considered debates give us reason to expect that the European Parliament and the European Commission see a more active role for the European Union than the Council of Ministers does. We therefore hypothesize that speeches by EP members and Commission members will display a bias toward the use of action verbs when dealing with the subject of the EU role in the Middle East peace process. We suggest that the Council's attitude toward the EU peace process remained reserved until the early 1990s: its members mainly spoke in terms of opinions about developments in the Middle East. Since then, the Council's position has moved more into line with the position of the Parliament and has shifted

Table 6.3
The 1980–1995 Average Ratio of Action Verbs to Stative Verbs in EP Debates
Regarding the Israeli-Palestinian Conflict

Level 1
(Ratio calculated for all six subject categories)
Commission 2.3:1 (124 action verbs to 53 stative verbs on 10,009 words)
Council 2.0:1 (136 action verbs to 69 stative verbs on 12,250 words)
Parliament 1.8:1 (449 action verbs to 249 stative verbs on 57,960 words)

(Ratio calculated for the subject category "we")
Parliament 1.3:1 (280 action verbs to 210 stative verbs on 57,960 words)
Commission 1.3:1 (36 action verbs to 27 stative verbs on 10,009 words)
Council. 0.9:1 (36 action verbs to 40 stative verbs on 12,250 words)

Level 2
(Ratio calculated for all six subject categories)
Spain 2.4:1 (29 action verbs to 12 stative verbs on 4,122 words)
Italy 2.1:1 (78 action verbs to 37 stative verbs on 10,363 words)
Germany 1.8:1 (60 action verbs to 34 stative verbs on 5,877 words)
France 1.8:1 (148 action verbs to 81 stative verbs on 19,431 words)
United Kingdom 1.7:1 (51 action verbs to 30 stative verbs on 6,602 words)
The Netherlands 1.1:1 (16 action verbs to 15 stative verbs on 3,699 words)

Level 3
(Ratio calculated for all six subject categories)
Communist group 3.0:1 (57 action verbs to 19 stative verbs on 7,608 words)
Socialist group 1.8:1 (103 action verbs to 57 stative verbs on 10,031 words)
Christian Democrats 2.0:1 (64 action verbs to 32 stative verbs on 8,114 words)
Liberals 1.0:1 (26 action verbs to 27 stative verbs on 3,647 words)
Conservatives 2.0:1 (66 action verbs to 33 stative verbs on 7,626 words).

Contributions to the analyzed debates by all other parties (1980–1995), including the Greens, who entered the arena of the European Parliament in 1990, were less than 400 lines.

---

toward a policy of joint action. Accordingly, the language of the Council's representatives has changed from predominantly descriptive to more active.

At *level 2* and *level 3*, previous research (De Landtsheer, 1998b) indicates that common European dispositions (similarities in political style) are most profiled at the level of the political groups (3). We therefore hypothesize that similarities in the use of action verbs when dealing with the subject of

Table 6.4
The European Commission's Use of Action Verbs versus Stative Verbs in EP
Debates Regarding the Israeli-Palestinian Conflict (1980–1995)

Year	Words	Action Verbs				Stative Verbs			
		Eu/T	Eu/A	We/T	We/A	Eu/T	Eu/A	We/T	We/A
1980	555.519	6	1.08	1	0.18	4	0.72	1	0.18
1981	370.346	7	1.89	0	0	2	0.54	0	0
1982	289.836	8	2.76	1	0.345	1	0.345	0	0
1983	499.162	1	0.2	0	0	0	0	0	0
1984	0								
1985	0								
1986	1,521.639	21	1.38	16	1.051	5	0.329	3	0.197
1987	933.916	10	1.071	0	0	5	0.535	1	0.107
1988	885.610	7	0.79	2	0.226	5	0.535	1	0.107
1989	611.876	13	2.125	4	0.654	4	0.645	2	0.327
1990	369.749	8	2.164	0	0	2	0.541	0	0
1991	538.915	5	0.928	2	0.371	2	0.371	0	0
1992	265.312	4	1.508	0	0	2	0.754	0	0
1993	638.407	5	0.783	0	0	4	0.627	3	0.47
1994	1,044.666	14	1.34	4	0.383	8	0.766	6	0.574
1995	1,484.125	15	1.011	6	0.404	9	0.606	7	0.472
	10,009.078	124	1.239	36	0.36	53	0.53	27	0.27

Verbs used in combination with the subject "Europe" (Eu) in general or with the subject
"We" (We).
T = total number of usages; A = average number of usages for 100 words.

the role of the EU in the Israeli-Palestinian conflict will be more considerable at level 3 than at level 2 or even level 1.

RESULTS AND CONCLUSION

Conforming to our expectations, the discourse in the EP on the role of
the EU in the Israeli-Palestinian conflict during the period 1980–1995
shows that the differences between political groups (Table 6.3, Level 3) and
between member states (Table 6.3, Level 2) are wider than the differences
between the European institutions (Table 6.3, Level 2). The positions of
political groups diverge most (see Table 6.3).

Of the three main European institutions, the Commission speaks about

Table 6.5
The European Council's Use of Action Verbs versus Stative Verbs in EP Debates
Regarding the Israeli-Palestinian Conflict (1980–1995)

Year	Words	Action Verbs				Stative Verbs			
		Eu/T	Eu/A	We/T	We/A	Eu/T	Eu/A	We/T	We/A
1980	2,954.720	30	1.015	7	0.237	13	0.44	5	0.169
1981	627.978	2	0.318	1	0.159	7	1.115	3	0.478
1982	644.080	6	0.932	0	0	2	0.311	0	0
1983	1,022.480	7	0.685	5	0.489	11	1.076	8	0.782
1984	0								
1985	0								
1986	861.457	6	0.696	1	0.116	2	0.232	2	0.232
1987	1,513.590	23	1.52	3	0.198	11	0.727	6	0.396
1988	0								
1989	0								
1990	0								
1991	1,401.180	14	0.999	5	0.357	6	0.428	5	0.357
1992	0								
1993	1,989.840	28	1.407	6	0.302	5	0.251	2	0.101
1994	0								
1995	1,235.180	20	1.619	8	0.648	12	0.972	9	0.729
	12,250.505	136	1.11	36	0.293	69	0.563	40	0.327

Verbs used in combination with the subject "Europe" (Eu) in general or with the subject
    "We" (We).
T = total number of usages; A = average number of usages for 100 words.

Europe using the most active terms. In addition, the Council uses more
action verbs in combination with the subject "Europe" than the Parliament
does. The fact that for the Council and Commission the ratio for all subject
categories together was higher than the ratio of the Parliament might be
caused by the nature of their parliamentary speeches. Besides debating with
the parliamentarians, representatives of the Council and the Commission
have to report on their activities. However, if only clauses including the
subject "we" are considered, which might paint a more representative picture ("we" by far exceeds the other categories), the Commission and Parliament show the same ratio of action verbs to stative verbs, whereas the
Council's ratio of stative verbs even exceeds the amount of action verbs.
This might indicate, as was expected, that the Council was fairly reserved

Table 6.6
The European Parliament's Use of Action Verbs versus Stative Verbs in EP
Debates Regarding the Israeli-Palestinian Conflict (1980–1995)

Year	Words	Action Verbs				Stative Verbs			
		Eu/T	Eu/A	We/T	We/A	Eu/T	Eu/A	We/T	We/A
1980	1,875.88	13	0.693	2	0.107	12	0.64	1	0.053
1981	5,885.28	36	0.612	28	0.476	25	0.425	25	0.425
1982	6,006.05	43	0.716	25	0.416	31	0.516	26	0.433
1983	4,395.85	39	0.887	25	0.569	15	0.341	13	0.296
1984	4,146.27	36	0.868	24	0.579	8	0.193	6	0.145
1985	4,991.62	51	1.022	40	0.801	24	0.481	23	0.461
1986	4,540.76	24	0.529	18	0.396	19	0.418	17	0.374
1987	2,173.77	13	0.598	4	0.184	7	0.322	7	0.322
1988	2,922.51	17	0.582	11	0.376	7	0.24	7	0.24
1989	1,924.19	17	0.883	11	0.572	7	0.364	5	0.26
1990	5,436.10	34	0.625	30	0.552	40	0.736	38	0.699
1991	2,023.00	16	0.791	4	0.198	11	0.544	4	0.198
1992	2,852.10	31	1.087	23	0.806	14	0.491	14	0.491
1993	3,100.83	24	0.774	12	0.387	10	0.322	9	0.29
1994	2,238.57	24	1.072	7	0.313	7	0.313	6	0.268
1995	3,447.00	31	0.899	16	0.464	12	0.348	9	0.261
	57,959.79	449	0.775	280	0.483	249	0.43	210	0.362

Verbs used in combination with the subject "Europe" (Eu) in general or with the subject "We" (We).
T = total number of usages; A = average number of usages for 100 words.

as far as the EU role in the peace process was concerned. Both the Commission and Parliament favored a much more active attitude. When comparing the first half and the second half of the period analyzed (1980–1987 and 1987–1995), it can be concluded that the position (ratio) of the Parliament remained constant. The Commission has, over time, used fewer action terms when discussing the role of Europe in the Middle East. The ratio for the Commission decreases from 2.5:1 to 2.0:1. Finally, the discourse of the Council has changed into a much more active one. The Council's ratio increases substantially from 1.6:1 in the first period to 2.7:1 during the second period (see Tables 6.4–6.9).

Italian and especially Spanish representatives use relatively few stative verbs per hundred lines with "Europe" as subject. Dutch parliamentarians,

Table 6.7
The European Parliament's Political Groups' Use of Action Verbs versus Stative
Verbs in EP Debates Regarding the Israeli-Palestinian Conflict (1980–1995)

Group	Words	Action Verbs		Stative Verbs	
		T	A	T	A
Com	7,608.20	57	0.749	19	0.25
S	10,031.88	103	1.027	57	0.568
PPE	8,114.19	64	0.789	32	0.394
L	3,647.10	26	0.713	27	0.74
LDR	3,592.52	30	0.835	15	0.418
ED	4,033.51	36	0.893	18	0.446
GR	2,129.00	10	0.47	13	0.611
	39,156.39	326	0.782	181	0.49

Verbs used in combination with the subject "Europe" (Eu) in general.
T = total number of usages; A = average number of usages for 100 words.
Political Groups: Communists (Com), Socialists (S), European People's Party (PPE), Liberals
    (L), Conservatives (LDR, ED), Greens (GR).

Table 6.8
The European Member States' Use of Action Verbs versus Stative Verbs in EP
Debates Regarding the Israeli-Palestinian Conflict (1980–1995)

State	Words	Action Verbs		Stative Verbs	
		T	A	T	A
Germany	5,876.95	60	1.021	34	0.579
France	19,430.87	148	0.762	81	0.417
Italy	10,363.49	78	0.753	37	0.357
The Netherlands	3,699.04	16	0.458	15	0.43
Spain	4,122.27	29	0.703	12	0.291
United Kingdom	6,602.11	51	0.654	30	0.385

Verbs used in combination with the subject "Europe" (Eu) in general.
T = total number of usages; A = average number of usages for 100 words.

Table 6.9

The European Institutions' Use of Action Verbs versus Stative Verbs in EP Debates Regarding the Israeli-Palestinian Conflict (1980–1995)

Year	A Action Verbs Eu/We			A Stative Verbs Eu/We		
	Council	Parliament	Commision	Council	Parliament	Commission
1980	0.237	0.107	0.18	0.169	0.053	0.18
1981	0.159	0.476	0	0.478	0.425	0
1982	0	0.416	0.345	0	0.433	0
1983	0.489	0.569	0	0.782	0.296	0
1984		0.579			0.145	
1985		0.801			0.461	
1986	0.116	0.396	1.051	0.232	0.374	0.197
1987	0.198	0.184	0	0.396	0.322	0.107
1988		0.376	0.226		0.24	0.452
1989		0.572	0.654		0.26	0.327
1990		0.552	0		0.699	0
1991	0.357	0.198	0.371	0.357	0.198	0
1992		0.806	0		0.491	0
1993	0.302	0.387	0	0.101	0.29	0.47
1994		0.313	0.383		0.268	0.574
1995	0.648	0.464	0.404	0.729	0.261	0.472
A	0.293	0.483	0.36	0.327	0.362	0.27

Verbs used in combination with the subject "Europe" (Eu) in general or with the subject (We). A = average number of usages for 100 words.

on the other hand, employ few action verbs per hundred lines. The prominent role of Germany in European political integration and the more distant attitude by The Netherlands and Britain seems to correspond with their use of action verbs. The average of the ratios of the nations considered (Germany, France, Italy, The Netherlands, Spain, and the United Kingdom) is similar to the previously mentioned ratio for the entire Parliament (1.8: 1) (see Table 6.3 and Table 6.8).

This psycholinguistic exploration of diverse positions within the European Union regarding an international diplomatic role for the EU might contribute to evidence for a democratic deficit in the European Union. It, again, shows that the political integration of the EU proceeds with the growing power of the EP. It further suggests that a more powerful European Parliament is the best guarantee for a confident and active role of the European Union in the Israeli-Palestinian conflict in particular as well as in international peace negotiations in general.

NOTE

We have benefited from the helpful comments of Dr. S. de Haan (Department of General Linguistics at the University of Amsterdam), and Ihab Saloul (MA in Political Science from Birzeit University and MA student in English Literature at the University of Amsterdam).

REFERENCES

Bellier, I. (1996). Une Culture de la Commission Europeenne? [About the culture of the European Commission]. In Y. Meny, P. Muller, & J. L. Quermonne (Eds.), *Politiques Publiques en Europe* [Public policies in Europe] (pp. 49–60). Brussels: L'Harmattan.

Billig, M. (1998). Rhetoric and the Unconscious. *Argumentation*, 12, 199–217.

Bomberg, E., & Peterson, J. (1998). European Union Decision Making: the Role of Sub-national Authorities. *Policy Studies*, 22, 219–235.

Chafe, W. L. (1970). *Meaning and the Structure of Language*. Chicago: University of Chicago Press.

Cogen, M., & François, A. (1995). Realising the Right to Self-Determination of the Palestinian People: The European Union and the Peaceful Settlement of the Israeli/Palestinian Conflict. In N. Sybesma-Knol (Ed.), *Naar een nieuwe interpretatie van het recht op zelfbeschikking* [Toward a new interpretation of the right to self-determination]. Brussels: VUB Press.

Corbin, J. (1994). *Gaza First: The Secret Norway Channel to Peace between Israel and the PLO*. London: Bloomsbury.

Crawford, M. (1996). *One Money for Europe? The Economics and Politics of EMU*. Basingstoke: Macmillan.

De Landtsheer, C. (1998a). Introduction to the Study of Political Discourse. In O. Feldman & C. De Landtsheer (Eds.), *Politically Speaking: A Worldwide Examination of Language Used in the Public Sphere* (pp. 1–18). Westport, CT: Praeger.

De Landtsheer, C. (1998b). The Political Rhetoric of a Unified Europe. In O. Feldman & C. De Landtsheer (Eds.), *Politically Speaking: A Worldwide Examination of Language Used in the Public Sphere* (pp. 129–145). Westport, CT: Praeger.

De Poot, C. J. (1996). *De sturende werking van het werkwoord in de vraag* [The steering function of the verb in the question]. Doctoral dissertation, Free University of Amsterdam.

European Parliament Secretariat. (1972). *The European Communities' Own Resources and the Budgetary Powers of The European Parliament*. Selected documents. Luxembourg: European Parliament Secretariat.

Feldman, O., and De Landtsheer, C. *Politically Speaking: A Worldwide Examination of Language Used in the Public Sphere*. Westport, CT: Praeger.

Grahl, J., & Teague, P. (1990). *1992—The Big Market*. London: Lawrence & Wishart.

McDowall, D. (1998). *The Palestinians*. An MRG International Report. London: Minority Rights Group.

Semin, G. R., & Fiedler, K. (1991). The Linguistic Category Model, Its Bases, Applications and Range. *European Review of Social Psychology*, 2, 1–30.

Van Dijk, T. (1997). What Is Political Discourse Analysis? In J. Blommaert & C. Bulcaen (Eds.), *Political Linguistics*. Special Issue of the *Belgian Journal of Linguistics*, 11 (pp. 9–52).

CHAPTER 7

National versus Global Public Discourse in the Era of Multi-channelism: The Introduction of Commercial and Cable Television in Israel as an Empirical Test of Habermas' Theory

MIRA MOSHE AND SAM LEHMAN-WILZIG

The "public sphere," as defined by Habermas (1989), constitutes a public stage for discourse regarding critical joint problems and topics of collective concern that are found in the public realm—especially as enunciated in the mass media, universities, and voluntary organizations. The "sphere of public discourse" is the intermediate area between the state and civic society, a space in which differences in power and social status are put aside, where in theory at least, each person has equal weight (Werman, 1997). Such rational public debate on political issues first occurred (in the modern age) within the "private" group discussions of the emerging bourgeoisie.

Habermas asks a critical question regarding our understanding of democracy: What are the social conditions for a substantive, rational discussion of public issues, carried out by private people who are willing to allow *argument* and not *status* to carry the day (Calhoun, 1992)? One of the conditions for enabling citizens to act as a "public" and become part of public activity is their being freed from force or other environmental pressures when dealing with public issues—thus enabling them to feel responsibility to the social collective and to give free expression to their ideas (Mukerji & Schudson, 1991). The capacity to do so is traced to the dissemination of literacy and enlightenment.

The second part of Habermas' major study describes the transformation—indeed, the decline—of the public sphere in advanced capitalist society. This is a structural transformation built into the developmental processes of Western society over the past few generations. He finds here a blurring of the lines between the private and public realms, the adoption of public tasks by private organizations, and the penetration of the state into private life. Simultaneously, the ideal of the general public interest has been supplanted by a picture of necessary compromise between opposing interests, and thus critical and rational discourse in the public sphere has been overtaken by negotiation. Moreover, active critical debate of cultural products has changed into passive consumption of mass culture, determined by forces outside the public sphere (Werman, 1997).

In opposition to Habermas, we believe that public discourse as a tool for engendering a "democratic dialogue" remains essential and continues to exist—this through creation of conditions for collective (not collectivist) thought and enlightened activation of democratic decision making (Dayan-Urbach, 1996). The political realm has an important job of "creation" in this regard; its job is to discover societal values and provide opportunities for deciding priorities. Such a public discourse must allow a free flow of information and criticism regarding governmental leaders and decision makers, in order to guarantee open channels of communication and to spark public debate on the burning issues of the day.

THE NEED FOR A MODEL

In the last few years, the academic communications community has adopted the idea of the "public sphere" and has dealt with different questions regarding the place and role of the mass media in this public sphere. Most of the scientific literature in this area, taking Habermas' lead, has focused on analyzing the historical process of its appearance and has further expanded upon philosophical and theoretical aspects of the subject. However, this preoccupation with the earlier stages of the phenomenon has steered the discussion away from Habermas' other argument that the public sphere is in decline.

The present chapter, therefore, represents an initial attempt to use empirical tools to determine whether, and to what extent, the public sphere has been weakened, using Israel as our case study: a country planning in conscious fashion a significant expansion of its electronic media. We have no doubt that the conditions for "pure" public discourse no longer exist in the contemporary world. On the other hand, we do believe that the intermediate public sphere between the individual and the polity does continue to work, to create, to listen, and to influence. Moreover, in moving from a theoretical discussion of the existence and function of the "public sphere" to a development of an applied, real-world examination, we continue to hold Habermas' opinion that the state—the "public authority"—is one of the prime factors determining the priorities in advancing the citizenry's welfare.

To that end, we have developed the "Funnel Model," a practical model that offers a mechanism for exhibiting the actual development of an open and true dialogue in the public space. This is an applied tool designed to aid in describing the dynamics of any one of the many possible public topics for discussion. It combines quantitative and qualitative analysis of the phenomenon. Use of the Funnel Model involves setting up a methodology for comparing the promised public discourse with the actual empirical consequences of the process.

THE MODEL

The proposed model creates a "funnel" through which the local various social, cultural, economic, and technological subjects pass. In the Habermasian version of the public discourse process, one would expect that local, particularistic topics take preference over regional/international ones, but this need not be true. In any case, our model is value-free, that is, it is based on the priorities of the specific country under discussion and does not determine a priori for any country what those priorities must be.

The central characteristic of our model is that it is dynamic; the following are the four major elements:

Determining the Parameters of the Main Subjects

The first order of business is defining the priority public discourse topics that are the focus for future nurturing.

Hierarchical Dynamism

The several public discourse subjects of importance need to be prioritized, giving the more important ones greater emphasis in the future public discourse. In that way, we can determine the hierarchy of priority.

Filling and Emptying the Funnel

"Filling the Ideational Funnel"

In this first stage the actors attempt to determine future public discourse. The funnel "fills up" with different public topics, based on the pronouncements of all those publicly involved in the expansion of the public sphere.

"Emptying the Funnel"

In the second stage, the funnel "empties out," as evidenced by the actual subjects that form the core of the public discourse. If the most prioritized subjects in the first (pre-expansion) phase emerge as the core subjects constituting the post-expansion discourse, then we have a case of FIFO—first in, first out. Conversely, if the actual public discourse revolves around the (pre-expansion) lower-priority subjects, then the process can be called LIFO—last in, first out.

Feedback

The proposed model is an open one, in constant interaction with the social, cultural, economic, political, and technological environment. Therefore, every change in expectation and aspiration in any of the listed subject areas over time may lead to internal changes in the "public sphere" and concomitant public discourse.

CASE STUDY: HISTORICAL BACKGROUND TO ISRAEL'S MEDIA EXPANSION

The decision to open up Israel's television broadcast system to competition received legislative expression in Amendment 4 of the Bezek (Telecommunications) Law in 1986, as well as in the law establishing the Second Channel Authority for Television and Radio in 1990. It is in the early and final stages of legislation that we find our Ideational Funnel being filled regarding the expectations for the country's future public discourse—through the hoped-for development of a "public sphere" that would nurture certain topics for public discourse. On the other hand, the actualization of the public discourse ("emptying the funnel") occurred after Channel 2 began broadcasting (late 1993), and it is this latter period that forms the basis of our analysis of the actual pubic discourse that emanated from this new multi-channel broadcast system.

METHODOLOGY

Our proposed model emphasizes the dynamic process of change and immediate interaction with the social environment as the core factor of change.

Stage 1: Filling the Ideational Funnel

We first identified the major subject areas raised by the various participants in the legislative and accompanying public debate process. This was done through an in-depth analysis of the following: the arguments and recommendations of the sundry "Commissions of Inquiry" (e.g., Kubersky in 1979; Bar-Sela in 1982; Karniel in 1993) set up by several Israeli governments for the purpose of receiving input as to suggested models; the applicable laws establishing the various broadcast agencies and the way they were supposed to work (Am. 4 to the Bezek Law, 1986; Second Channel Law, 1990); collections of relevant regulations related to the auction of broadcast licenses, such as the programming obligations of the licensees, (for example, as listed in the official *Reshumot*, November 12, 1987: 110–148) and speeches on the part of members of the Knesset (MKs), across the political spectrum, involved in legislating the new communications map of Israel.

The next task was prioritizing the "public discourse" subjects to be nurtured. We broke these down into four categories of hierarchical importance, in a systematic fashion in line with several (occasionally inchoate) attempts on the part of the actors themselves (Ericson, 1996). In order to ensure a systematically empirical analysis, this prioritizing task was based on the obligatory demands placed on the Channel 2 and CATV licensees as found in the respective *legislation* and *ordinances* exclusively—and not on the more amorphous speeches and commission recommendations expressed to the legislative/bureaucratic outcome.

Stage 2: Emptying the Ideational Funnel

After the establishment of the expanded broadcast system, we arrive at the point where we can analyze the public discourse de facto. Our method was to return to the same actors involved in stage 1, for their feelings of success or failure regarding the desired public discourse (as expressed in the earlier hierarchy of subjects). Such a research typology, then, is based on a double research focus (Lin, 1976): the first stage's intentions constituted the intended *means*, while the second stage's results are the *ends* whereby the latter are evaluated in light of the former. To do this, we turned to the following sources: speeches by several Ministers of Communications who dealt with the process over the years; once again, speeches on the part of MKs; interviews conducted by one of the authors with "key informants" (Tremblay, 1982)—ministers, MKs, members of parliamentary committees, and experts deeply involved in the process; and the State Comptroller's annual reports.

The State Comptroller's Report is an important adjunct to this type of research because it is the only source among all those mentioned with a relatively "neutral" stance. While the office is beholden to the legislative branch (the State Comptroller is elected by the Knesset), historically these annual and special reports are almost universally accepted in Israel as being objective (the present and previous comptrollers formerly were Supreme Court justices). Indeed, the scope of this office in Israel and elsewhere (usually called State Ombudsman) has transformed it into a central institution guaranteeing the stability and proper functioning of the nation's democratic system (Friedberg, 1990). In the Israeli case, the main purpose of the State Comptroller's office is to gather data and information on public institutions and to compare their functioning with the legislative mandate (including ordinances, etc.) underlying their existence and work. Thus, these reports were designed from the outset to do in general what we have chosen to do in the particular subject area under discussion, and provide significant assistance—not to mention corroboration—of our findings with regard to the gap between original intent and subsequent fruition.

We chose to divide all the subject areas into three classifications from the standpoint of such a "gap": (1) lack of fit, (2) minimal to partial fit, and (3) large to complete fit. It should be noted that the "fit" refers only to the degree in which each "promise" was fulfilled and not to the amount of "fit" relative to the other subject areas. In other words, a category could score 100 percent total fit, which might indicate that it received *too much* attention, given its low ranking among the prioritized "promised" subject areas.

For illustrative purposes, we offer an example here of the second classification ("minimal to partial fit"). One of the desired intentions of the new television legislation was to enable local community expression. However, the State Comptroller's Report of 1994 found that "the regional advisory committees [mandated by law] *were hardly active* from their establishment; from 1992 only two such committees were active. Due to their inactivity, the subject of community broadcasts was not advanced. . . . In November 1993 the [Second Channel] Council turned to a professional consultant in the area of programming and he will work on developing a policy in the area of local community broadcasts."

Most of the original intended "promises" were carried out in one degree or another, with very few not showing any results at all. One rare example of the latter was the intent to enable broadcasting to linguistic and religious minorities. Although the new cable television system did provide satellite broadcasts from Russia and Morocco, the intent could be said to have been *completely unfulfilled* insofar as these local groups having any control of such broadcast programming was concerned. Overall, however, virtually all the "promised" subject areas did find some expression in the second, post-expansion stage, enabling us to clearly show which had greater expression and which had less.

Findings

Filling the Ideational Funnel

After studying all the sources of the pre-expansion, legislative stage, we were able to reduce all the announced "promises and intents" of future multi-channel broadcasting to four basic categories, each of which had several specific policies and intended outcomes. The following four categories are presented in descending order of prioritized importance (i.e., from the most important priority, as declared by the sources, to the least important): (1) social, cultural, and local public discourse; (2) economics and technology; (3) democracy and values; and (4) global/international trends (see Figure 7.1). The following MK citations are representative of the political debate on the related subjects.

Figure 7.1
Filling the Funnel

Mapping the "Promises" of the Future Public Sphere

Priority 4:
Lowest-Level Priority Promise
Nurture and Develop Globalization (36%)

Priority 3:
Low-Level Priority Promise
Nurture and Develop Democracy and Values (32%)

Priority 2:
High-Level Priority Promise
Nurture and Develop Economy and Technology (20%)

Priority 1:
Highest-Level Priority Promise
Nurture and Develop Society, Culture, and Local Ties 912%)

Social and Cultural Promotion and Development

Encouraging original Israeli and Hebrew works: Many shared the view that increasing the number of television broadcasting channels would encourage thought and creativity. As early as the 1980s, MK A. Rubinstein, Minister of Communications, made provisions for "the promotion of original Israeli and Hebrew works" (DK, 18.5.87). At the beginning of the 1990s, various MKs pursued the same course. MK N. Arad thought that "competition would help the creative network in Israel" (DK, 18.2.91). MK R. Rivlin worried that "local creative works are nonexistent today; only a second channel can enhance and enrich the nation with true and original Israeli creative works" (DK, 18.2.91).

Encouraging cultural rapprochement: Minister of Communications, MK G. Yaakobi, viewed communications as a medium that "brings nations closer together, and also brings remote areas of Israel closer, and gives them some leeway for accelerated development" (DK, 23.5.88). He saw many advantages to the adoption of satellite broadcasting: "The advantages of satellites are bringing other cultures closer, receipt of information, and the opportunity to develop a better understanding of occurrences beyond Israel's borders" (DK, 20.7.88).

Permitting the public to influence the content of broadcasts: Minister of Communications MK A. Rubinstein believed that "it is essential that the news agency be separate, and that the public will have an independent representative therein, and that it not be composed of representatives of the broadcasting authority—representatives of the parties" (DK, 18.5.87). His successor, MK G. Yaakobi, promised that "we will soon set up regional advisory committees in order to allow the public to influence the content of broadcasts" (DK, 19.6.89).

Providing a platform for residents of the geographical periphery: MK Y. Bibi believed that "a second channel could serve more communities in the country (speakers of other languages).... The North need not be deprived" (DK, 19.6.89). MK A. Dayan inveighed against the existing discrimination "in channel two, whose broadcasts do not get to our areas because of the limited scope of the budget, and because of opposition on the part of the Broadcasting Authority management" (DK, 19.6.89). The Minister of Communications, MK M. Shahal, also "recognized the particular needs of residents of the periphery in the North and the South, who don't enjoy an excess of other information, culture and entertainment resources, and therefore are especially in need of these broadcasts."

Providing a platform for peripheral ethnic or national groups of the periphery: MK M. Nefa'a denounced the failure to adopt the idea of providing a platform for national or ethnic groups by way of multi-channel television broadcasts. In his view, "there is no justification for the limited time devoted to Arabic language broadcasts on Israel television.... The Arab population has the right to that!" (DK, 28.5.91). MK R. Cohen also requested "that some of the cable television programs be in Arabic. It is important for the society and for economic diversity" (DK, 9.11.92).

Providing a platform for linguistic minorities: MK A. Burg hoped "that the second channel would be fair and egalitarian minority groups in Israel—not necessarily ethnic minorities, but minorities in terms of language. ... The second channel should be available for other languages as well" (DK, 22.7.92). Minister of Communications MK M. Shahal also wanted "a channel that is fair and equal toward the entire population, including speakers of other languages and new immigrants" (DK, 22.7.92).

Creating a platform for the religious periphery: MK S. Yahalom, a member of one of the religious parties in Israel, wondered whether "there would also be interesting programs for minorities" (DK, 2.7.92). MK C. Biton also viewed as important the expansion "of tools of mass communications primarily for the protection of minority groups like women, religious minorities and other groups that are vulnerable and deprived" (DK, 18.2.91).

Giving expression to community life: MK M. Goldman was satisfied with the thought that increasing the number of broadcasting channels gives expression to community life: "The time has come for Israel, after 42 years, to have more than one channel.... The second channel broadcast from Kfar Tavor, and caused quite a stir" (DK, 18.2.91). There was no doubt among various members of Knesset that "a community channel is important also for local authorities and for residents of the smaller cities" (S. Buhbut, DK, 25.1.93).

Fostering and Development of Globalization Trends

Strengthening the process whereby Israel is becoming part of the global village: MKs from various factions lent their support to the words of MK D. Tichon, that "the world is becoming smaller and smaller" (DK, 20.7.88). MK R. Pinhasi also saw how "modern communications are turning the world into a small global village" (DK, 28.5.91). Thus, as noted by MK R. Cohen, "electronic communications are turning the world into a global village" (DK, 11.2.92).

Diversifying the airwaves: MK A. Rubinstein's conception has become more and more true: "The sky above Israel is opening up more and more and the country's communications network is becoming more and more diversified. . . . We are a free country. The sky is the limit" (DK, 20.7.88). And in truth, "the sky cannot be closed down by laws and fines" (DK, 20.7.88). It is clear, as stated by MK D. Tichon, that "the airwaves must be diversified, they must be opened for every citizen of Israel" (DK, 19.6.89).

Helping to make Israel part of the new age: MK Y. Tsidon saw "great importance in the field of communications, in terms of national infrastructure. . . . The post-industrial age we have entered is an age in which the smooth and rapid flow of information has replaced highways, railroad lines and ports" (DK, 19.6.89). "The field of communications," according to MK A. Solodar, "is perhaps one of the most important fields in the modern era" (DK, 28.5.91). MK R. Cohen also acknowledged that communications is the "key to the next century" (DK, 22.7.92).

Building block in the creation of an advanced mass communications network: Minister of Communications MK G. Yaakobi declared that "one of the primary goals of our communications policy is the creation of an advanced mass communications network, with well-developed, advanced and free foundations, to be accomplished primarily via private and public—but not government—investment" (DK, 19.6.89). His replacement, MK R. Pinhasi, also saw in the promotion of the Israeli communications satellite project, Amos, "a catalyst for further improvement in communications and broadcasting. . . . Promotion of the option of broadcasting by satellite to the Soviet Union and thence to Israel . . . [offers] a flexible means of communication that changes to meet the needs of the current generation and to be in sync with advanced technology . . . the combined system—satellite broadcasts for direct reception and for transmission purposes, as is employed in the most advanced countries in the world" (DK, 28.5.91).

Fostering and Developing of Democratic Values

Expectations regarding enhanced democratization: According to the views of Minister of Communications MK G. Yaakobi, "The principal goals of our communications policy are the creation of an advanced mass communications network, built upon well developed, advanced and unrestricted foundations, to be accomplished primarily via private and public—but not government—investment. . . . Free choice of sources of information, diversified radio and television, will strengthen our democracy, increase the competitive strength of the Israeli economy, and render the society more stable" (DK, 19.6.89).

Preventing centralization: The issue of centralization of all the television broadcasting channels in Israel has a number of aspects. MK Y. Goldberg attached great importance to the fact that there should be a number of channels, in light of the security situation. "Cable television in Kiryat Shmonah and Metulla is part of the organization of these communities in a fluctuating security situation. . . . It is very important that there be two television channels, particularly at such times, so that people will not be stuck on one channel" (DK, 28.5.91). MK H. Corfu (Chairman of the Special Committee on the Second Television and Radio Authority Law) tried to increase the number of broadcasting competitors, in order to avoid the problem of centralization. "The number of participants in each franchise will be far greater, and will tend to prevent the concentration of ownership of commercial communications media in a limited number of persons" (DK, 11.2.92).

Reducing attempts to obtain political influence over the media: MK Y. Levy saw how "the second channel has turned into a focus of controversy between Likud and Labor. . . . Among the public, the opinion is broadly held that if a second channel is created, the Minister of Communications will control it, and thereby serve as an alternative to Mekel [Director-General of the Broadcasting Authority]" (DK, 19.6.89). MK O. Namir believed that the proposed law fell apart on the point they cannot get away from—"who will oversee the news department. . . . Neither of the large parties comes to this with clean hands. . . . If the politicians don't manage to overcome the desire for personal publicity, and the struggle to control the news, then the second channel won't be created as a serious channel" (DK, 19.6.89).

Breaking up the Broadcasting Authority's monopoly: MK A. Rubinstein wanted to see an end to the monopoly of the Broadcasting Authority and requested the Israeli public's support: "The Israeli public desires to bring an end to the destructive monopoly of the Broadcasting Authority" (DK, 20.7.88). Moreover, according to Rubinstein, "the opening of a news agency will bring an end to the destructive monopoly that has existed with regard to everything having to do with television and radio broadcasting" (DK, 11.2.92).

Economic and Technological Support and Development

Encouraging economic growth: Minister of Communications MK G. Yaakobi welcomed the economic initiative he saw in the changes in television broadcasting. "Communications brings countries together, and also brings the distant corners of Israel together, giving them space for breathing and accelerated development. . . . The investment required for laying down the infrastructure, building studios, and acquiring broadcasting equipment will total $400 million over the next five years, supplied by private and public sources (DK, 23.5.88). "The proposed law is designed to ensure that the system has the capacity to function financially," explained MK D. Ben Meir (DK, 20.7.88).

Increasing competition: The accelerated processes in the field of communications were understood by the Minister of Communications, MK G. Yaakobi, as processes with "broad-ranging ramifications for society, culture and the economy. . . . The free choice of sources of information, a range of television and radio programs, etc. . . . will strengthen democracy, increase the ability of the Israeli economy to compete" (DK, 19.6.89). MK M. Wirshuvsky agreed with this view and emphasized the notion that "people need to have a choice between Channel One and Channel Two" (DK, 19.6.89).

A communications revolution: "Throughout the world, and in Israel as well, a communications revolution is taking place, as part of the computer and information revolution. . . . The age of the communications revolution is upon us, and with it an increase in new organizations and new media: cable television, direct satellite reception," as MK G. Yaakobi proclaimed (DK, 23.5.88). MK D. Tichon protested that "the Knesset does not understand the communications revolution that is taking place around the world; and it is setting down impediments to all the laws regarding the creation of a second, a third, and a fourth channel" (DK, 19.6.89).

These are but a few of many sundry quotations from the Knesset debates on the subject of Israeli TV programming, and they are presented here to offer a taste of the spirit of those debates, At the end of the legislative process several laws and ordinances were passed and issued, and it is on the basis of these more concrete and measurable expressions that we turn to an analysis of the relative success or failure in shaping the public discourse.

Emptying the Ideational Funnel

After the introduction of cable and commercial television, the intentions and promises of the pre-expansion sources could be measured through what we call "emptying the funnel": an examination of which prioritized categories were actually carried out in the new multi-channel situation. As noted earlier ("Methodology" section), we scored each of the categories on a tripartite basis: (a) "lack of fit," (b) "minimal to partial fit," and (c) "large to complete fit." The major—and quite unexpected—finding of this study: the fit of the four major categories was in inverse (!) proportion to the priority each received in the first (pre-expansion) stage. The actual percentages of "fit" (a, b, and c), as felt and described by the post-expansion sources we studied are offered in the following description of our findings.

Priority 1: Society, Culture, and Local Ties (a = 33%; b = 67%)

The high hopes for a social, cultural, and local community-based public discourse were strongly dashed in the ensuing multi-channel reality. As the peripheral sectors—national, linguistic, and (ultra-) religious—were not given significant expression, collective public discussion could not take place because these groups did not become partners in any "joint collective public discourse." In complete contradistinction to the hopes that a rich cultural discourse would take place, few tools or venues were developed for an open dialogue based on mutual recognition and respect among Israel's sundry population groups.

Priority 2: Economic and Technological (a = 13%; b = 13%; c = 74%)

The link between intention and execution turned out to be far stronger regarding the second priority category. Overall, one can see that in large measure a public atmosphere of economic and technological growth was created, and even more pronounced was the emphasis on the importance of encouraging economic expansion in Israel of the communications realm. On the other hand, the development of a public discourse on the parameters and nature of such growth did not meet expectations. As a result, ongoing standard and clear rules of public discussion and control did not evolve for these new communications industries.

Priority 3: Democratic Values (b = 20%; c = 80%)

The relatively low priority originally given to this category was not reflected in its actual expression in the multi-channel environment. Quite the reverse. All the "promises" were kept in large measure: establishing the foundation for, as well as inculcating the relative concepts of, a democratic public discourse.

Priority 4: Globalization and Internationalization (c = 100%)

This last category was given very low priority, and yet in the new multi-channel environment it gained a very large amount of public attention. Thus, the public dialogue was turned on its head: instead of a serious *intra*-Israeli discussion of internal matters, the dialogue instead had a clear *inter*-national perspective!

In short, the post-expansion period, that is, after the introduction of multi-channel television in Israel, presents a mirror image of the hopes and aspirations of those who set the priorities in the course of its establishment. The higher the priority given a category, the lower its actual expression in the new media environment—and vice versa. In Habermasian terms, a sphere of public discourse did emerge, but not necessarily the one that he

Table 7.1
Success and Failure in Developing the Sphere of Public Discourse

Category	Stage 1: Designing the Future Public Sphere of Discourse	Stage 2: Fulfilling the Actual Public Sphere of Discourse
1–Society, Culture, and Local Ties	Step 1–Joint, collective sphere of discourse	Step 1–Failure
	Step 2–Pluralistic, collective cultural sphere	Step 2–Failure
	Step 3–Particularistic, community cultural sphere	Step 3–Failure
2–Economics and Technology	Step 4–Public atmosphere for economic and technological growth	Step 4–Success
	Step 5–Public discussion as to the parameters and nature of economic and technological growth	Step 5–Minimal success
3–Democratic Values	Step 6–Creation of a joint democratic public sphere of discourse	Step 6–Success
	Step 7–Inculcating its concepts and ideals	Step 7–Success
4–Globalization and Internationalization	Step 8–Inculcating the idea of an external transnational public dialogue	Step 8–High level of success

would have preferred. Table 7.1 summarizes the success and failure in developing the sphere of public discourse.

DISCUSSION

In the following discussion we shall offer four possible reasons for this anomalous outcome. First, the politicians attempted to determine not merely the agenda for "political debate" but rather the much wider "sphere of *public* debate," leading to the public's attempt to free itself from the long arms of political influence in order to create an "*independent* public sphere." Second, in the civic society the "marketplace of social reality" and the "marketplace of ideas" tend to be synchronous and influence one another. In other words, the public sphere is an active and *real* one, and not merely verbal and divorced from reality. Third, the growing "individualization" and "privatization" of Israeli society might have led the average Israeli citizen to leave the "political sphere" and withdraw into a "private sphere." Finally, the role of Israel's print press may have also influenced the nature of the electronic media's public discourse prioritized agenda.

Creation of an "Independent Public Sphere"

Until recently, Israel did not nurture a Habermasian environment in which all citizens had access to the public sphere. Even the public authorities (including the state bureaucracy) were not obligated to divulge information, a requisite for the proper functioning of public discourse in a democracy. It is only when the public authorities are obligated to "full disclosure" that the public sphere gains a measure of influence over the government through the judiciary (Mukerji & Schudson, 1991). Moreover, public opinion is created through informational transparency and journalistic publication, and without trustworthy and independent reporting the public is unaware of how public resources are being (ab)used (Friedberg, 1990). To this we can add the fact that the State of Israel has demanded of its citizenry intensive participation and involvement in the creation of Israeli society. The overall result: a virtually identical "political sphere" and "public sphere"—almost universal agreement on the important subject areas or, in other words, the political and the civic are one and the same.

During the 1980s, however, a privatization process commenced in which government-owned companies moved into private hands, or at least began to be run on a profit basis. This occurred simultaneously with the development of a "public sphere" in which attention was diverted to wider issues of greater public interest.

This trend received its greatest push in the changeover to a multi-channel system, as these media are truly "mass" and highly influential. However, many times the developing relationship between the new media and the government leaves the former integrally tied to the latter (Garnham, 1992). In the Israeli case, the legislation setting up multi-channelism attempted to ensure that the political establishment would continue to determine the public agenda. But the by-now "mature" Israeli public demanded an "authentic" discourse, that is, a debate relevant to its needs and desires. Thus, Israelis did not take upon themselves the "ideal role" which the authorities tried to foist upon them—and which Habermas called for. Instead, many Israelis decided not to use the new media as a tool for creating (or strengthening) their, or the country's, self-identity. This is line with Meyrowitz's argument (1985) that the electronic media, and especially television, lead to the reconstruction of social reality through the diminution of the value of social situations.

Perhaps Habermas is correct in arguing that the public sphere in its pure state has been sacrificed; however, we think that we can identify an attempt by the public to escape the constricting atmosphere of the nation-state into a wider, more "global" public sphere.

Mutual Influence between the Marketplaces of Reality and Ideas

The law reflects and represents the public discourse on the basis of society's fundamental cultural values (Broekman, 1996). However, already at the early legislative stage towards multi-channelism we can discern that the legislative process was operationally "realistic" in that it tried to resolve disagreements by taking account of divergent views (Ericson, 1996). As a result, even in the early stages of the development of a "sphere of public discourse" one can see the gradual blurring of lines between the "public sphere," the "state," and the "marketplace" (used here not only in the economic sense of the term). As opposed to Habermas' "ideal" prescription of a "pure" (i.e., conceptual, ideational) public sphere, the public was unwilling to divorce the marketplace of reality from the marketplace of ideas. Quite the reverse: the internal "dialogue" between these two spheres intensified.

In Israel, internal and external conflicts have not been resolved over the years. This complex marketplace of national reality exists through an array of political and social checks and balances that many times necessitate *avoiding* coming to grips with questions of national Israeli-Jewish identity (including the internal Arab-Israeli conundrum) as well as not trying to resolve totally the sundry social cleavages. Among other things, this is expressed in the unwillingness to use public channels of communication as a means of opening up these questions to serious public debate. The fear of the heavy social (and perhaps national-existential!) price to pay prevents any real internal coming to grips with Israel's almost unique problems. This may explain in part the "over" emphasis that we found on an external, trans-national public dialogue—a way of avoiding social "root canal" work. Put simply, in Israel's "sphere of public discourse" we find ongoing give-and-take around different *weltanschauungen*, but always taking into account the heavy "price" if matters cut too close to the bone. The marketplaces of reality and of ideas operate in an open system—one with feedback and equilibrium—but the main goal is ensuring the continued survival of the system as a whole.

Decreasing Civic Participation in the Political Sphere and Withdrawal into the Private Sphere

The existence of the State of Israel and Israeli society is without a doubt to the credit of the Zionist revolution (Dror, 1997). Its raison d'être was the physical salvation of the Jewish people qua nation and not of individual Jews per se (Rotenstreich, 1991). This is the central reason for our study's legitimate expectation that we would find trends nurturing a "*joint* (unified) sphere of collective discourse". Moreover, in Israel the "nation" is perceived as a natural ethnic community, a sort of highly extended family—one that not every individual can join and that a person cannot completely leave (once joined) because of an organic connection to the group. Thus, the interests of the individual and of the general community are considered identical (Liebman, 1990).

Unfortunately, the collective success of establishing the state and defending its existence (literally) in the conflict-ridden region of the Middle East proved to be a heavy burden for the individual citizen (Gorny, 1986). In addition, the breakdown of ideology as a unifying mechanism in Israel and the general decrease of attractiveness of ideological movements around the world only intensify this tendency (Almog, 1993). This is an indication of withdrawal from collective politics and a turn to individualistic self-expression.

Another reason for civic "withdrawal" into the private sphere can be found in Israel's evolution into an "Information Society." First, when television gradually becomes society's main means for news and information, then in the very use of this "home" medium the user strengthens privacy at the expense of collectivity (Garnham, 1992). The paradox here is not only Israeli, but rather universal: Worldwide media systems "push" the individual viewer back into hearth and home (Negrine and Papathanassopoulos, 1991). Israeli research has found that in subscribing to cable television (it had a very high "penetration" rate from the start), the new media environment encouraged a reorientation to individualistic values as well as global ones (Adoni and Nossek, 1997). In sum, through television the individual removes himself from the "political sphere" and attempts to create an "independent public sphere" while simultaneously withdrawing into a "private sphere."

Israel's Print Journalism as the Last Bastion of the Public Sphere

Habermas' characterization of the public sphere's evolution involved the rapid development of social communication networks, print media, lending libraries, publishing houses and the like, but mostly the rapid growth of the print media. The rise of a reading public and their gathering together for discourse in social settings (e.g., salons) was what gave the "publicness" to the "public sphere." Simultaneously, the role of the private reader emerged as well. While bookstores, cafes, and reading rooms offered space for different forms of "public assembly," subscribers' lists and pen pal associations were a form of non-personal communication, not to mention the fact that receiving printed material usually meant solitary consumption. The idea that one can view society as a series of private individuum, or that the individual takes priority over the social collective, draws more from a *reading* public than a listening one (Eisenstein, 1991). One way or the other, the field of modern intellectual criticism in the contemporary world regarding democratic discourse and political dialogue is to be found mainly in the medium of writing within newspapers, journals, and books (Kellner, 1995).

Therefore, it is possible that the real main forum for the sphere of public discourse is to be found in print and not the electronic medium of television. In Israel one can find a rough division of labor between print journalism and the broadcasting media, the latter specializing in collecting and reporting news while the former emphasize commentary and opinion formation to a much greater extent. Despite the expansion of television and radio in Israel over the last few years (the multi-channel revolution), the country's print media has maintained its important position in Israeli society (Caspi & Limor, 1992). Given the very high level of newspaper readership (about 85% of the adult population read a paper on an almost daily basis), there was very little need for any expansion of the public sphere.

As a result, despite the politicians' (and other interested parties') aspirations to have the multi-channel revolution expand the public sphere, the Israeli public saw little need for this. What the average Israeli *did* want was to expand the country's entertainment menu as a means for escaping (if only for a few hours each day) from the pressurized reality of daily life, and certainly not to have deal with it in yet another (expanded) medium! We find support for this hypothesis in the explosive growth of pirate cable television in the 1980s, which offered video movies almost exclusively to an entertainment-starved public. Further research into the "public discourse" as found in Israel's newspapers should be able to disprove or corroborate this last explanation for the lack of serious and open public discussion on the burning issues of the day in Israel's expanded, multi-channel television environment.

CONCLUSION

To a great extent, technology determines the dialogue between the citizenry and their elected representatives (Jacobson, 1993). The question of whether to adopt a new technology, therefore, is a very significant one in the evolution of a sphere of public discourse. Given the similarities of media development among the nations of the developed world and the omnipresence of the global market, it is our belief that the "funnel model" outlined in this article is applicable to most nations and cultures in which a "communication sphere" has evolved. Moreover, the accelerated trend toward a (somewhat) unified international lifestyle, the cross-cultural exchange between different cultures, and growing structural similarities among the advanced nation-states that were quite different in the recent past—all these trends tend to submerge traditional values and particularistic beliefs which gave each culture its particular coloration. This is especially the case among those countries with a high level of immigration and with those nations characterized by a high level of persecuted or repressed cultural and religious minorities. For these countries, our funnel model serves a useful purpose and constitutes an efficient tool for analyzing the gap between legitimate expectations from technological communications innovation and the actual success/failure of these media in the creation of a direct and authentic public discourse. If our central finding is replicated elsewhere, it would indicate that Habermas' argument of decline in the "sphere of public discourse" in the contemporary world is right and wrong—correct in that such discourse may no longer primarily revolve around national, societal matters as in the past; incorrect in that a new paradigm of discourse is taking its place—internationalist and global in perspective.

REFERENCES

Adoni, C., and Nossek, H. (1997). "I," "Israeli" and "World Citizen": Cable Television and Its Ramifications on Social Relationships [Hebrew]. In Dan Caspi (Ed.), *Communications and Democracy in Israel*. Tel Aviv: Van Leer Institute and Kibbutz Meuchad.

Almog, O. (1993). From the Era of the Famous to the Hour of the Common Celebrity [Hebrew]. *Politikah*, 48, 52–54.

Broekman, J. M. (1996). Communicating Law. In David Nelken (Ed.), *Law as Communication* (pp. 45–62). Aldershot: Dartmouth.

Calhoun, C. (1992). Introduction: Habermas and the Public Sphere. In Graig Calhoun (Ed.), *Habermas and the Public Sphere* (pp. 1–50). Cambridge, MA: MIT Press.

Caspi, D., and Limor, Y. (1992). *The Mediators* [Hebrew]. Tel Aviv: Am Oved.

Dayan-Urbach, I. (1996). The Democratic Model and Freedom of Expression [Hebrew]. *Iyunei Mishpat*, 20, 377–437.

Divrei haKnesset (18.5.87). *319th session of the 11th Knesset* [Hebrew]. Jerusalem (pp. 2681–2705).

Divrei haKnesset (24.5.88). *330th session of the 11th Knesset* [Hebrew]. Jerusalem (pp. 2926–2936).

Divrei haKnesset (20.7.88). *462nd session of the 11th Knesset* [Hebrew]. Jerusalem (pp. 3875–3879).

Divrei haKnesset (19.6.89). *75th session of the 12th Knesset* [Hebrew]. Jerusalem (pp. 2559–2580).

Divrei haKnesset (18.2.91). *168th session of the 12th Knesset* [Hebrew]. Jerusalem (pp. 2295–2302).

Divrei haKnesset (28.5.91). *301st session of the 12th Knesset* [Hebrew]. Jerusalem (pp. 3797–3816).

Divrei haKnesset (11.2.92). *383rd session of the 12th Knesset* [Hebrew]. Jerusalem (pp. 2894–3897).

Divrei haKnesset (22.7.92). *5th session of the 13th Knesset* [Hebrew]. Jerusalem (pp. 165–177).

Divrei haKnesset (9.11.92). *21st session of the 13th Knesset* [Hebrew]. Jerusalem (pp. 325–350).

Divrei haKnesset (25.1.93). *55th session of the 13th Knesset* [Hebrew]. Jerusalem (pp. 2757–2777).

Dror, Y. (1997). *Renewing Zionism* [Hebrew]. Jerusalem: World Zionist Organization Publishing.

Eisenstein, E. (1991). The Rise of the Reading Public. In D. Crowley and P. Meyer (Eds.), *Communication in History, Technology, Culture, Society* (pp. 94–102). New York: Longman Publishing Group.

Ericson, R. V. (1996). Why Law Is Like News. In D. Nelken (Ed.), *Law as Communication* (pp. 195–230). Aldershot: Dartmouth.

Friedberg, A. (1990). The Characteristics of Public Audit in Israel [Hebrew]. In A. Friedberg (Ed.), *Public Auditing in Israel, De Facto* (pp. 140–154). Jerusalem: Akademon.

Garnham, N. (1992). The Media and the Public Sphere. In C. Calhoun (Ed.), *Habermas and the Public Sphere* (pp. 359–376). Cambridge, MA: MIT Press.

Gorny, J. (1986). *The Search for a National Identity* [Hebrew]. Tel Aviv: Am Oved.

Habermas, J. (1989). *The Structural Transformation of the Public Sphere*. Cambridge, MA: MIT Press.

Habermas, J. (1991). The Public Sphere. In C. Mukerji & M. Schudson (Eds.), *Rethinking Popular Culture: Contemporary Perspectives in Cultural Studies* (pp. 398–404). Berkeley: University of California Press.

Habermas, J. (1992). Further Reflections on the Public Sphere. In C. Calhoun (Ed.), *Habermas and the Public Sphere* (pp. 421–461). Cambridge, MA: MIT Press.

Jacobson, R. (1993). Reciprocity versus Interactivity: Principles of Democracy Control for the Information Age. In S. Splichal and J. Wasko (Eds.), *Communication and Democracy* (pp. 197–206). Norwood, NJ: Ablex Publishing Corporation.

Kellner, D. (1995). Intellectuals and New Technologies. *Media, Culture & Society*, 3, 427–448.

Liebman, C. (1990). The Concept "State of Israel" and the Way It Is Viewed in Israeli Society [Hebrew]. In *Government and Politics in the State of Israel: A Reader*. Tel Aviv: Open University.

Lin, N. (1976). *Foundations of Social Research*. New York: McGraw-Hill.

Meyrowitz, J. (1985). *No Sense of Place*. New York: Macmillan.

Mukerji, C., & Schudson, M. (1991). *Rethinking Popular Culture: Contemporary Perspectives in Cultural Studies*. Berkeley: University of California Press.

Negrine, R., & S. Papathanassopoulos. (1991). The Internationalization of Television. *European Journal of Communication*, 6, 9–32.

Rotenstreich, N. (1991). *Between Fundamental Assumptions and Reality* [Hebrew]. Tel Aviv: Am Oved.

Tremblay, M-A. (1982). The Key Informant Technique: A Non Ethnographic Application. In R. G. Burgess (Ed.), *Field Research: A Sourcebook and Field Manual* (pp. 98–106). London: George Allen & Unwin.

Werman, D. (1997). Habermas' Public Sphere: An Intellectual Experiment or Historical Experience? [Hebrew]. *Devarim Achadim*, 1, 34–45.

CHAPTER 8

Mythical Thinking, Aristotelian Logic, and Metaphors in the Parliament of Ukraine

SERGIY TARAN

This chapter deals with the semantic figures of political language such as political metaphors as well as mythical and logical types of reasoning. The theoretical part presents a comparative analysis of the basic assumptions of Aristotelian logic and mythical thinking, two types of reasoning. It concentrates on the origin and nature of modern political discourses and their connection with modern myth creation. The focus is on the main assumptions of mythical thinking (synthetism, operating with images, possibility of contradictions, dramatization, and so-called cyclic time and non-equal time). These assumptions are examined in the context of political discourses and contrasted with the assumptions of Aristotelian logic (analytism, operation with concepts/terms, impossibility of contradictions, neutrality, and linear and equal time). The case study includes a sample of Ukrainian parliamentary debates devoted to economic issues (specifically, to the budget policy of Ukraine). It reveals how different political groups of the Ukrainian parliament use the political tribune to strengthen their impact on the audience through manipulation achieved with different types of reasoning.

The case study shows which elements of mythical thinking and Aristotelian logic are prevalent in the language of members of the Ukrainian parliament and how they are related to the use of metaphors. It further reveals which and how different political groups tend to use the assumptions underlying Aristotelian logic and mythical thinking. The conclusions and discussion concentrate on the existence and a possible explanation for the persuasive power of mythical thinking and Aristotelian logic in the modern political language of particular political groups.

ARISTOTELIAN LOGIC AND MYTHICAL THINKING

Myth is a traditional story that usually involves supernatural or imaginary persons and embodies popular ideas about nature and social phenomena (Robertson, 1993: 599). It is "a fable, an allegorical fiction originating in certain real events, re-created through wish and imagination in such a way that starting from a fact, it ends representing and meaning something else" (Montero, 1995: 52). According to Montero, the "term 'myth' is used with the connotation of falseness or to indicate that something is unreal"; thus it is related to the domain of human beliefs rather than to the domain of rational reasoning. Myth is the most ancient outlook that explains the world and determines human behavior (Alexandrov, 1987: 17), but, in spite of its "archaic" connotation, underestimating its role in human history might be a mistake. Mythical thinking played a crucial role in human culture as part of the religious mode of thought.

Science replaced religion during the European Enlightenment, and as such science started to play the role of religion in society (Mannheim, 1992: 59). According to the Enlightenment idea of Reason, scientific outlook applies to the normative, or formal logic. Basic axioms/assumptions of formal or normative logic were formulated by Aristotle (Feyerabend, 1994: 113–147). What are the differences between the mythical outlook, which operates within mythical thinking, and the scientific outlook, which operates within Aristotelian logic? Mythical thinking is the "logic of myth"; it can be distinguished from Aristotelian formal logic, says Goloskover (1987). Weinberger came up with a similar idea about "two types of argumentation: objective argumentation which deals only with the relation of arguments to the probandum, and pragmatic argumentation which views at the subjective reactions of the audience" (Weinberger, 1995: 37–47). The criteria used by Goloskover, Weinberger, and others to distinguish between Aristotelian logic and mythical thinking show how two types of reasoning are used in political language to persuade the audience. The distinction between two types of reasoning is to some extent socially constructed: Neither of the two modes of thought exists in pure form in one speaker. However, revealing the elements of both types of thinking in political discourse may be an important clue to the understanding of the unconscious/conscious intentions of a politician.

SYNTHESISM AND ANALYTISM

Mythical thinking arranges the world into one *singular universe*. It looks at the world *synthetically*. The different appearances of the world are united in certain organic parts of this world. These parts are represented very often by superhuman persons who embody different phenomena of the "cosmos" in themselves (Huizinga, 1994: 156). According to Cassirer, the emotional principle of myth fuses reality and ideal, things and images, body and attributes (Meletinskij, 1979: 54). Aristotelian logic aims at *analysis*. Analytical outlook splits the world into different components and investigates the relationships among them. From an analytical point of view, the world is not an organic singular universe, but unknown matter that must be split and explored *rationally*. Political discourse can create its own semantic web world, which is prohibited for critical analysis. For example, in Soviet political discourse it was impossible to criticize or analyze in depth notions like "workers and peasants," "building of communism," and "proletariat" (Marcuse, 1994: 74–82). In Western societies it is prohibited to question, or analyse, from a *non-democratic* point of view, notions like "human rights," "individual," "democracy," and "election." Political discourse, thus, is a synthetically undivided unity of once given notions. It is inconceivable to change these relationships because it can destroy the "cosmos harmony" of discourse.

According to Foucault: "In every society the production of discourse is at once controlled, selected, organized and redistributed by a certain number of procedures whose role is to ward off its powers and dangers, to gain mastery over its chance events, to evade its ponderous, formidable materiality." Restrictive practices in discourse are implemented through certain semantic formations of communication, which according to Foucault are divided into "forbidden speech," "the division of madness," and "the will to truth" (Foucault, 1984: 109–113). Such "semantic locks" are the essential part of mythical thinking, since myth contains "resistance to the analytical attempts, which leads to the appearance of internal forms of opposition and to present a monolithic front to criticism, either internal, or external" (Montero, 1995: 53). However, the locked political discourse may have to employ Aristotelian logic in order to prove "the truth" of the political discourse within the *once fixed* semantic structure. Notably, the negative labels for critics of the ideology of political discourse may be summarized as "irrational": "mad," "fool," "non-truth" (Foucault, 1984: 113). The assumptions of Aristotelian logic here play a purely propagandistic role. In order to be persuasive, political discourses have to be extended into all areas of social life. According to Mannheim, political discussion strongly differs from scientific discussion; as political discussion penetrates much deeper into the existential foundations of one's thinking, it aims to destroy the internal ideological base of the opponent (Mannheim, 1992: 65). Therefore, there are no closed social areas for political discourses. For instance, it is apparent that in democratic societies "to be a good citizen" means to be democratically oriented in each social area: personal (issues about gender), economic (issues about equal opportunities for everybody), and political (issues about human rights). Penetrating all spheres of human life, political discourse creates a singular universe within which both types of reasoning may be employed.

TERMS (CONCEPTS) AND IMAGES

Aristotelian logic operates with terms (concepts). The *term* is a basic attribute of science. Each term has a definition with concrete specific meaning. Terms have definite and logically arranged relations between each other. *Myth* rests on images, or symbols, which unlike terms are based on beliefs or creativity (imagination), but not on reason. Each myth contains a lot of images and symbols. In ancient myths images and symbols are usually related to the forces of nature. Images and symbols of myths may be translated into mythologems: "that is narration which incorporates the total, or part of the mythical thinking representations so expressed" (Montero, 1995: 52). Images and symbols have a lot of meanings, which may contradict each other.

Key notions of political discourses may have strong attributes of images rather than of terms (concepts). Terms (concepts) that are used in political discourse have usually come from the social sciences, where they are strictly defined and arranged among each other. However, the same political discourse may not have strict definitions and logic connections with other definitions or with the reality they describe in actual political discourse. According to Orwell, many political notions are similarly abused:

The word *Fascism* has now no meaning except in so far as it signifies "something not desirable." The words *democracy, socialism, freedom, patriotic, realistic, justice,* all have a different meaning which cannot be reconciled with one another. In the case of a word like *democracy,* not only is there no agreed definition, but the attempt to make one is resisted from all sides. It is almost universally felt that when we call a country democratic we are praising it: consequently the defenders of any kind of regime claim that it is a democracy, and fear that they might have to stop using the word if it were tied down to any one meaning. (Orwell, 1995: 428)

According to Lotman, rhetorical constructions belong to signs and symbols. They always have a double meaning (Lotman, 1994: 71). For example, metaphors, "figures of speeches, in which a word (group) symbolises an idea by the use of an implicit comparison, rather than by directly stating the idea" (De Landtsheer, 1998: 32), have real manipulative power to persuade an audience. The power of metaphors "to mystify or clarify things" can be widely used by politicians: They "often use incorrect analogies, thereby transmitting certain desirable but inaccurate connotations" (De Landtsheer, 1995). Another important aspect of notions of political discourses is the fact that they are historically determined. "The same notion in one case contains the evaluation, or purpose, in another one does not. . . . The ontology of a notion itself is historically determined, but it usually remains unexamined" (Mannheim, 1992: 81). Images in politics can promote the re-emergence of ancient personifications of political (ex-nature) forces. Such persons as Uncle Sam (United States) or Mother-Motherland (Russia) serve the idea of an emotionally unified nation. This personification can create an ancient cult with idols. The burning of the stuffed bourgeoisie in the former Soviet Union in the 1930s can be an example of such a cult.

CONTRADICTIONS

Within Aristotelian logic, contradictions are impossible. It is absurd to assume the existence of *A* and *non-A* at the same time. For example, Aristotelian logic regards it as inconceivable to be in a room and outside a room at the same time. Within myth, contradictions are possible. In the ancient myths immortal gods can die, the mythical hero is able to be in different places at the same time, or suddenly have or lose paranormal abilities. Within mythical thinking, obvious contradictions can exist and do not hinder each other (Goloskover, 1987: 48). Considering the role of political discussion for ideological issues, Mannheim emphasized: "A word 'ideology' implicitly presumes that collective unconsciousness can hide reality in a certain situation in order to stabilize a society" (Mannheim, 1992: vol. 1, 66). According to Mannheim, the cultural roots of visible contradictions within political discourse can be found in the essayistic and experimental thinking of the scientists of the 17th and 18th centuries (Mannheim, 1992: vol. 1, 81). Mythical thinking can create a specific situation in mass communication that evokes an impression that everything is possible within political discourse. Like in ancient myths, in which immortal gods could die or the mythical hero could be in several places at once or suddenly have or lose paranormal abilities, political discourse can arrange semantic constructions that contradict themselves. There are examples of such semantic "self-contradictory" constructions in the history of Soviet political discourses: "socialistic pluralism," "scientific communism," and "five-year plan—during four years." Formally, it is impossible to assume the existence of "socialism," which is based on mono-ideology and "pluralism" at the same time. It is impossible to combine notions like "communism" (certain ideology) and "scientific" (politically neutral outlook) in one notion (Pocheptzov, 1994). It is impossible to implement a "five-year plan" that is supposed to be done "during four years." Nevertheless, the mentioned semantic constructions were accepted by the audience. Moreover, visible contradictions create what I would call an "effect of miracle"—the contradictory semantic construction that makes the audience believe in the impossibility and, as a result, strongly support the one who can create the uttered impossibility. In this respect, "miracles" created by gods of any religion may be considered the cultural roots and precursors of modern contradiction in political discourse.

MYTHICAL TIME

Line Time

From Aristotelian logic, we can extract the features of scientific conceptions of time that have to be contrasted with the assumptions of mythical thinking. In my view there are two basic assumptions of normative, scientific time:

The Past Is Always before the Future

According to normative logic, if A ⇒ B, and B ⇒ C, we can conclude that A ⇒ C. In other words, A happens before C. We can state that the past happens before the future. Thus, scientific time is "linear," successively ordered.

All Pieces of Time Are Objectively Equal

For instance, one hour is always one hour, at any point in time: at night or in the day, in winter or in summer, at times of war or at times of peace.

Cyclic Time

Confused Time

Mythical time is built according to the natural order (Meletinskij, 1979: 12–48); therefore, it has a *cyclic succession*. Everything can or must be repeated. For that reason, confused non-linear mythical time assumes that past can come after future, or future before present. For instance, we can know a predicted future of our activity and unavoidably move toward this future.

Political discourse may confuse time. The past or the future can be more important than the present in political discourse, if that is required for current propagandistic purposes. The importance of the future can create a situation in which everyone can live "for the future," as in the former Soviet Union. Moreover, political discourse presents the future as a positive result as one that has already been achieved: "In the Soviet Union the building of a factory plant was presented in such a way as to make people feel it already existed and produced real goods." Discussing the future is safe in the sense that nobody can check on the future (Pocheptzov, 1994: 20).

On the other hand, the past can become the present through political discourse. "Dead" events attain a second life and can be re-lived many times. There are examples: Past battles can be performed for a mass audience without taking into account the present international context. The discovery of the Americas by Columbus can be turned into a performance without consideration for the native Americans and the consequences this event had for them.

In order to prolong the influence and power of past glories, heroes of the past become "saints," or their bodies are mummified (Mao and Lenin, or in ancient religious cults). Political myth needs a kind of "mythical genealogy" that gives to the current politicians the role of descendants of past heroes (Montero: 1995: 59). In my opinion, the special attention in modern politics to political rituals (Hariman, 1995: 80–94) and traditions is an attempt to save certain aspects of the past for current political discourse.

Cyclic succession in mythical thinking is used to persuade each participant of political discourse that some good events are unavoidable. "We always were winners and we will win in this battle again" appears to be a general principle of this kind of propaganda.

Another persuasive capacity of the mythical cyclic succession of time is the obvious conclusion that there is no reason to find out something new in political discourse: Everything has already been decided, and nobody has any option but to take this once-determined way.

Applying cyclic succession in mythical thinking grows in times of crisis: "When the sense of progress is checked by depression or recession, or by war or social disruption, we may reassure ourselves (somewhat) either with the idea of cyclical time ('long waves', 'Kondatieff cycles', etc.) as natural phenomena to which we must perforce adapt, or dredge up an even more compelling image of some stable universal propensity (such as innate human quarrelsomeness) as the perpetual counterpoint to progress" (Harvey, 1990: 202).

"Unequal" Time

Mythical time is divided into "sacral" and "normal" time. For instance, in Christian myth the birthday of Christ is more important than other days of the year. In other words, time is marked (or divided) according to subjective will, not according to the physical objective succession.

Time in political discourse is also divided into sacral and normal time. For instance, the period of the Russian Revolution (October, 1917) was proclaimed as the "beginning of a new epoch" in Communist political discourse. Obviously, the period of Greek democracy is more significant for the political discourses of modern democratic countries than, for instance, the period of the Byzantine Empire. National holidays of modern states became more important days for these states than other days of the year. Thus, pieces of time equal from a scientific point of view are not equal within the logic of political discourse. Time is not equal; it is marked according to subjective will. Each ideological unity (national state, European Union, or international political movement) is looking not only for common visual symbols but also for common sacral time. That time can be found both in the past (sacral periods of history) and in current time (for example: the birthday of the Queen or elections in democratic Europe or party congresses in the former Soviet Union).

DRAMATIZATION AND NEUTRALITY

Myth presents the world as an area of *dramatic* battle between good and evil. Watching and experiencing the mythical drama, people are supposed to realise what it means to be "good" or "bad." Mythical thinking thus paints the world in "black" and "white" and in such a way imposes a certain meaning of morality.

From the point of view of Aristotelian logic, reality is the result of various factors that are ethically heterogeneous. Any event is presented as a natural result of ethically neutral reasons. For example, spring comes not because of the victory of the forces of spring over the forces of winter (mythical thinking), but as a consequence of the rotation of the Earth around the Sun.

Dramatization of the world within political discourse creates an important dimension of mythical thinking. According to Montero, dramatization of events is an essential part of political myth, since reality is viewed as the "result of the struggle between different forces. Good versus evil; sacred versus profane; pure versus impure" (Montero, 1995: 52). Since political myth strives not only to explain reality but also "to justify specific power practices" (Lasswell, 1949: 9), the division of events into "right" (white) and "wrong" (black) creates ethical values for pragmatic purposes. Therefore, it is very difficult for politicians to be entirely neutral as long as they have any pragmatic intentions.

METAPHORS

The case study of this research investigates how assumptions of mythical thinking and Aristotelian logic are connected to the use of metaphors. The investigation of political metaphors contains the cognitive issues that are similar to an examination of mythical thinking and Aristotelian logic in political discourse. For example, the impossibility of a differentiation between object and subject in mythical thinking (Montero, 1995: 52) can be aligned with the need to analyze the subject and his or her application of the metaphor (object) (De Landtsheer, 1994: 69). Political metaphors, like mythical thinking, can allow logical contradictions between different elements of political language, since they do not have strict relations between words and ideas. Finally, the operation of images within mythical thinking may be juxtaposed with the fact that metaphors are images (Dobrzynska, 1995: 597) and not notions, since they can connect different unfixed semantic elements and thereby provide an aesthetic effect for the audience. Besides the mentioned similarities between mythical thinking and metaphors, there is an important point about the increase of metaphorical language in times of crisis (De Landtsheer, 1994: 69), which can also be said about mythical thinking, in particular about mythical "cyclic time" (Harvey, 1990: 202).

Metaphors can also penetrate the realm of Aristotelian logic. A metaphor is the "backbone of social science writing" (Richardson, 1994: 519) and as such, it may be widely used in political discourse, since politicians apply to the theoretical approaches of the social sciences. Richardson makes the following important examples of metaphorical usages in political science that elicit the importance of metaphors in political science and political discourse:

Consider *functionalism, role* theory, *game* theory, *dramaturgical analogy, organicism, social evolutionism,* the social *system, ecology, labeling* theory, *equilibrium, human capital,* the *power elite, resource mobilization,* ethnic *insurgency, developing* countries, *stratification,* and *significance* tests. Metaphors organize the sociological world and affect the interpretations of the "facts"; indeed, facts are interpretable ("make sense") only in terms of their place within a metaphorical structure. The "sense making" is always value constituting—making sense in a particular way, privileging one ordering of the "facts" over others." (Richardson, 1994: 518–520)

Metaphors thus are an essential part of political science. As was shown by Richardson, they may even become terms or concepts of social sciences. Therefore, metaphors are embedded in two types of reasoning. The case study shows how they are correlated with the assumptions of Aristotelian logic and mythical thinking and which political groups utilize them.

THE PARLIAMENT OF UKRAINE

The current political discourse of Ukraine is the model for my research. Particularly, samples of debates in the Ukrainian parliament were examined (Table 8.1). Ukraine appeared as an independent state in 1991. However, independent Ukrainian political discourse appeared before the country's actual political independence. Indeed, political discourse created an ideological background for the nationalist movements and signified the creation of a new national elite.

Initially Ukrainian political discourse was dominated by the key words "independence" (1988–1991) and, later, "state building" (1991–1994). Gradually, however, the discourse became preoccupied with the term "economic reforms." The semantic structure of the "economic reforms" discourse is a significant example of how certain "positive" notions (Marcuse) can restrict alternative ways of communication within political discourse.

The political program of "economic reforms" was initiated by President Kuchma during his pre-election campaign and presidential activity. It was

Table 8.1
Sample of Debates on Budget Policy in the Parliament of Ukraine (1991–1996)
(Protocols of Debates in *The Bulletin of the Parliament of Ukraine*)

Date	Title	Issue No.	Size (27 lines in one page, 10 words in one line)
December 19, 1991	Discussion on draft of state budget of 1992	*Bulletin* 55, pp. 3–65	62 pages: **16,740** words
May 19, 1992	Discussion on state budget of 1992	*Bulletin* 68, pp. 2–49	47 pages: **12,690** words
February 1, 1994	Discussion on state budget of 1994	*Bulletin* 11, pp. 3–73	71 pages: **19,170** words
December 21, 1995	Discussion on the results of budget policy of 1994 and on the adoption of state budget of 1995	*Bulletin* 62, pp. 40–93	52 pages: **14,040** words
December 18, 1996	Discussion on the report on the result of state policy in 1994 and 1995	*Bulletin* 65, pp. 56–86	30 pages: **8,100** words
			Total: **70,740** words

accepted as a general program for all areas of political, economic, and social life. The economy of Ukraine is nevertheless still in deep crisis. Notions and semantic links among key notions of "economic reforms" discourse restrict all other possible ways of thinking and, therefore, all other possible ways of practical reformation of the Ukrainian economy. For instance, the fixed interactions among the notions of "voucher privatization," "strict monetary politics," and "strong presidential power" limit the discussion about alternative ways of privatization, finance policy, and reformation of the political system. Weak attempts to establish such discussions are considered a mistake or as opinions against "economic reforms" as a whole. All basic attributes of "economic reforms" must therefore be accepted wholesale. Notably, opinions against reforms are considered "inconvenient" and "irrational."

In spite of a gap between the reality (economic crisis) and the proclaimed ideology of "economic reforms," the President of Ukraine is a quite popular politician. In my view, this is a consequence of the mythical belief that reforms are really provided by the governing elite of Ukraine. The case study examines how assumptions of two types of reasoning are fluctuating within the restricted political discourse and how they are connected to the usage of metaphors. The topic of the sample of debates in the Ukrainian parliament is the budget policy.

Operationalization

Examining political speeches, I answered the following questions, which were arranged according to the main assumptions (axioms) of Aristotelian thinking and mythical thinking. Thus, I brought the internal semantic structure of a sample into correlation with the following elements (axioms) of Aristotelian logic and mythical thinking. For each set of assumptions, I marked the speeches with the associated variables.

Analytism and Synthetism

Does the political language of a given politician present the political reality as a unitary universe or as one that is made up of different elements? Is it possible to extract (exclude) any elements of a politician's political language from the whole web of notions of his or her political speech? If reality in a political speech (or a part of a speech) is presented as a unitary universe, I marked the speech with variable SY. If reality in political speech (or a part of a speech) is presented as a matter for analysis, I marked it (or its part) with variable AN.

Concepts and Images

Do the key notions of the political speech have only strict meanings, or do they have many meanings? Do key notions of the political language include semantic tautologies? Examples of semantic tautologies are the following: *We need to give more power to the president because it is necessary for the reformation of the finance system,* and *We need to reform the financial system because we have to give more power to the president.* Key notions of political speech that do not have strict meaning were marked with variable IM (images). Key notions that do have strict meaning were marked with variable CN (concepts).

Contradictions/ Non-contradictions

Does the political language of a given politician contain internal contradictions? If a political speech (or a part of a speech) contains internal contradictions, I marked the speech (or its part) with variable CT. If political speech (or a part of a speech) does not contain internal contradictions, I marked the speech (or its part) with variable NC.

Interpretation of Time

Does the political language of a given politician consider any events "unavoidable"? Does political language allow alternative models of the future?

Can any periods of the past, or any future events (periods) be considered as more important than the present situation? If a political speech (or a part of a speech) of given a politician considers any events as "unavoidable," I marked the speech (or its part) with variable TC ("cyclic time"). If a political speech (or a part of a speech) allows different alternative models of the future, I marked the speech (or its part) with variable TL ("linear" time). If any periods of the past or any future events (periods) are considered more important than the present situation, I marked the speech (or its part) with variable TN. If the present is considered more important than any periods of the past and/or future events (periods), I marked the speech (or its part) with variable TE.

Dramatization and Neutrality

Is the reality viewed as a result of struggle of opposite forces? Is there any "labeling" of events along the lines of "black" and "white" in a speech (good versus evil)? If the reality is viewed as a result of struggle of opposite forces and/or there is any "labeling" of events along the lines of "black" and "white" in a speech, I marked the speech (or its part) with variable DR. Does a political speech of a given politician consider the world to be the result of various factors that are ethically heterogeneous? If a political speech of a given politician considers the world to be the result of various factors that are ethically heterogeneous, I marked the speech (or its part) with variable NE.

Concepts and Formulas

The following formulas, which I constructed for mythical thinking and Aristotelian logic variables, are based on the model that De Landtsheer conceived for the calculation of the metaphorical coefficient (De Landtsheer, 1994: 69–72). In addition to calculating mythical thinking and Aristotelian logic variables according to the coding scheme represented in Table 8.2, I examined the same political speeches and calculated their metaphorical coefficient. The "metaphorical coefficient" is the total of the metaphorical variables "frequency," "intensity," and "content," which are indicators of the metaphorical power of a text (De Landtsheer, 1994: 63). In order to calculate mythical thinking and Aristotelian logic variables, each element of mythical thinking and Aristotelian logic was assigned a value ranging from 1 to 3, depending either on the level of strength (low, medium, strong) or on the expansion of the element (expanding on one issue of a topic, on the whole topic, on the situation in the country). As a consequence, each assumption of mythical thinking and Aristotelian logic received a coefficient that is the sum of the values (points) of an assumption divided by the total frequency of the assumption. The *frequency* of an assumption is calculated as the number of the assumption in 100 words.

Table 8.2
Coding Scheme for Mythical Thinking versus Aristotelian Logic

Category	Dimensional Range (Values)
Synthetism (variable SY)	on the issue of the topic (SY-1) on the whole topic (SY-2) on the situation in the whole country (SY-3)
Analytism (variable AN)	on the issue of the topic (AN-1) on the whole topic (AN-2) on the situation in the whole country (AN-3)
Images (variable IM)	low (IM-1); medium (IM-2); strong (IM-3)
Concepts (variable CN)	low (CN-1); medium (CN-2); strong (CN-3)
Contradictions (variable CT)	on the issue of the topic (CT-1) on the whole topic (CT-2) on the situation in the whole country (CT-3)
Non-contradictions (variable NC)	on the issue of the topic (NC-1) on the whole topic (NC-2) on the situation in the whole country (NC-3)
Cyclic time (variable TC)	on the issue of the topic (TC-1) on the whole topic (TC-2) on the situation in the whole country (TC-3)
Non-equal time (variable TN)	low (TN-1); medium (TN-2); strong (TN-3)
"Linear" time (variable TL)	on the issue of the topic (TL-1) on the whole topic (TL-2) on the situation in the whole country (TL-3)
"Equal" time (variable TE)	low (TE-1); medium (TE-2); strong (TE-3)
Neutrality (variable NE)	on the issue of the topic (NE-1) on the whole topic (NE-2) on the situation in the whole country (NE-3)
Dramatization (variable DR)	low (DR-1); medium (DR-2); strong (DR-3)

The factors C(Myth) and C(Logic) show a general degree of the existence of mythical thinking and Aristotelian logic in a sample. C(Myth) and C(Logic) are calculated as the product of the other variables and the frequency of the assumption:

$$C(Myth) = C(sy) \times C(im) \times C(cn) \times C(tc) \times C(tn) \times C(dr) \times F(Myth)$$
$$C(Logic) = C(an) \times C(cn) \times C(nc) \times C(tl) \times C(te) \times C(ne) \times F(Logic)$$

The sample was divided into five groups according to the five political preferences Extreme Right, Right, Center, Left, and Extreme Left. Using the previously described methodology, I compared the degree of the presence of mythical thinking, or C(Myth), Aristotelian logic, or C(Logic), and metaphorical coefficient in the each group and compared the groups with each other. In addition, the degree of the presence of different assumptions of Aristotelian logic and mythical thinking in different political groups was compared.

RESULTS

The results of the sample analysis are shown in Table 8.3 and Figure 8.1. The metaphorical coefficient is high in Extreme Right and Extreme Left groups. The lowest degree of the presence of metaphorical factors can be observed in the Center group. However, the difference between the groups Center and Right is not as much as the difference between groups Center and Left. It also may be concluded that Right-oriented groups in the Ukrainian parliament tend to use metaphors with a high intensity (I) variable, while Left-oriented politicians use less intense metaphors, but the frequency (F) of the metaphorical usage among the left wing is higher.

The highest degree of elements of mythical thinking is observed in the group Extreme Right (Table 8.4). The second highest level is indicated in the group Extreme Left. Notably, the difference of degree between Left and Extreme Left is much smaller than between Right and Extreme Right. The smallest level of the application to mythical thinking is observed in the group Center. Synthetism, C(sy), of mythical thinking is higher on the margins of the political spectrum. Images C(im), are used mostly among right-oriented politicians. Variable contradiction, C(cn), is relatively insignificant in all groups of the political spectrum. It also has the smallest frequency, F(cn). The variable Cyclic time (TC) has the highest frequency and intensity among left-oriented politicians and is still high among others. However, the usage of the assumption defined by the variable "non-equal time" (TN) has a low frequency among all political groups. "Dramatization" has the highest frequency in all groups. That is the most popular assumption observed in the sample. The highest level of dramatization, C(dr), demonstrates Extreme Left, Extreme Right, and Left groups of politicians.

Applying the assumptions of Aristotelian logic is more common than applying mythical thinking in all political groups (Table 8.5). The language of Center and Right groups contains the highest degree of assumptions of Aristotelian logic. Extreme Left and Extreme Right have the lowest degree of these assumptions.

Analytism (variables F(an) and C(an)) is preferred in the groups Center and Right. However, Concepts (variables F(cn) and C(cn)) are more popular among politicians who have left-oriented preferences. The frequency

Table 8.3
The Evolution of the Use of Metaphors: Frequency (F), Intensity (I: w, n, s), Content (D: p, n, po, d, sp, m), and Metaphorical Coefficient (CM) in the Language of Five Groups of the Ukrainian Parliament (1991–1996)

| Group | Metaphor/words | F | I | | | | D | | | | | | | CM |
			w	n	s	I (total)	p	n	po	d	sp	m	D (total)	FxIxD
Extreme right	31/4860	0,637	5	19	7	2,06	12	0	11	5	1	2	2,645	3,470
Right	58/16470	0,352	22	23	13	1,844	25	0	23	9	0	1	2,344	1,521
Centre	52/24165	0,215	23	25	4	1,634	27	2	21	2	0	0	1,961	0,688
Left	76/13500	0,562	28	41	7	1,723	29	4	28	13	2	0	2,407	2,330
Extreme left	83/11745	0,706	33	31	19	1,855	16	3	36	21	2	5	3,060	4,007

Figure 8.1
The Presence of Metaphors in the Rhetoric of Political Groups in the Ukrainian
Parliament (1991–1996)

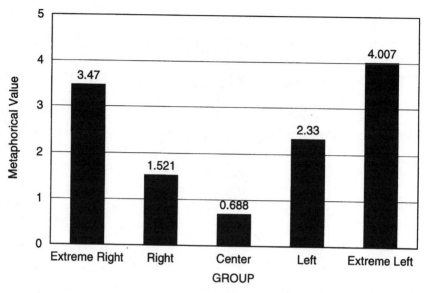

of the variable Non-Contradiction has the highest degree in the group Center. However, the differences between variables of Non-Contradiction (F(nc) and C(nc)) among other groups is not crucial. The assumption Linear Time has a higher degree of presence in Right-oriented than in Left-oriented groups. Variables of Equal Time (F(te) and C(te)) are relatively equally presented in all groups. However, the frequency of Equal Time (F(te)) is low in the Extreme Right group, but the coefficient of Equal Time (C(te)) is higher here than in other groups, because of the high intensity of the used assumption. The coefficient of neutrality is highest in the Center group and declines on the margins of the political spectrum (see Figure 8.2).

There is a direct correlation between the coefficient of mythical thinking (C(Myth)) and the metaphorical coefficient (CM). At the same time, there is a reverse correlation between the coefficient of logical thinking (C(Logic)) and the metaphorical coefficient (CM): more logical thinking, fewer metaphors (Table 8.6). In mythical thinking, the most frequent and significant assumptions are Dramatization, Synthetism, and Images. They are in direct correlation with the metaphorical coefficient. The most frequent and significant assumptions of Aristotelian logic are Neutrality, Concepts, and Non-Contradiction. They are in inverse correlation with the metaphorical coefficient.

Table 8.4
The Evolution of the Use of Assumptions of Mythical Thinking in the Rhetoric of
Members of the Ukrainian Parliament (1991–1996)

Group	Synthetism (SY)			Images (IM)			Contradictions (CN)		
	sy/words	F(sy)	C(sy)	im/words	F(im)	C(im)	cn/words	F(cn)	C(cn)
Extreme right	9/4860	1,185	2,33	18/4860	0,370	2,50	3/4860	0,061	1,66
Right	7/16470	0,042	1,57	44/16470	0,267	2,29	4/16470	0,024	1,25
Center	8/24165	0,033	1,12	26/24165	0,107	1,50	3/24165	0,012	1,33
Left	16/13500	0,118	2,06	13/13500	0,096	1,84	2/13500	0,014	1,50
Extreme left	12/11745	0,102	2,16	15/11745	0,127	1,73	3/11745	0,025	2,33

Table 8.5
The Evolution of the Use of Assumptions of Aristotelian Logic in the Rhetoric of
Members of the Ukrainian Parliament (1991–1996)

Group	Analytism (AN)			Concepts (CN)			Non-contradictios (NC)		
	an/words	F(an)	C(an)	cn/words	F(cn)	C(cn)	nc/words	F(nc)	C(nc)
Extreme right	13/4860	0,267	2,23	10/4860	0,205	1,70	21/4860	0,432	2,47
Right	59/16470	0,358	2,64	53/16470	0,321	2,36	64/16470	0,388	2,72
Center	103/24165	0,426	2,77	126/24165	0,521	2,82	124/24165	0,513	2,61
Left	28/13500	0,207	1,86	68/13500	0,504	2,80	58/13500	0,429	2,48
Extreme left	25/11745	0,213	1,84	48/11745	0,409	2,62	44/11745	0,374	2,32

Cyclic time		(TC)	Non-equal time (TN)			Dramati-zation		(DR)	Myth.		
tc/words	F(tc)	C(tc)	tn/words	F(tn)	C(tn)	dr/words	F(dr)	C(dr)	Myth/words	F (Myth)	C (Myth)
16/4860	0,329	2,62	4/4860	0,082	2,25	28/4860	0,576	2,78	78/4860	1,604	254,17
51/16470	0,309	2,50	5/16470	0,030	2,20	39/16470	0,236	2,28	150/16470	0,910	51,28
24/24165	0,099	2,46	4/24165	0,016	2,25	34/24165	0,140	1,14	99/24165	0,409	7,13
42/13500	0,311	2,83	5/13500	0,037	2,40	76/13500	0,562	2,64	154/13500	1,14	116,22
38/11745	0,323	2,92	6/11745	0,051	2,33	73/11745	0,621	2,86	147/11745	1,251	211,94

Linear time		(TL)	Equal time (TE)			Neutrality		(NE)	Logic		
tl/words	F(tl)	C(tl)	te/words	F(te)	C(te)	ne/words	F(ne)	C(ne)	Myth/words	F (Logic)	C (Logic)
7/4860	0,144	2,57	5/4860	0,102	2,40	14/4860	0,289	1,92	70/4860	1,440	159,6
18/16470	0,109	2,39	24/16470	0,146	2,87	48/16470	0,291	2,73	266/16470	1,615	512,5
39/24165	0,161	2,41	33/24165	0,136	2,73	105/24165	0,434	2,86	503/24165	2,081	798,3
12/13500	0,089	1,91	21/13500	0,156	2,62	26/13500	0,192	2,34	213/13500	1,577	238,5
13/11745	0,110	2,07	10/11745	0,085	2,80	12/11745	0,102	1,08	152/11745	1,294	91,1

Figure 8.2
The Evolution of the Assumptions of Mythical Thinking and Aristotelian Logic
in the Rhetoric of Political Groups in the Ukrainian Parliament (C (Myth) and C
(Logic)) (1991–1996)

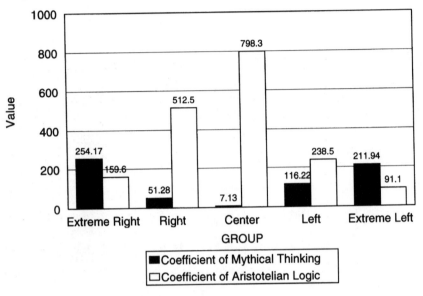

CONCLUSION AND DISCUSSION

Two types of reasoning, mythical thinking and Aristotelian logic (Go-loskover), or "pragmatic" and "objective" argumentation (Weinberger, 1995) do not exist in pure form in political language. Nevertheless, the examination of how these types of reasoning are floating in political language may serve as a clue to the unconscious and conscious preferences or intentions among politicians. For example, the case study reveals that the metaphorical coefficient and the coefficient of mythical thinking of the groups Right and Center are closer than for other groups. However, only recently, after the election of the Ukrainian parliament in 1998, the politicians and their parties generally presented in these groups created a close coalition during the election of a new speaker. Officially these groups (Center represented mainly by pro-presidential politicians and Right mainly represented by right-oriented "Rukh") had never created a united political movement; moreover, "Rukh" has proclaimed a so-called constructive opposition toward the president. Nevertheless, it might be argued that through examining the political language of these two groups, it would be possible to predict the intention or the possibility to create a political coalition when it comes to important questions about power such as, in our case, the election of a new speaker. The study of political language may

Table 8.6
The Evolution of Assumptions of Mythical Thinking, Aristotelian Logic, and Metaphors in the Rhetoric of Members of the Ukrainian Parliament (1991–1996)

Group	Logic Myth/words	F(Myth)	C(Logic)	Myth. Myth/words	F(Myth)	C(Myth)	CM F x I x D
Extreme Right	70/4860	1,440	159,6	78/4860	1,604	254,17	3,470
Right	266/16470	1,615	512,5	150/16470	0,910	51,28	1,521
Center	503/24165	2,081	798,3	99/24165	0,409	7,13	0,688
Left	213/13500	1,577	238,5	154/13500	1,14	116,22	2,330
Extreme Left	152/11745	1,294	91,1	147/11745	1,251	211/94	4,007

reveal more information than does content analysis because of its unconscious character (Sapir, 1949, 432–433; De Landtsheer, 1998: 130).

The correlation between the coefficient of mythical thinking and the metaphorical coefficient may imply that application to myth as well as to metaphors (De Landtsheer, 1994: 12) increases in times of crisis. This research also confirms the political-semantic analysis of metaphorical discourse within the European Parliament (1991–1993), which concluded that metaphorical coefficient increases on the margins/extremes of the political spectrum (De Landtsheer, 1998: 140).

Politicians who belong to the margins of the political spectrum tend to use more metaphors and elements of mythical thinking. For them, any current situation appears to be critical. Being in an extreme position in the political spectrum, they are the least satisfied with the current political situation. They therefore try to destroy the semantic construction of the current discourse. We can say they try to destroy the *logic* of the current situation, the fixed links between notions and concepts that placed them on the political margins. Referring to the nature of the elements of mythical thinking, past or future became more important than the present; the world is overwhelmed with the dramatic contradictions and may be perceived as such in the whole.

The capability of mythical thinking to destroy the semantics of a current political discourse may be juxtaposed with the ability of metaphors to permit the audience to escape from reality, which increases when politicians deliberately use incorrect or inaccurate connotations (De Landtsheer, 1995: 9). The aesthetic power of metaphors de-formalizes discourse, makes it more understandable for the audience. Mythical thinking also aims at causing an immediate impression without any further rational explanation (Barthes, 1993: 130).

Politicians of the center of the political spectrum prefer logical thinking. Politicians who carry power try to preserve it by establishing a formal discussion. Therefore, they apply terms (concepts), "analytism," non-contradictory conclusions, and emphasize the importance of the current situation. Thus, politicians can fix or "hermetically seal" (Marcuse) the political discourse at the current stage, not only by using elements of mythical thinking but also by using Aristotelian logic. It is important to be aware that both Aristotelian logic and mythical thinking *in political discourse* are used to affect the audience. The difference between politicians who use Aristotelian logic and those who use mythical thinking lies not only in the fact that from the current perspective the first are considered "right" and the latter as "wrong" but also and much more in the *means* they use. For the political center or governing elite, Aristotelian logic seems to be more appropriate, while for the opposition or extreme, mythical thinking is more suitable. Here I would refer to Weinberger: "political argumentation—even if it may have a sound tendency to use objective argumentation—it is in principle mainly pragmatic argumentation" (Weinberger, 1995: 51). From this perspective it is clear why reasoning arranged by Aristotelian logic may also restrict discourse when it turns into *political* discourse.

Mythical thinking is an ontological presumption of religion and art. Aristotelian logic became an essential part of science because it had formed the methodological apparatus for any science. During the Enlightenment, however, mythical thinking was embedded in the social sciences, creating modern images and myths about social reality. The creation of myths about any society is vital for each political system, since it defines the meaning of "who are we" and "who are others." Within social myths, however, we can observe both mythical thinking and Aristotelian logic.

In this chapter it is shown how oppositions employ mythical thinking to destroy a current political discourse. In contrast, ruling politicians use Aristotelian logic to stabilize political discussion and thus avoid change. If, however, the ruling elite applies mythical thinking, it makes strong reference to the rational background. For example, cyclic, repetitive succession of time in present Ukrainian discourse ("economic reforms") is designed to prove that the current reforms are the only way for national development: "All Eastern European countries went through economic reform and we should do the same." This motto of "economic reforms" is supposed to impose cyclic time onto political discourse and therefore to divert attention from the nature and reality of economic reforms (Taran, 1995: 16). Thus, cyclic time, an assumption of mythical thinking, is used to refer to a rational background in the past—the logic and success of economic reforms in Central Eastern European countries. The opposition employs mythical thinking without reference to the rational background, since it obviously attempts to create something new that would deny that which was made by the governing politicians.

Political discourse creates a semantic web that explains and justifies the current policies. At the same time, the web will describe the opposition to political discourse as something "bad" or "evil," since the opposition resists current policies. The paradox, however, lies in the fact that the opposition will operate with the same semantic web, even while being "against" current policies. Therefore, the opposition will have no chances to have a decisive impact on the audience if it applies only the adopted system of "dissent" ("good") political values arranged with the current semantic web. The opposition will always be viewed as "evil" and thus it risks to be in opposition all the time. Considering this, I believe that, seeking success, opposition political movements should go not *against* but *beyond* the current semantic web. The opposition has to create a new political discourse with a new semantic web that would move the opposition away from the marginal situation of a political discourse.

The political discourse *beyond* does not necessarily need to be proclaimed within the opposition. It may be established within governmental parties as well, if there is a feeling of exhaustion of the old system of values. For example, "economic reforms" discourse was developed in 1994 within the ruling elite presented by Kuchma, who was prime minister at that moment. "Economic reforms" were *not against* the ideology of the previous political discourse presented by the key term "state building." "Economic reforms," however, ideologically was *not in favor* of "state building" as well, considering those using this slogan as "being too political" and paying too little attention to the economic situation in the country. The "economic reforms" discourse has been created *beyond* the ideological struggle between supporters of "state building" ("good") and those who struggle for rebuilding the Soviet Union ("bad"). The creators of "economic reforms" developed their own semantic web, which put them in the center of a political discourse that eventually led to their success and the election of their leader Kuchma as president of Ukraine. Notably, communist and radical right opposition remained in the opposition in both "state building" and "economic reforms" discourses, because they followed the logic of discourses proclaimed by the ruling elites of these discourses.

Two types of reasoning, Aristotelian logic and mythical thinking, play a crucial role in the creation of new images and saving old ones regardless by whom they are employed. The nation state and political discourse, which during Enlightenment substituted aristocratic order and biblical interpretations, did not destroy people's desire for miracles and worshipping the one who can create this miracle. Skilled argumentation enables the speaker to create a miracle in language rather than in reality, which often is quite enough to satisfy the audience.

REFERENCES

Alexandrov, A. (Ed.) (1987). *Introduction into Philosophy*. Moscow: Progress.
Anderson, R. D., Jr. (1997). *On the Irrelevance of Culture to Politics*. Los Angeles: University of California.
Barthes, R. (1993). *Mythologies*. London: Vintage.

Camus, A. (1942). *Le mythe de Sisyphe: Essai sur l'absurde* [The myth of Sisyphus: Essay on the absurd]. Paris: Editions Gallimard.

De Landtsheer, C. (1994). The Language of Prosperity and Crisis: A Case Study in Political Semantics. *Politics and the Individual*, 4, 63–85.

De Landtsheer, C. (1995). Political Communication. In C. De Landtsheer (Ed.), *Political Communication*. Special Issue of *Politics, Groups and the Individual. International Journal of Political Psychology and Political Socialization* (pp. 1–20). Norderstedt, Germany: APP Verlag.

De Landtsheer, C. (1998). The Political Rhetoric of a United Europe. In O. Feldman & C. De Landtsheer (Eds.), *Politically Speaking: A Worldwide Examination of Language Used in the Public Sphere* (pp. 129–145). Westport, CT: Praeger.

Dobrzynska, T. (1995). Translation Metaphor: Problems of Meaning. *Journal of Pragmatics*, 24, 595–604.

Dreyfus, H., & Rabinow, P. (1983). *Michel Foucault: Beyond Structuralism and Hermeneutics*. Chicago: University of Chicago Press.

Ellul, J. (1973). *Propaganda*. New York: Vintage.

Feyerabend, G. (1994). *Against Method*. London, New York: Verso.

Foucault, M. (1984). The Order of Discourse. In M. J. Shapiro (Ed.), *Language and Politics* (pp. 108–138). Oxford: Basil Blackwell.

Goloskover, J. (1987). *The Logic of Myth*. Moskow: Nauka.

Hariman, R. (1995). *Political Style: The Artistry of Power*. Chicago: University of Chicago Press.

Harvey, D. (1990). *The Condition of Postmodernity*. Oxford: Blackwell Publishers.

Huizinga, J. (1994). *Homo Ludens*. Kyiv: Kyiv University Press.

Lacoue-Labarthe, P., and Nancy, J. (1995). *Nacistcký Mýtus*. Bratislava: Camenius University Press.

Lasswell, H. (1949). The Language of Power. In H. Laswell & L. Nathan (Eds.), *Language of Politics: Studies in Quantitative Semantics*. New York: G. W. Stewart.

Levi-Strauss, C. (1994). La structure des mythes [The structure of myth]. In C. Levi-Strauss, *Anthropologie Structurale*. Paris: Plon.

Lotman, J. (1994). *Rétorica* [Rhetorics]. In J. Lotman, *Text a kultúra* [Text and culture]. Bratislava: Camenius University Press.

Mannheim, K. (1992). *Ideology and Utopia*. Moskow: Moskovsky University Press.

Marcuse, H. (1994). *One-Dimensional Man*. Kyiv: Kyiv University Press.

Meletinskij, J. (1979). *Poetica mýtu* [Poetry and Myth]. Bratislava: Camenius University Press.

Montero, M. (1995). The Psychological Construction of a Political Myth. *Politics, Groups and the Individual*, 5, 51–65.

Orwell, G. (1995). Politics and the English Language. In R. Jackall (Ed.), *Propaganda*. New York: New York University Press.

Pocheptzov, G. (1994). *Totalitarian Man*. Kyiv: Kyiv University Press.

Richardson, L. (1994). Writing: A Method of Inquiry. In N. Denzin & Y. Lincoln (Eds.), *Handbook of Qualitative Research*. London: Sage.

Robertson, D. (1993). *Dictionary of Politics*. London: Penguin Books.

Rosenau, P. (1991). *Post-Modernism and the Social Sciences*. Princeton, NJ: Princeton University Press.

Sapir, E. (1949). *Selected Writings in Language, Culture and Personality*. Berkeley, CA: Mandelbaum.

Shapiro, M. (1982). *Language and Political Understanding: The Politics of Discursive Practices*. New Haven, CT: Yale University Press.

Sweetser, E. (1995). Metaphor, Mythology, and Everyday Language. *Journal of Pragmatics*, 24, 585–593.

Taran, S. (1995). Impact of Mass Media on Ukrainian Policy Making. *Politics*, 23, 13–15.

Weber, M. (1963). *Sociology of Religion*. Boston: Beacon Press.

Weinberger, O. (1995). Argumentation in Law and Politics. *Communication and Cognition*, 28, 37–54.

Wilson, A. (1997). *Ukrainian Nationalism in the 1990s*. London: Cambridge University Press.

PART III

Speech Aimed at Encouraging Citizen Participation

CHAPTER 9

Raising the Social Status of Intellectuals and Prescribing Ideal Behavior for Chinese Citizens: Press Images of Model Intellectuals under Economic Reform

MEI ZHANG

Following the death of top Party leader Mao Zedong in 1976, the Chinese Communist Party started policies of economic reform and opening up to the Western world in 1978 in the nationwide efforts to modernize China. Reform boosted the Chinese economy, promoted consumption, raised the standard of living, and widened political participation. However, reform also led to increasing inequality, corruption, money fetishism, and indifference to Party affairs. The post-Mao reform has been widely hailed as a "second revolution" comparable to the communist revolution that brought about the founding of the People's Republic. In the early reform years, one fundamental policy change was the Party's emphasis on developing science and technology as the key to catching up with advanced nations in the West. The new constitution of China recognized intellectuals as a major driving force for modernization.

The official Chinese media, especially Party organs such as the *People's Daily (Renmin Ribao)*, played a crucial role in promoting new policies and opening doors to reform. In addition to publishing official speeches, Party documents, and editorials, the Party newspaper used stories of model Chinese to further encourage engagement in reform. Models stood for "principle in action" (Munro, 1977: 138), and their stories aimed at "appeal and participation value" (Liu, 1971: 145). Persuasion by depicting role models had a long history in China dating back to Confucian times, and the Communist Party continued this tradition with its unique ideological control of model images and nationwide campaigns for socialist model emulation (Sheridan, 1968; Munro, 1977). According to Kenneth Burke's *A Rhetoric of Motives* (1969), persuasion resulted from identification between the rhetor (producer of messages) and the audience (receivers of messages)

(p. 20). Burke defined rhetoric as "the use of words by human agents to form attitudes or to induce actions in other human agents" (p. 41). The official stories of role models continued to function as Chinese political rhetoric designed to induce ideal citizen behavior in the reform era.

This chapter studies the functions of model intellectuals in the early 1980s in the *People's Daily* by examining four major model themes: courage to pursue research, hard work and sacrifice, love of the Party, and relationship to others. The chapter argues that the Party used the images of model intellectuals to promote new policies, to prescribe ideal attitudes and behaviors for Chinese citizens, and to provide model ways of conflict resolution on issues involving the moral life of the citizens. By using the qualitative method of rhetorical criticism informed by Burke's theory of identification, the chapter suggests that the Party continued its strategies of identification with Chinese audiences as well as adding new ways to relate to them. This chapter contributes to political communication through a case study of the Chinese elite Party's rhetorical presentation of intellectuals, the special social group it had always attempted to reform and educate, as national role models for all Chinese to help with the Party's radical policy shift from class struggle to economic development.

IDENTIFICATION AND CHINESE POLITICAL CULTURE

According to Burke (1969), identification resulted from consubstantiality when the rhetor and the audience were united in substance or action such as common ideas, attitudes, and material or spiritual possessions. While Burke discussed both conscious and unconscious levels, the Chinese Communist Party's identification with its citizens constituted conscious and deliberative efforts to secure communist control and develop socialism. The Party's strategies in Mao's era set up structures of hierarchy and equality and singled out class enemies as scapegoats for policy failures and public frustrations.

The Party organized Chinese society politically under totalitarianism and a hierarchy of classes. As the absolute and supreme ruling elite, the Communist government maintained tight political control of all state apparatuses under central planning by eliminating private ownership and by restricting citizens' job and residence mobility. Class struggle became a defining characteristic of Chinese politics as evidenced by constant political movements ranging from the Anti-Rightist Campaign to the Cultural Revolution, when numerous Chinese, especially intellectuals, were constantly labeled, purged, jailed, and even tortured to death. Class determined an individual's political and social standing, opportunities in education and employment, and access to honorary titles in society. The Party's national role models had the appropriate class status since they hailed from the working class, the Party's most reliable force for the communist revolution.

Role models' class background facilitated identification from working-class Chinese. Non–working-class citizens were told to follow model actions by these exemplars from the working class to reform themselves. In addition, the Party set up a hierarchy of model workers in increasing order of importance at the work unit level, at the city level, at the provincial level, and at the national level. The most important, such as model soldier Lei Feng, received written citations from top Party and government leaders and had their stories covered in news media across the country. The Party required uniform behavior from all Chinese through stories of role models in the mass media and through political meetings and study groups. All models shared similar qualities only to be differentiated by their respective occupations and different honorary titles. Such a hierarchy of models left room of perfection for everyone to try harder to be a model worker at a higher level of recognition.

Meanwhile, the Party showed equality between role models and their audiences by selecting models from the working class and emphasizing adaptation to audiences in news coverage. As workers and peasants, role models were born into poverty and reportedly regarded the Party as the savior who relieved their families from sufferings in the Old Society. Defined by their family background and eager to follow the Party, role models all professed to love the Party and actively engaged in socialist construction. By defining the Chinese political system as proletarian dictatorship, the Party identified the goals of the Party with the needs of the working class for a better life and used stories of role models' daily lives to guide proper behavior during the progress to communism, where all needs would supposedly be satisfied. The Party indicated equality between the role models and the Chinese audiences by selecting models at the grassroots levels, which suggested that audiences could acquire model behavior if they had the will to strive as hard. Role model coverage served "to increase conformism" and "to appeal to people's motives and expectations" (Liu, 1971: 145). The Party journalism emphasized service to the masses and the importance of identifying model images with Party agendas at different periods and with audiences' interests and desires (Guo, 1983).

A third technique of the Party's identification with the Chinese was the creation of scapegoats to unite all people. Stories of sufferings before 1949 correlated with mass political rallies where role models condemned hardship in the Old Society under Chiang Kai-shek's Nationalist Party before 1949 and sang praises of happiness in the New Society after 1949 under Mao's Communist Party. The Old Society became an easily available scapegoat, and the Party emerged as victor to deliver the Chinese from evil and suffering. Such public storytelling constantly reminded attendants of the benefits of socialism. The other type of scapegoat was those who lost the factional struggle in the top Party leadership and were purged out of the Party, such as Liu Shaoqi (head of state before his downfall) and Lin Biao

(Mao's acknowledged successor before his failed coup). By identifying enemies in the central leadership and encouraging nationwide criticism of their supposed crimes, the Party emerged as infallible victor and made individual deviants within the Party responsible for all Party mistakes, thus providing victimage to rid itself of any affiliated guilt. Those who had fought against "evil" Party leaders became heroes after the Party victory, and their stories helped the Party to implement subsequent political campaigns and to sustain and reinforce people's trust in the Party.

PARTY JOURNALISM AND THE *PEOPLE'S DAILY*

The political function of modern Chinese journalism could be traced back to the late 19th century, when intellectual reformers published newspapers to resist foreign aggression and promote reform in the late Qing period, the last dynasty of China. In the early 20th century, progressive newspapers and magazines played a significant role in the Republican Revolution that overthrew the Qing government, the May Fourth Movement against foreign privileges, and the New Culture Movement against feudal establishments in China. The Chinese Communist Party started newspapers in major cities such as Beijing, Shanghai, Wuhan, and Guangzhou soon after it was founded in 1921 to rally support for its revolutionary cause (Chang, 1989: 7–13). After the communist takeover of mainland China in 1949, Party newspapers and institutional publications helped the communist government to secure national integration. Even though newspapers in China were mostly a medium for literate and urban readers, collective newspaper reading sessions and group discussions of Party policies constituted the Party's strategy to "link newspapers with face-to-face communication among the masses" (Liu, 1971: 139). The political language in the newspapers organized reality into a single Party perspective and performed the function of political socialization, especially for urban Chinese, by providing model politically "loyal" utterances and action in a nation constantly engaged in class struggle and political persecution during Mao's tenure (Liu, 1971: 143–144).

The formal theory of Party journalism emerged in the communist headquarters in Yanan in 1942 during a rectification campaign, which defined and reinforced Party control of journalism by weeding out rival ideology and "bourgeois" thinking from intellectuals. The Party Central Propaganda Department issued a circular on the restructuring of Party newspapers in 1942 that stated, "The principal responsibilities of newspapers are to propagandize party policies, carry through party policies, reflect the party's work, and reflect the life of the masses" (p. 162). In 1943, Lu Dingyi's seminal talk on news reiterated the importance of political direction of journalism and the class nature of news coverage (Lu, 1986). This emphasis on journalists' political responsibility continued not only into post-1949

Mao's China but also into the post-Mao era of economic reform, as evidenced by official speeches on Party journalism. In 1985, Hu Yaobang's keynote address reiterated the importance of journalism as the Party's mouthpiece and urged journalists to follow the Party's leadership and guidance in their daily news reports (Hu, 1986).

The most important Party newspaper, the *People's Daily*, was established on June 15, 1948, after the former Party organ *Liberation Daily (Jiefang Ribao)* stopped publication in 1947 following the evacuation of communist forces from Yanan to avoid direct confrontation with the Nationalist forces. The *People's Daily* operated at the Party's North China Bureau in Xibaipo Village, Hebei Province until 1949, when Beijing was liberated. The paper then moved to the capital city of Beijing and became the official organ of the Party Central Committee (Chang, 1989: 92–93). In light of the ultimate importance of formalized language and political terminologies in Chinese politics (Schoenhals 1992), the *People's Daily* provided Chinese citizens with politically attuned formulations and actions ever since the founding of the People's Republic. Economic reform led to certain degrees of political relaxation and commercialization in the Party newspaper as reflected in the increasing number of informational and entertainment pieces, exposure writings, and commercial advertisements to combat competition from new popular press and relate to audiences in the new era. However, the *People's Daily* remained the most authoritative voice of the Party for its policy transmission and ideological dissemination to legitimize socialism and market economy.

IMAGES OF MODEL INTELLECTUALS

Model intellectuals whose stories appeared in the *People's Daily* were mostly professionals in industries and research institutes, doctors, professors, and school teachers and press coverage of them was repetitive across different occupations. National models encompassed all the key qualities of those at regional levels with more panoramic pictures and more extensive media coverage. Therefore, the following analysis focuses on Jiang Zhuying and Luo Jianfu, the two most significant national model intellectuals whose stories initially appeared in local newspapers and finally made their way into the *People's Daily* in November 1982.

In February 1983, the State Council of China designated Jiang, Luo, and Zhao Chun'e (a coal-mine worker) as national model workers. The State Council cited them as "outstanding representatives of the working class" because of their "extraordinary contributions" in their respective fields and called upon all government employees to follow their examples to modernize China (Xinhua, 1983: 1). The images of Jiang and Luo transcended their profession and became ideal images for the whole nation to follow. The simultaneous designation of two intellectuals and one worker indicated the importance of intellectuals and the Party's special efforts to raise the social political status of Chinese intellectuals in the early 1980s in the nationwide efforts to end class struggle and develop science and technology to modernize China.

The editorial "They Are the Most Beloved People" in the Party's theoretical organ *Red Flag* best illustrated the importance of the two model intellectuals in December 1982.

Every historical period has its own most beloved people. Zhang Side, Liu Hulan, and Dong Cunrui were among the most beloved people in the Revolutionary War years. It was their fight and their sacrifice that brought about the birth of New China. Peaceful construction is also a battle, another form of military battle. In the sixties, we had most beloved people like Jiao Yulu and Lei Feng. Today, in the fight for socialist modernization construction, we in turn have most beloved people like Jiang Zhuying and Luo Jianfu. Their names should be written into the heroic history of the great Communist practice of our country with gold words. (p. 31)

By comparing Jiang and Luo to combat heroes during the Communist Revolution, this historical analogy pointed out that model intellectuals as heroes of the reform era were essential in modernizing China just as revolutionary fighter heroes were in bringing about Communist China. The quote clearly indicated the Party's efforts in promoting its new assessment of intellectuals and the significance of Jiang and Luo as outstanding intellectuals and national role models.

The names of Jiang and Luo frequently appeared together in news and editorials. The initial simultaneous reports of Jiang and Luo side by side in the *People's Daily* in November 1982 reinforced the image of sacrifice by intellectuals (Li, 1982: 4; Xinhua, 1982: 4). A senior optics research scientist in the Changchun Precision Machinery Research Institute in Northeastern China, Jiang died of complications of multiple diseases on June 15, 1982, at the age of 43. An engineer at Lishan Microelectronics Company in Shanxi Province in Northwestern China, Luo died of cancer on June 16, 1982, at the age of 47. Jiang and Luo shared similarities because their jobs both emphasized research, they both worked in less developed regions of China compared with big cities such as Beijing and Shanghai, and they both died in their middle age in June 1982. Meanwhile, they were also different in many ways. Jiang was born into a non–working-class family, became a Party member posthumously, held a senior-level academic position with a graduate degree, and died of multiple diseases. Luo was born into a poor peasant family, became a Party member in 1959, had a middle-level academic position, and died of cancer. The brief biographical accounts of Jiang and Luo already projected an image of model intellectuals working until their last breath for the Party in different regions of China.

Courage to Pursue Research

Jiang was born into an office worker's family, and his father was put in prison because of "political problems" in 1954. He never gave up on his research during the Cultural Revolution, despite experiencing difficulties resulting from his family background and from the political label of being "expert" without being "red" (Chen, 1982: 5). Similarly Luo was openly criticized because of his concentration on research. When told to do self-criticism by discussing his own mistakes, Luo said, "We do research . . . not for myself, not for you, but for the country, for the Party" (Qiu, Liu, Pang, & Tang, 1982: 4).

This courage to pursue knowledge at the risk of political consequences indicated to readers that Jiang and Luo were heroes in the most adverse circumstances because of their courage to fight against the influence of the "Gang of Four" (the four persons in central Party leadership headed by Mao's wife Jiang Qing before their arrest in 1976) with their dedication to scientific research at a time when engaging in class struggle and being "red" or following the Party's political instructions superseded being "expert" or attaining professional expertise. By identifying Jiang and Luo's images of pursuing knowledge during the pre-reform years with active pursuit of knowledge that the Party wanted to promote in the reform years, the small segments of the stories told readers that Jiang and Luo more than satisfied the professional demands placed on them because they were already ahead of most people in their work. The image of their courage and dedication to scientific research in connection with the campaign attacking the "Gang of Four" across China enabled them to emerge as heroes against the common enemy of the nation. By pitting Jiang and Luo against the nation's scapegoat, the stories helped the Party to promote the social status of intellectuals by showing that Jiang and Luo's conscientious actions were precisely what the Party wanted the Chinese to do under economic reform. Such images could serve to encourage readers to follow Jiang and Luo's examples and study science and technology wholeheartedly when the Party had purged the "Gang of Four" out of the Party's central leadership.

Hard Work and Sacrifice

The stories of Jiang and Luo constantly related their research successes to hard work and sacrifice. Jiang helped to develop a project regarding color distinction that changed the color television industry in China. He often worked till midnight even during the Cultural Revolution. After his children were born, he would get up at five every morning and managed to concentrate on his study in the evening despite his children playing in the same room for lack of space (Chen, 1982: 5). In the electronic industry, Luo and his coworkers made several breakthroughs that won awards at the National Science Conference in 1978. When his research required continuous observation, he would often work in his office for up to seven days in a row, eat only bread and water, and sleep on the floor when feeling tired (Qiu et al., 1982: 4). The following paragraph further illustrates Luo's concentration on his work with every free minute he had.

He concentrated on and was deeply involved in his work. After leaving Xinhua bookstore, he would begin to read as soon as he got on the bus. He often forgot to get off the bus on his way back just as he did on his way to the bookstore. When he went to the bathroom at midnight, he thought about his work while taking off his coat. It was not until he could not find any place to put his coat on that he realized that he was only in the bathroom, not in his room. (Qiu et al., 1982: 4)

This was a defining image of a hard-working model intellectual always deeply concentrated on work in the reform years, as similar stories appeared in media coverage. The quote vividly portrayed Luo's dedication to work without attention to the difference between day and night or work and rest.

The Party had always maintained an ambivalent relationship with Chinese intellectuals because the need to use their talent conflicted with the desire to control their "bourgeois" ideology. Thought reform and political campaigns constantly required intellectuals to suspend their privileged mental work in offices and remold themselves by learning from the working class and doing manual labor. Hence this new image of professional dedication in the reform era constituted a sharp departure from the key image of model workers in pre-reform days, especially during the Cultural Revolution from 1966 to 1976, when politics dominated all aspects of work and life and "there was no place for intellectualism or professionalism" (Grieder, 1981: 354). At that time, models were all defined by their enthusiastic reading of Mao's works to show their loyalty to the Party and to engage in class struggle. Mao's writings constituted the major source for socialist technical innovations in the right political direction (Goldman, 1981: 137). Politics dominated university curricula and class background constituted the key criteria for college admission as workers and peasants became college students without academic examinations.

The model image of hard work and sacrifice aiming at research success served to promote the new policy change from domestic political struggle and international isolation to economic development and opening up to the West. Presenting Jiang and Luo as model intellectuals for the nation clearly showed that professional expertise in science and technology no longer occupied an inferior position but gave correct political orientation concrete manifestation. The stories of hard work and sacrifice told Party cadres that intellectuals like Jiang and Luo were unsung heroes in that they had taken the lead in scientific development by contributing to the country anonymously without much public attention until the reform years. This image of dedication to work served to promote the pursuit of knowledge and the new policy on intellectuals as members of the working class. The image further served to tackle the traditional cadre bias and suspicion of intellectuals as being "tricky" when they did not talk and as "arrogant" when they did talk (Shao, 1981: 4) because Jiang and Luo spent all their time on their research.

The image of Jiang and Luo further benefited economic reform because it not only served to inspire Chinese citizens to pursue knowledge under the new policy but also showed them the right way to come to terms with the Cultural Revolution. Those who were disillusioned because of their personal tragic experiences and youth who read negative writings about the period all had to find ways to resolve the disillusionment, disappointment, and problems facing China. Such concerns appeared frequently in the discussions on "outlook on life" in *Chinese Youth* and *Workers' Daily* in 1981. Jiang and Luo underwent political pressure and criticism for their dedication to research, but they kept working hard instead of procrastinating or complaining. Their model action showed that the right way to make up for personal and professional loss in the past was to strive hard, learn science and technology, and improve their technical skills to modernize China and live a better life. The emphasis on professional dedication also told the audiences that Jiang and Luo were not born geniuses because their accomplishments resulted from persevering in hard work, which had the potential to encourage others to work and study hard.

The model image of hard work further came with the sacrifice of time for family happiness and personal health. Jiang kept postponing the trip to take his two teenage children to a nearby scenic spot, Nan Hu, because he gave top priority to work in daily life (Chen, 1982: 5). After he found out that his own death was imminent because of cancer, Luo said, "Please tell me how much time I have left. Do not tell my wife. Do not do a biopsy. Every minute is precious to me. . . . I have too much work waiting to be done." After being transferred to a hospital in Shanghai, he returned to work in Lishan within a month (Qiu et al., 1982: 4). This image of sacrifice showed that model intellectuals worked hard and sacrificed not only their free time but also time to be with family members and time to receive medical treatment to possibly prolong life. This again reinforced the new reform policy promoting the importance of professional contribution to replace the sole dominance of politics and class struggle in pre-reform years. Before economic reform, model workers all sacrificed themselves to follow Mao's call for "self-reliance and hard struggle" to develop the Chinese economy with its emphasis on human will guided by Mao's teachings rather than scientific knowledge. The new image told Chinese audiences how model intellectuals dealt with the relationship between work for the country, family, and individual self and encouraged them to contribute their share in the modernization process by studying science and technology. The image further benefited reform in light of the repeated media coverage of political social bias against intellectuals. Some cadres considered intellectuals as reaping the profits of revolutionary cadres' sacrifice during the Communist Revolution and posed a serious obstacle for the official policy change from "uniting, educating, and reforming" intellectuals to "treating them equally without discrimination, giving them a free hand in their work, and caring for them in their lives" ("Luoshi Zhishifenzi Zhengce," 1983: 1). The stories of Jiang and Luo told cadres that their sacrifice was comparable to that of revolutionary Party cadres and fighter heroes who left their families and risked their lives to ensure communist victory. Since intellectuals like Jiang and Luo sacrificed everything they had to work for the country, the stories urged Party cadres to take care of them in the familiar metaphor of a big socialist family in the reform era.

Love of the Party

Politically Jiang loved the Party and never gave up faith in the Party whatever the circumstances. Though he was denied Party membership every time he applied because of his father's "political problem," he never stopped loving the Party and was instead forever grateful. This was reflected in his hard work, his words, and his applying for Party membership time and again. "My parents gave me life but it was the Party who educated me." After his father was proven innocent in 1981, he was eventually allowed to fill in an application form. He wrote down, "A person should live on faith. Life is finite but the Party's cause is infinite. I am willing to give all my life to the various tasks of the Party." Jiang became a Party member posthumously (Chen, 1982: 5). Luo joined the Party in 1959 and was never afraid of those who attacked his research during the Cultural Revolution because he always regarded his research as contributing to the country and the Party (Qiu et al., 1982: p. 4).

This love for the Party served to maintain and legitimatize China's socialist political system in the reform era. Despite all that had happened to intellectuals in Mao's China, model intellectuals Jiang and Luo always kept faith in the Party. This image told Party cadres that Jiang and Luo's hard work resulted from their correct political motivation to make China strong since their actions suggested their conviction that the Party represented people's interests in leading China to modernization. This image of love for the Party further promoted the new policy of recognizing intellectuals as members of the working class. The stories showed Party cadres that Jiang and Luo never used Party membership as a stepping-stone for promotion or subsequent benefits accorded to Party cadres. They were fully devoted to the Party with no "bourgeois" interests to sabotage socialism, as intellectuals were charged with during the Cultural Revolution. This told cadres that Jiang and Luo were truly members of the working class and supported the Party's new policy to admit more intellectuals to the Party and recruit intellectuals to management positions to strengthen the corps of cadres from workers and peasants.

This image of love of the Party further benefited reform because it showed the Chinese audiences that the correct political attitude and the proper way to resolve their doubt of the Party and their disillusionment with the Cultural Revolution were to keep faith in the Party despite the decade of political turmoil. Their model image showed intellectuals' unselfish motive in that loving the Party entitled them only to extra effort for the country's modernization. Jiang and Luo never complained nor attempted to capitalize on their past to bargain for personal gains, which served to provide model attitude and action for audiences. Politically attuned and professionally accomplished Party members and intellectuals like Jiang and Luo served to restore audience confidence in the Party in light of public indifference to Party affairs and encourage audiences to have high political aspirations to motivate their concrete contribution to the country.

Indifference to Benefits, Willingness to Help Others

Jiang and Luo never attempted to reap any benefits at work such as salary raises, academic promotion, administrative position, or the opportunity to visit abroad. While Jiang was studying in West Germany, he saved money to purchase research equipment for his research institute instead of buying modern electronics for his family before returning to China (Chen, 1982: 5). Luo often let colleagues go to conferences and asked them to be first authors for a team project award and in academic publications (Qiu et al., 1982: 4).

Passive reception of benefits had always been the Party's ideal moral value for Chinese citizens in its promotion of altruism, collectivism, and group interests against individual private desires. Mao's "Serve the People," among others, emphasized the importance of selfless devotion and sacrifice to serve the people and the Communist revolution wholeheartedly. Constantly associating model intellectuals' actions with their altruistic dedication to serving the people helped to raise the political social status of intellectuals by highlighting their sacrifice and urged the cadres to be more concerned about the living and working conditions of intellectuals. Indeed, there was much news coverage of intellectuals' poor working and living conditions. For example, in China's largest center of scientific research in Beijing, five to six researchers normally shared one office and it was common for families to have only one room each for total living space (Yu & Gong, 1980: 2).

This value took on further significance in the reform era, which officially encouraged citizens to get rich and strive for material prosperity. By promoting the image of model intellectuals' ideal way of possible conflict resolution for collegial interpersonal harmony in the workplace, the stories reminded Chinese audiences of the socialist orientation of economic reform and the proper way to deal with the relationship between striving for a better life and helping others to prosper first when not enough resources were available.

Jiang and Luo's sense of selflessness also consisted of their willingness to help colleagues with their work. Jiang was always ready to help others with their research problems by sharing his notes, sometimes even handcopying notes for them and helping the library of his research institute to index optics information. He was forever forgiving to those who mistreated him during the Cultural Revolution, as shown in his willingness to help a colleague who had acted against him with a research article problem. Jiang said to him, "Let bygones be bygones. It was not your fault. Let us work well together" (Chen, 1982: 5). Similarly Luo would send all his research notes when a colleague asked for an equation (Qiu et al., 1982: 4).

This image of helping colleagues highlighted altruism by sharing one's knowledge and emphasized group professional progress and communal harmony at the workplace, including the ideal forgiving way to address interpersonal conflicts of the past and treat those who made mistakes during the Cultural Revolution. Such emphasis on helping others with one's professional expertise served to promote the new policy on the importance of intellectuals in society and the importance of professional knowledge in the reform era. The story told cadres that intellectuals were like ordinary workers and were willing to help others in times of need and showed audiences the ideal interpersonal relationship at the workplace.

Finally, Jiang and Luo also cared about others in many other ways unrelated to their work. The following illustrated Jiang's miscellaneous volunteer jobs:

Jiang was always concerned about everything inside or outside his research institute. When the cooling machine broke down and slowed down research work, he would go to fix it with several others even though it was not his duty. The manual printer broke down in the information room, he went to repair it. . . . When a colleague in his office was sick, Jiang would go to see him in heavy rain. When another colleague needed powdered milk for his child, Jiang would ask his friend to send it from another city and would deliver it in person. In the old apartment building where he lived once, when the toilet of the bathroom ten families shared broke down, he would go to make the toilet flush again, becoming the well-recognized "volunteer janitor." (Chen, 1982: 5)

This quote clearly refuted the political bias against "arrogant" intellectuals by showing that Jiang made no distinction between mental work at research and manual labor at various volunteer tasks. While Mao's China constantly emphasized the importance of manual work to reform intellectuals' "bourgeois" outlook on life and their supposedly elitist detachment from the working class, this image of Jiang's being always ready to solve mechanical problems at work, to help colleagues with their daily necessities, and to work as a "volunteer janitor" in his apartment building vividly showed that intellectuals were every bit like workers and peasants in their skills and devotion to non-academic affairs. Model intellectuals were politically well ahead of other fellow Chinese with their socialist consciousness of voluntarism for community benefits. Model intellectuals like Jiang and Luo regarded it as their individual duty and responsibility to work hard and sacrifice for the country not only in terms of research success but also in helping others and doing volunteer work. This image of sacrifice at work and beyond urged Party cadres to change their bias against intellectuals and provided ideal behavior for Chinese citizens under the context of the Party's endorsement for a better personal life in the reform era.

Such images of Jiang and Luo as defined by their hard work and selfless sacrifice for the country shows the Party's use of traditional socialist rhetoric to promote the new policy on intellectuals and to encourage Chinese to pursue professional expertise. Unlike model workers in pre-reform years who read Mao's writings intensely and actively engaged in class struggle, Jiang and Luo spent every minute on their research while aiming at scientific breakthroughs to help China catch up with the rest of the world. With the Party shifting its focus from class struggle to economic development, family background no longer defined a person. Birth into a poor working-class family no longer constituted an essential quality of role models, which served to tell the audiences that the Party welcomed everyone and that reform called for their concrete contribution to the country.

IMAGE VARIATIONS AMONG MODEL INTELLECTUALS

As mentioned earlier, images of model intellectuals at lower levels than Jiang and Luo were repetitive in form and were similar to those of Jiang and Luo, even though various occupations called for dedication in different ways. For example, model doctors were dedicated to treatment of patients and model teachers were dedicated to students. However, there also existed variations between the images of Jiang and Luo and some other local model intellectuals. For the following analysis, we will study the images of Wang Jiyong, who became a model doctor after developing leukemia as reported in a 1983 story in the *People's Daily*. The page-long coverage of Wang led to active audience responses, ranging from expressing admiration and determination to live a meaningful life to sending gifts and providing medical referrals as summarized by the Party paper ("Yi Fengfeng Laixin," 1983: 2). Wang shared the qualities of the national role models Jiang and Luo, but his images also differed in several ways as shown in his weakness, need for family support, love of life, and pursuit of hobbies.

First of all, Wang had his share of weaknesses as an average doctor before he developed leukemia.

When asked about how he could achieve so much without paying attention to imminent death while a seriously ill patient himself, his answer was surprising. "This has to 'thank' my illness." This of course was put in jest. He was referring to his illness as an important turning point in his life. He said to the reporters, "As you know, I am the child of high-ranking officials and the son of a general. . . . Before I turned twenty-seven, I always felt superior to others . . . as if entering college and joining the Party meant the end of taking over the Revolutionary cause. To tell you the truth, I seldom thought about doing ordinary things or hard work. I often looked down upon others. . . . I did not want to work hard. Rather I wanted to find an easy way to fame. This illness not only changed my blood, but also changed my thinking." (Cong, Lu, & Jian, 1983: 7)

As this quote indicated, models did not have to be perfect all their life like Jiang and Luo. Wang was not a highly motivated doctor before the fatal leukemia struck him, even though he was already a Party member and not an irresponsible doctor, either. He was fallible like other ordinary people. Born into a family of high officials, he felt elitist and did not have the initiative to work harder beyond regular job requirements. Furthermore, unlike Mao's era when Party instructions were the key to changing any individual or even role model's weakness, the cause of Wang's change was the non-political illness that taught him human mortality and shortness of life.

Second, Wang valued his life and was afraid of death. Unlike Luo Jianfu, who did not show any fear and only thought about his work when he learned about his cancer, Wang panicked with desperation and even cried.

That bright red blood, that was his life! He felt as if he were falling off a galloping horse. Shock, fear, desperation. Would he never be able to stand up from now on? He was only twenty-seven years old. . . . As a doctor, he knew the time of life leukemia had left for him. . . . For the first time, Wang Jiyong realized that he was so sentimentally attached to life. . . .

Mother came. What should he say to Mother? Looking at the head of gray hair that grew sparse day by day, Jiyong's heart sank and could not helping crying, "Mother, you brought me up in vain." (Cong et al., 1983: 7)

Apparently Wang thought about many things he wanted to do in life but might not be able to do. He also thought about his mother and was afraid that he would not be able to measure up to her expectations. Such mental and emotional conflict was a departure from Mao's role models, who thought only about the Party, and also from post-Mao model intellectual Luo Jianfu, who thought only about his work before his death.

Third, Wang drew support from his family to sustain his courage to fight the disease. The following quote showed that his mother gave him strength and encouraged him to hold firmly onto life: "Mother cleaned his tears and managed to keep a firm tone. 'How can you say this, Jiyong! You are a Party member. You have just graduated from college. You are so young. But you want to fall down?!'" (Cong et al., 1983: 7).

Hence, Wang's mother reminded him that he was a Party member, who should never be afraid of death. If the Party's strength did not disappear in the news report, other types of non-political strength such as family support also played a significant role in Wang's life. After all, it was his mother who reminded him of his Party membership. The report further talked about his family support. "He has a warm home, a mother who constantly and quietly gives him strength as if her strength were endless and boundless." The report went on, "He has an attentive wife, who married him after he got cancer. She was not afraid. Wang Jiyong said that she gave him half of his life" (Cong et al., 1983: 7). Wang's need for family support differed from Mao's role models' regarding the Party as their sole savior and most important parent and was different from the image of Jiang and Luo, who always put work first and never seemed to need any emotional support from their families.

Fourth, Wang took care of himself physically and lived life to its fullest with his various hobbies:

Did Wang Jiyong only have work on his mind without paying attention to his illness? Of course not. He paid special attention to his illness. For twelve years, he never forgot to take his medicine, to do regular check-ups and lab tests, or to seek immediate medical treatment for other illnesses. To stabilize his mood, he refrained from reading sad literature or seeing sad movies. He knew that a person's emotions—joy, anger, and sadness—could worsen or lessen cancer. (Cong et al., 1983: 7)

Though he would forget about himself when patients needed him even after work, Wang was at least reported as paying attention to himself whenever possible. This was a different image from that of Luo, who insisted on going back to his work before his death, which showed the Party media coverage's recognition of role models as normal human beings who needed special attention to their health for further contribution to the country. Wang also reportedly liked cooking and learned carpentry and painting. He cared about his son's future and liked to discuss his vision for his family (Cong et al., 1983: 7). Unlike Jiang, who never found time to be with his children, Wang showed his love of his son as part of his joy of life and his parental responsibility.

Such images of Wang Jiyong suggested the Party's endorsement of a variety of images of role models. As a regional model intellectual, Wang had weaknesses, was afraid of death, and took good care of himself whenever time was available, had different hobbies, and had a strong sense of family values. Simply put, Wang was reported as having moments of doubt and enjoying life if possible. This was different from the depiction of the majority of model intellectuals who were fully dedicated to work, did not fear death, paid little or no attention to family or selves, and had virtually no life other than work. On the other hand, the story of Wang did not suggest that his images were opposed to those of Jiang or Luo because Wang's priority was also work and patients. The difference was that Wang would do something else if possible when time permitted and his life had other dimensions. It remains unclear whether it was the Party's intention or the reporters' initiative that contributed to this new dimension. Nonetheless, the story of Wang added a new level of identification in role model coverage by acknowledging realities in people's daily life, and readers seemed to identify with him more than they did with Jiang and Luo, as indicated by the case of numerous letters to the editor summarized by the *People's Daily*. The story of Wang suggested to audiences that they did not have to deny themselves the pleasures of life as long as they put their work and life into proper perspectives.

CONCLUSION

This chapter has shown that the images of model intellectuals in the early post-Mao reform years served to raise the social status of intellectuals and to encourage Chinese citizens to actively engage in the pursuit of knowledge and development of science and technology to modernize China. By identifying model actions with the traditional socialist values of political loyalty and altruism and by identifying their active pursuit of knowledge during and after the Cultural Revolution with the new requirements of the reform era, the Party promoted intellectuals as pioneers of the new era from a class to be reformed to national heroes for all Chinese. The communist socialist rhetoric as embodied in the stories of model intellectuals' professional and personal lives suggested the Party's continued indoctrination of new socialist values in the reform era to legitimatize its political system while introducing elements of market mechanism to the nation's economy. Official political rhetoric in the *People's Daily* perpetuated the undemocratic nature of the Party press in that it allowed no space to challenge the Party's supremacy and rule in China.

However, with the end of class struggle and new emphasis on economic development, there was less political hierarchy and more equality between citizens in terms of model selection and model emulation. Role models no longer enthusiastically read Mao's writings but devoted themselves to professional development and practical results. Presentation of model intellectuals showed that persuasion by role model in the reform era constituted a less coercive way of political control for desirable actions with the increasing multiplicity of model images and decreasing frequency of political study sessions for model emulation. Role models no longer exhibited unified qualities solely defined by their political aspirations. Model intellectuals ranged from national models Jiang Zhuying and Luo Jianfu, with all-inclusive panoramic qualities, to the regional model Wang Jiyong, with his unique personal pursuits, to numerous model intellectuals, with their single professional technical breakthroughs. Such a multiplicity of images indicated the loosening of political control and the declining pervasiveness of politics on citizens' personal lives. The multiple qualities of model intellectuals at different levels suggested space for individually defined action of model emulation and encouraged audiences to follow models to the best of their abilities and political consciousness in the hierarchy of model actions from hard work and professional contribution to altruism and self-sacrifice in public interests. In this regard, role models became easier for audiences to identify with since role models were more like ordinary people with hobbies and desires in addition to work.

This eclectic approach, as evidenced by model intellectuals' image variations at different levels of honor, reflected China's middle-of-the-road approach to developing a market economy while maintaining a socialist political system. This type of new identification with the citizens' lives after work by presenting the human dimensions of role models could be expected to be more common as China went deeper into economic reform. However, as long as the Party remained in power, the stories of model Chinese in the Party press would continue to constitute Chinese political rhetoric to signal the political direction of China and the "changing boundaries of permissible political discourse and behavior" (Schell, 1988: 247).

REFERENCES

Burke, K. (1969). *A Rhetoric of Motives.* Berkeley: University of California Press.
Central Propaganda Department. (1986). Circular from the Central Propaganda Department Concerning the Restructuring of Party Newspapers. *Chinese Sociology and Anthropology*, 18, 162–163.
Chang, W. H. (1989). *Mass Media in China: The History and the Future.* Ames: Iowa State University Press.
Chen, Y. S. (1982). Wei zhonghua jueqi er xianshen de guanghui bangyang [Glorious model of sacrifice for the revitalization of China]. *People's Daily*, December 1, p. 5.
Cong, L. Z., Lu, N., and Jian, W. Y. (1983). Shengming de jiazhi [The value of life]. *People's Daily*, January 10, p. 7.
Goldman, M. (1981). *China's Intellectuals: Advise and Dissent.* Cambridge, MA: Harvard University Press.

Grieder, J. B. (1981). *Intellectuals and the State in Modern China: A Narrative History.* New York: The Free Press.

Guo, Q. S. (1983). Lun dianxing [On role models]. In Editorial Board of China Journalism Yearbook (Ed.), *China Journalism Yearbook* (pp. 97–101). Beijing: China Social Science Press.

Hu, Y. B. (1986). On the Party's journalism work. *Chinese Sociology and Anthropology,* 18, 174–198.

Li, A. D. (1982). Jilin shengwei jueding kaizhan xiang Jiang Zhuying xuexi huodong [The Party Committee of Jilin Province decided to launch the activity of learning from Jiang Zhuying]. *People's Daily,* November 16, p. 4.

Liu, A. P. L. (1971). *Communications and National Integration in Communist China.* Berkeley: University of California Press.

Lu, D. Y. (1986). Our Basic Viewpoint Concerning Journalism. *Chinese Sociology and Anthropology,* 18, 164–173.

Luoshi zhishifenzi zhengce haiyaozuo henduo gongzuo [Much more work needs to be done to implement the policy on intellectuals]. (1983). *People's Daily,* February 24, p. 1.

Munro, D. J. (1977). *The Concept of Man in Contemporary China.* Ann Arbor: University of Michigan Press.

Qiu, W. Z., Liu, J., Pang, W. Q., & Tang, Z. X. (1982). Luo Jianfu. *People's Daily,* November 30, p. 4.

Schell, O. (1988). *Disco and Democracy: China in the Throes of Reform.* New York: Pantheon Books.

Schoenhals, M. (1992). *Doing Things with Words in Chinese Politics: Five Studies.* Berkeley: University of California Press.

Shao, Q. (1981). Haiyao jixu jiuzheng dui zhishifenzi de zhengzhi pianjian [Continue to change the political bias against intellectuals]. *People's Daily,* January 27, p. 4.

Sheridan, M. (1968). The emulation of heroes. *China Quarterly,* 33, 47–72.

Tamen shi zuikeaideren [They are the most beloved people]. (1982). *Red Flag,* 24, 31–33.

Xinhua News Agency. (1982). Xuexi Luo Jianfu de gongchanzhuyi xianshen jingshen [Learn from Luo Jianfu's Communist spirit of sacrifice]. *People's Daily,* November 16, p. 4.

Xinhua News Agency. (1983). Shouyu Zhao Chun'e Luo Jianfu Jiang Zhuying quanguo laodong mofan chenghao [Conferring the title of national model worker to Zhao Chun'e, Luo Jianfu, Jiang Zhuying]. *People's Daily,* February 21, p. 1.

Yi fengfeng laixin yi pianpian xin [Letter after letter, heart after heart]. (1983). *People's Daily,* February 15, p. 2.

Yu, Z. R., & Gong, D. F. (1980). Yao qieshi guanxin keyan renyuan de jiku [Show concrete concern for scientific research personnel's suffering]. *People's Daily,* January 24, p. 2.

CHAPTER 10

Non-oratorical Discourse and Political Humor in Japan: Editorial Cartoons, Satire, and Attitudes Toward Authority

OFER FELDMAN

Political humor is a form of linguistic expression consisting of jokes, comedy, satire, or caricatures that are publicly directed at the power structure, including the political system, institutions, political leaders, and other decision makers. It draws upon the semantics and pragmatics of political language, contextual information, and the political culture of a given society (Bryder, 1993; Langeveld, 1981).

This chapter examines, in a highly selective and personal manner, some aspects of political humor in Japan. It focuses particularly on political cartooning: a form of non-oratorical discourse that is usually synonymous with editorial cartooning [*fuushi manga*]. In this chapter I use the terms "political cartoon" and "editorial cartoon" interchangeably.

"Political cartoon" is defined here as a representational or symbolic drawing that makes a satirical, witty, or humorous point. It typically takes the form of a single, non-continuing panel that makes an independent statement or observation about political events or social policy. As a form of visual and persuasive communication, political cartoons visually symbolize, satirize, or caricature some topic, action or person. They provide visual images of ideas or issues that might otherwise only be thought of in terms of verbal abstractions.

The present chapter explores the nature and major characteristics of political cartoons that appeared in two Japanese national daily newspapers: the *Yomiuri Shimbun* (with a circulation of 14.5 million for both morning and evening editions) and the *Asahi Shimbun* (12.9 million). Every day for the past decade, both papers have published editorial cartoons in a prominent place on their political pages. This chapter focuses especially on the way these dailies, which represent both conservative (*Yomiuri*) and progressive (*Asahi*) editorial orientations, portray Japan's national political leader, the prime minister.

DEMOCRACY AND POLITICAL HUMOR

Democracies, by their nature, seem to welcome and indeed encourage open expression of humor (Galnoor & Lukes, 1985; Paletz, 1990). Political and critical humor evolve along with the freedom of opinion and expression that democratic culture permits and inspires. Such humor may be created and circulated with the assumption that it satisfies a need for relief from the trivial or from the fears and anxieties of political life. Political humor may also be seen as a weapon of social criticism, as well as an outlet that helps individuals cope with their dislike of or frustration with political institutions, political parties, policies, elected politicians, and the judiciary system (Bryder, 1993; Schutz, 1995).

Even to the casual observer, Japan offers endless potential targets for social criticism and dissatisfaction, to the extent that political leaders, decision-making processes, and the system as a whole may become targets of laughter. Consider, for example, the worsening recession economy, increasing unemployment and job insecurity; deregulation and the yen's appreciation; increasing incidence of administrative corruption and political scandal, including extramarital affairs involving Diet members; lack of leadership, integrity, and competence among politicians—particularly prime ministers; politicians' relations with syndicated crime; increasing apathy and disgust with politics; and the public's growing cynical contempt for the government and its ability to handle important issues like political reform.

Despite the wealth of potential material here, one finds significantly fewer expressions of political humor in Japan than in many Western societies.[1] Jokes about leading politicians, Diet members, the prime minister, or government bureaucrats are rare. Jokes about the Emperor are unthinkable. One seldom sees politically oriented messages in public places such as walls or fences around public institutions, on the street, or in public toilets. Political satire is extremely rare. Some would cynically explain the scarcity of satire by saying that satire mainly thrives in an open and democratic environment, whereas the unusual nature of "Japanese-style democracy" discourages healthy critique. Others suggest that there is no need for satire in Japan because political reality—including the increasing number of political scandals and the way politicians go unpunished despite their involvement in corruption—already seems like a parody (Feldman, 1993a).

In either case, Japanese seem to prefer laughing at anecdotes and episodes related to politics and politicians rather than making jokes about their governing institutions and individuals. The difference, of course, is that anecdotes are purportedly true stories that belong more to a category of folklore that we might label "gossip and hearsay," containing narratives of interesting or amusing incidents. Japanese often find these to be a source of laughter.

To illustrate: there is a famous anecdote about a public figure shouting at an opponent. Former prime minister Shigeru Yoshida once commented that "a speech wouldn't be a real speech without heckling" ["*yaji ga nai to enzetsu ni naranai.*"]. But a heckling brought down his administration. In March 1953, in response to an opposition question during a meeting of the Lower House's most powerful committee, the budget committee, Yoshida shouted, "You damn fool!" ["*bakayaro!*"], an utterance that became quite famous. The opposition quickly moved to discipline the prime minister, and the plenary session then passed a no-confidence resolution. In what is known as the "bakayaro dissolution," Prime Minister Yoshida chose to dissolve the Lower House rather than resign.

Another well-known anecdote has the same prime minister looking particularly robust. When asked, "Prime Minister, what have you eaten?" Yoshida answered, "I ate a human being." This famous story became a joke in Japan because his choice of words—"*hito wo kutta*"—sounds arrogant. Few Japanese would speak that way, but it was very typical of that particular prime minister. Like many other anecdotes, this story loses a great deal in translation.

Prime Minister Shigeru Yoshida was not the only politician whose remarks made Japanese laugh. Yoshio Sakurauchi was appointed foreign minister and served in that post for one year from November 1981. He stunned U.S. reporters during a visit to the United States in March 1982 by saying "My name is Cherry." ("*Sakura*" means cherry.) When asked "What do you think of Japan–U.S. economic friction?" he answered, "Cherry blossoms will eventually bloom on Japan–U.S. relations." During that visit he shouted loudly, "*America banzai!*" ["Long Live America!"]. Whenever he met with Washington officials, he introduced himself by saying, "I am Japanese Yul Brynner," while pointing at his bald head.

Another anecdote concerns a visit to Washington by Tsutomu Hata, a former finance minister who later became prime minister. While visiting the U.S. capital as chairman of the ruling Liberal Democratic Party's agricultural policy research council in December 1987, Hata claimed, "We Japanese have longer intestines than you Americans" to explain why Japanese had difficulty coping with red meat and needed to hold off U.S. exports of beef to Japan (cf. Kumon, 1988). It is worth noting that a large number of well-educated Japanese take this "intestine difference" to be gospel truth (e.g., Sakaiya, 1994: 91).

Former Prime Minister Toshiki Kaifu tried hard to win concessions and even to change policies in response to aggressive U.S. moves related to trade, earning him personal praise from President George Bush. Political observers in Japan complained that Kaifu would not do anything without first consulting with President Bush. Therefore, they called the telephone in Kaifu's residence a "Bush-phone" instead of a "push-phone" (Japanese for push-button telephone).

One last example relates to Prime Minister Ryutaro Hashimoto trying to show his commitment to administrative reform when he formed his second cabinet in November 1996. He said "I will accomplish this even if I become engulfed in flames" ["*Hidaruma ni natte mo yaru*"]. "Daruma" refers to a round-bottomed doll representing Boddhidharma, the founder of Zen Buddhism, sitting cross-legged in meditation. The doll is viewed as a symbol of good luck because its weighted bottom always returns to an upright position even if it is tipped. "Hidaruma," however, means a ball of flames. Because of Hashimito's expression, the mass media called his new cabinet the "ball-of-flame Cabinet" ["*hidaruma seiken.*"]

JAPANESE SENSE OF HUMOR

There are fundamental reasons why political jokes and satire are not as widespread in Japan as they are in Western societies. Political humor lies hidden deep within a society's psyche, drawing on common experiences, images, and stereotypes from that society and its culture. It also reflects general attitudes that citizens have toward political authority, institutions, and the political system as a whole.

In societies like the United States or Israel, in which domestic and foreign affairs are of major concern to citizens and interest groups and the psychological involvement of individuals in politics is relatively high, jokes can serve as a means of relaxation from political tension, routine life, and social and economic insecurity, as well as an opportunity to attack political authority (Freud, 1905/1960; Keith-Spiegel, 1972; Schutz, 1977; Ziv, 1988). This is not the case in Japan, however, where politics is not generally perceived to be as important or central as it is in other societies. Public opinion surveys have shown a gradual decline in public interest in domestic policies and a low level of general concern with international affairs (Feldman, 1993b). A famous Japanese proverb—"Number one in economy, number three in politics" [*keizai ichiryu seiji sanryu*]—reflects both the greater importance that Japanese attach to economics relative to politics and the psychological distance they feel from politics.

The dearth of political humor in Japan can also be attributed to the fact that politicians, along with other authority figures such as medical doctors, lawyers, and teachers, are granted an unusually large measure of social prestige. They are generally addressed respectfully as "*sensei,*" which means literally "born before." In Japan, one rarely sees the level of suspicion, criticism, or hostility toward these public figures that one finds displayed in Western countries, regardless of what negative feelings Japanese may feel toward them. Japanese attitudes toward civil authority and workplace superiors resemble attitudes directed only toward God in the West (De Vos, 1992).

There is a saying in Japan: "A monkey remains a monkey even if it falls from the tree, but a Diet member who loses his seat becomes a mere human being" ["*saru wa ki kara ochitemo saru daga, kokkaigiin wa senkyo ni ochireba tada no hito da*"]. Nevertheless, no one would tell jokes even about a legislator who failed to be re-elected. Rather, people would continue to demonstrate respect, calling the person "sensei" despite the loss of political position and providing support until he or she is re-elected.

The Japanese lack of political humor might also reflect general attitudes not only toward the political system and politicians but also toward humor in general. Since politics is part of society, the question here is the extent to which social humor exists in Japan. Indeed, one prevalent view is that there is little humor in Japanese society. This view claims that children are the only people in Japan who are allowed to laugh at any time. Adults have few chances to laugh; they are supposed to feel some kind of social pressure that keeps them from laughing and makes them very self-conscious about such behavior (Sotoyama, 1976: 141–156). This attitude is attributable to three factors.

First, laughter has been traditionally perceived as implying impudence, imprudence, cruelty, and/or complicity that hurts others and causes them discomfort. Because Japanese tend to be cautious about the feelings of others in order to avoid giving offense and avoid "loss of face" (loss of self-respect and dignity for both speaker and listener) due to public humiliation or embarrassment, individuals were not supposed to laugh at all in front of other people (Fukusaku, 1977: 27–29).

Second, laughter was traditionally viewed as a threat to the harmony and conformity of the community—two elements that Japanese greatly value and strive for in every social interaction (Feldman, 1997). For example, extended families used to live together in one house. The small size of this house and its thin wooden or paper dividing walls allowed talking, and especially laughter, to be easily heard from one end of the house to the other. These sounds often interrupted the peaceful, quiet atmosphere of the home. Therefore, Japanese developed a particular sensitivity to laughter as something having the power to disrupt the peace and tranquility of one particular house and the community as a whole (Fukusaku, 1977: 31–32).

The last reason is related to the vertical structure of Japanese society. Japanese social relations are hierarchical, based on superior-subordinate relations such as boss-employee, master-follower, or senior-junior. This superior-subordinate structure is the primary basis of social order in Japan, shaping attitudes and behavior and affecting character, personality, and ability (Johnson, 1993). Japanese consider activities involving humor, such as telling jokes, to be appropriate only among equals. For an inferior to tell a superior a joke would be presumptuous; for the superior to tell one to an inferior might be inviting unwanted intimacy. In Japan, most people are not equals. Therefore, exchanging jokes is less prevalent in Japan than it is in other, less hierarchical, societies.

Until late in the 19th century, Japanese society was strongly dominated by vertical relations defined by status, class, and authority. This made it imperative for people to maintain strict social codes. The rigid social hierarchy of the time required that members of each social caste—samurai, farmer, artisan, merchant, or untouchable—behave in a manner befitting their status. As members of the highest group, samurai were expected to exhibit the most exemplary behavior. Samurai warriors valued taciturnity, staidness, and solemnity; laughter was construed as a vice that was offensive to others, which thus had to be suppressed as much as possible (Inoue, 1984: 176). Because people in those days were always conscious of one another's position or authority, laughter was perceived as an insult that was sometimes sufficient cause to start a fight.

Samurai believed it was a virtue not to reveal any thoughts or emotions through facial expressions, including smiling (Sotoyama, 1976: 141–142). In fact, most Orientals, including Japanese, tend to keep a poker face—not necessarily meaning to deceive, but simply due to a cultural habit of avoiding expression of emotion (Haga, 1979: 76). Even after the samurai era, Japanese soldiers were forbidden to laugh, and any who did laugh in front of a superior would be subject to severe punishment.

In the latter years of the Edo period (1603–1867), satire and other forms of popular entertainment languished as a result of governmental pressure. Before the Meiji Restoration of 1868, the Tokugawa Shogunate feared the potentially subversive effects of popular entertainment forms that looked critically at the ills and oddities of society. Political authorities were afraid that satire, which exposes society's structural flaws and troubling social relationships, might have a demoralizing effect on the public and encourage immoral acts. Therefore, the Shogunate attempted to control public opinion through a series of edicts that regulated popular entertainment. An edict issued in 1816, for example, denounced lighthearted material as unsuitable for viewing and of little socially redeeming value (Sekine, 1967). Even after the Meiji Restoration, officialdom viewed some types of popular entertainment with suspicion. The new Meiji government issued many edicts against such entertainment, similar to those formulated by the Tokugawa Shogunate.

Whereas some observers underline the sociohistorical aspects that oppress humorous expression in Japan to the extent that it is not as widespread there as it is in Western societies, others will assert that the Japanese do not totally lack a sense of humor. They do exchange jokes, albeit not nearly as frequently as Westerners do, and they do have means for publicly expressing humor and satire through rakugo, manzai, kigeki, and senryu.

Rakugo is a popular form of comic monologue in which a storyteller (*rakugoka*) creates an imaginary drama and portrays various characters through episodic narration and skillful use of vocal and facial expressions. Typically, the storytellers—who are almost always male—use no scenery; their only musical accompaniment is a shamisen, flute, or brief drum roll heard as the rakugoka, dressed in a plain kimono, enters and sits on a cushion at center stage. There he remains, delivering comic monologues or telling funny stories, often taking the roles of two or three people and using only a small towel and a fan as props. He begins with an introduction that provides a context for the narrative to follow. The rakugoka discusses social events, episodes involving a married man and his wife or his lover, and anecdotes related to society in general.

Manzai is a dialogue containing comical wording and gestures. It is usually performed by a team of two or three comedians. They act out humorous incidents or tell a series of loosely connected funny stories. Very often one of them asks questions, which the other answers. Their dialogues reflect all kinds of current affairs, from family matters to social events. *Kigeki* are comic plays performed by troupes of comedians. They reflect common social situations involving neighbors, police, gangsters, and family members.

Senryu, or satirical verse, are humorous poems consisting of 17 syllables in three lines. Senryu deals primarily with everyday people in everyday situations. One need not be a specialist to compose it; in fact, the national newspapers, including the *Asahi*, the *Yomiuri*, and the *Mainichi*, publish almost daily senryu composed by readers. The qualities that give literary value to senryu are the light, witty realism of its expression and its penetrating, intuitive observations of human foibles and events that are generally overlooked by poets in other genres. At its best, senryu's keen insights into social mores and daily life make for excellent satire, but its inclination toward sharpness sometimes causes it to take an irresponsibly negative view of humanity and society and lowers it to the level of mere sarcasm and scandal-mongering (*Kodansha Encyclopedia of Japan*, 1983; Spellman, 1997). Examples of senryu from the Yomiuri Shimbun are: *"Tenmei no sori ga tsuzuku choju-koku"* [The Japanese live long, but life as prime minister is short]. This refers to the fact that although the life expectancy of the Japanese is the highest in the world, in late 1980s and early 1990s there were frequent changes of prime ministers in Japan, with six prime ministers assumed office within five years) (cited in Spellman, 1997: 12); *"Heisei no kodomo ichi-hime han-taro"* [The average Heisei family: first a girl, then half a boy]. This refers to the fact that in an ideal family, the firstborn child is a girl and the second a boy. But in the Heisei era, started from 1989, the average family has 1.57 children (cited in Spellman, 1997: 42). And, *"Koyaku ga ichiban ukeru shigatsu baka"* [Politicians' public promises are an April Fool's day favorite] (cited in Spellman, 1997: 17).

Some of those who say that Japanese do not totally lack a sense of humor assert that there is a need to make a "regional distinction" between "the humor of the East and the humor of the West" (Inoue, 1984). The East here refers to the Tokyo region [*Kanto*] and the West to the Osaka region [*Kansai*]. Now, of course, Tokyo and Osaka are only three hours apart by train. Since the end of World War II, the development of television and other mass media has helped standardize information, knowledge, and culture in Japanese society to the extent that there are no longer major differences between the speech, dress, or lifestyles of people living in rural areas and those of people who live in large cities. Lifestyles and attitudes have become homogeneous, and the class structure has disintegrated to the point that 90 percent of the population regards itself as belonging to the middle class (Tsuruki, 1982). Even so, differences between eastern and western Japan persist, as Kanto has retained the culture of the samurai, while Kansai has retained the culture of merchants.

As discussed earlier, in the samurai culture that Tokyo retained, people were highly conscious of one another's social position, and laughter was construed as a form of offense, insult, or dishonor. In the merchants' culture that continued in Osaka, however, laughter was viewed as something that smoothes human relations and makes people feel closer to each other. One major concern for merchants is how to develop favorable horizontal relationships. As a merchant's livelihood depends on wholesalers as well as regular and prospective customers, the ability to get along with fellow townspeople is extremely important. This requires skill at negotiation, verbal ingenuity, and a knack for lightening the atmosphere with comic remarks (Inoue, 1984: 204). Thus, humor came to play an important role in daily life. This environment was also ideal for the natural development of senryu, representing the hopes and aspirations of the common people. Senryu, which is often very bitter or caustic, attempts to expose the pretensions of the privileged classes, including samurai and Buddhist monks.

Today, the Kansai region of Japan is still a thriving commercial center where various arts of laughter have been cultivated for centuries. Osaka boasts more comedians than any other city in Japan. Osaka differs from Tokyo in its comedians' style and selection of materials: Osaka comedians use the everyday Osaka dialect and generally work from an extended or exaggerated vision of everyday life. Their material seems deeper and more sophisticated, whereas comedians from Tokyo use standard Japanese and tend to play set roles, seldom revealing their true character. Tokyo entertainers typically favor carefully controlled topics; their comedy tends to be lighter and simpler (Inoue, 1984: 42–53).

Perhaps one comic form that speaks in the same manner to people in both areas of Japan is political cartoons. Let's now examine this type of Japanese humor.

POLITICAL CARTOONS

Editorial Cartooning

In recent years, editorial cartoons have become an important form of political communication within Japanese news media. Since the 1980s, a growing number of weeklies, monthlies, and other periodicals have devoted extensive space to cartoons that illustrate political figures and situations on the domestic and international scenes. Addressing subjects that are also treated verbally in political stories and editorials, editorial cartoons visually inform readers and interpret political affairs for them. As a mean of sharp social and political satire, editorial cartoons try, through simple graphic metaphors or comically distorted drawings, to guide readers' thinking about the issues of the day.

Political cartoons also reveal the essence of a situation, person, or issue and reinforce viewpoints or reflect nuances of political reality. They serve to attract readers to the editorial page and remind readers of the achievements and flaws of the political process.

The power of pictures sets cartoons apart from other editorials. Their graphic imagery can convey messages that would be unacceptable if spelled out in words (Seymour-Ure, 1986: 170). The concentrated information contained in cartoon drawings facilitates comprehension better than photographs (Ryan & Schwartz, 1956). And, unlike their verbal counterparts, ideographs can be made to speak to members of a culture in a variety of ways: through addition, omission, or distortion of component elements (Edwards & Winkler, 1997).

Thus, visual representations can be effective in shaping people's understanding of political reality and can influence the beliefs and behavior of the public and politicians—sometimes even more powerfully than verbal messages (McGee, 1980: 5; Gamson & Stuart, 1992; Langeveld, 1981; Bohrmann, Koester, & Bennett, 1978; Edwards & Winkler, 1997: 305). Gombrich (1982: 138–140), for example, asserts that while language is superior to pictures alone at conveying information and formulating arguments, the visual image is "supreme" in its ability to arouse emotions.

This notion is particularly significant in a society that uses a written language like Japanese, in which meaning is visually conveyed through ideographs, rather than alphabetic symbols. Japanese would therefore presumably find the use of graphics to convey information more compatible than would a society that uses an abstract alphabetic script (Beniger & Westney, 1981). Indeed, Japanese seem especially adept at instantly grasping the large amount of information presented in images such as photographs or cartoons and are able to perceive and distinguish between minute imagistic nuances (Feldman, 1993a).

Japanese newspapers, for example, place particular emphasis on the visual aspects of page layout in order to allow readers to rapidly absorb large amounts of information by simply scanning headlines, which usually consist of short strings of Chinese ideographs with highly concentrated message content.

The purpose of this chapter is to analyze the content and nature of editorial cartoons. More specifically, this chapter aims to detail the manner in which the national political leader, the prime minister, has been depicted in the political cartoons that appeared in two major dailies and the roles that cartoons played in shaping perceptions about politics.

The time period chosen for this analysis was the first 100 days after the inauguration of eight prime ministers. Many subscribe to the view that, when a new Cabinet is formed after an election, reporters traditionally give the new ministers a honeymoon [goshugihyo, literally, "congratulatory gift"]. In other words, there is said to be a grace period of two or three months during which reporters voluntarily refrain from criticizing the Cabinet, instead lending support through favorable reporting that gives the new administration time to get established.

This chapter also identifies the way the two national dailies portrayed prime ministers during their first terms in office and analyzes the extent to which the content and orientation of editorial cartoons changed as new administrations got under way.

Methodology

To study these issues, content analysis was performed on editorial cartoons that appeared regularly on the political pages of the *Yomiuri Shimbun* and the *Asahi Shimbun* for the first three months of the terms of eight of the past ten prime ministers: Zenko Suzuki (inaugurated July 17, 1980), Yasuhiro Nakasone (November 27, 1982), Noboru Takeshita (November 6, 1987), Toshiki Kaifu (August 8, 1989), Kiichi Miyazawa (November 5, 1991), Morihiro Hosokawa (August 5, 1993), Tomiichi Murayama (June 30, 1994), and Ryutaro Hashimoto (January 11, 1996). Two prime ministers, Sosuke Uno and Tsutomu Hata, were excluded from the study because they only remained in office for 69 days (June 2 to August 8, 1989) and 64 days (April 28 to June 30, 1994), respectively.

Coding sheets, developed in pilot studies, were used to compile information about people who appeared in the cartoons. Content was first characterized as being mainly oriented to either domestic or foreign/international issues. Dominance was measured by first considering whether the prime minister was shown alone or with other people. If he was shown with others, attention was given to the role that the prime minister played in the cartoon: Was he the main figure or did he play a secondary role, subordinate to others? Was he depicted as bigger than, equal to, or smaller than other figures?

In addition, the cartoon-version prime ministers were analyzed according to the types and degrees of exaggeration or deformity with which they were drawn. Illustrations of prime ministers were measured along ten dimensions, such as Strong, Sociable, Decisive, or Active (the full list appears in Figure 10.2). This list of items was developed in a previous study of Japanese political cartoons (Feldman, 1993a). In order to observe how prime ministers appeared in the cartoons, a seven-interval semantic differential scale was constructed for each of the ten items, ranging from "applied very much" (to the prime minister in the cartoon) to "does not apply at all."

In order to explore the nature of the cartoons, three classical psychological and philosophical categories of humor were selected: aggression, superiority, and incongruity (Berlyne, 1969; Sheppard, 1977). Aggression-related themes included hostility, violence, or threats; superiority (incompetence) themes illustrated individuals as inept, bungling, or unable to comprehend their own situation; incongruity was characterized by the juxtaposition of incompatible elements. Each cartoon was coded if it belonged to one of these three categories. The effectiveness of these types of humor was then evaluated using a 5-point scale, where 1 is very funny and 5 is not funny at all.

The object of analysis for all coding was an editorial cartoon depicting the shape, face, or figure of whichever prime minister was in office at the time. The prime minister was coded only once in each cartoon. Earlier data that has been analyzed and discussed elsewhere (Feldman, 1993c, 1995) served as the basis for the present study. A well-trained graduate student worked closely with the author on the coding. Any questions that arose during the coding were discussed with the author and immediately resolved.

Findings and Discussion

Subject Matter of the Cartoons

A total of 1,378 political cartoons appeared in the two newspapers during the study period. Prime ministers were depicted in 657 of these cartoons. In other words, approximately 47.7 percent of the cartoons that appeared in the political pages of the *Yomiuri* and the *Asahi* portrayed the national leader. This high proportion reflects the prime minister's position at the center of national government news coverage. The large amount of coverage is not necessarily related to the prime minister's real political power, however, or to his ability to establish national priorities or to solve important problems. Rather, it is related to the fact that because politics is personal in Japan, newsgathering efforts focus on people, and most intensely on a few top figures including the prime minister.

Instead of focusing on policy, the wisdom of various positions, or moral and ideological issues, politics is seen in terms of personal, factional, and strategic power games. Outcomes are of interest because they reflect and demonstrate the shifting fortunes of key power brokers and help readers keep track of winners and losers. Political events are presented through the activities of selected political leaders: what people in key positions do and think. The political climate in Japan is thus reflected best in stories that tell why and how political leaders—particularly the prime minister—create and manipulate events (Feldman, 1993d: 103).

Thus, editorial cartoons mirror the content of political articles by frequently portraying the prime minister. In these cartoons, the prime minister's figure represents several distinct forces. At times he stands for political power, the government, or the ultimate policy maker. At other times he symbolizes the ruling party or the leadership of the ruling coalition of parties. Frequently he represents all Japanese people or the "regular" Japanese, the person on the street. Alternatively, his figure may appear as an icon of the traditional, conservative values of Japanese society.

Editorial cartoons depicting the prime minister tended to contain more incongruity, resulting from the juxtaposition of incompatible elements. Sometimes the prime minister was shown in unusual forms such as a fish, bird, or snake with a human head; his face might be on the slope of an active volcano; or he might be a complex building or have other people on his shoulders. When evaluating the various types of humor on the 5-point scale (1 = very funny; 5 = not funny at all), caricatures containing an aggressive element averaged 3.20; those with superiority/ incompetence themes rated 2.27; and incongruity scored 2.05. Not only did incongruity-related cartoons appear most often, they were also the funniest.

Observing these three types of humor becomes more meaningful when they are examined relative to the length of time each prime ministers had been in office. Table 10.1 reveals an obvious increase in relative humor in all three types (aggression, incompetence, incongruity) as time passed. In other words, the longer a prime minister was in office, the funnier the cartoons became. This trend held true for all the prime ministers, without exception. There was a growing tendency to depict the national leader in funnier fighting situations—engaged in football collisions, down for the count in boxing matches, at war—struggling in increasingly humorous situations against typhoons or dragons, being hurt by falling objects, or trying to command a boat in the midst of a stormy ocean.

Differences between the Two Dailies

The two newspapers carried approximately the same number of cartoons showing a prime minister's figure or face. The *Asahi* had 322 (49% of the total cartoons) and the *Yomiuri* had 335 cartoons (51%). In fact, it is

Table 10.1
Means and Standard Deviations of Funniness by Type of Humor of Editorial Cartoons

	Aggression			Superiority			Incongruity		
	Mean	SD		Mean	SD		Mean	SD	
First Month	3.25	1.80	(42)	2.42	1.61	(56)	2.14	1.59	(45)
Second Month	3.26	1.74	(39)	2.35	1.62	(45)	2.01	1.54	(29)
Third Month	3.16	1.74	(58)	2.09	1.49	(59)	1.98	1.49	(45)
Total	3.22	1.76	(139)	2.27	1.58	(160)	2.05	1.54	(119)

Based on 5-point scale ranging from 1 = very funny to 5 = not funny at all.
Note: Figures in parentheses indicate the number of editorial cartoons in which a certain type of humor appeared in the period examined.

significant that cartoons depicting the prime minister appeared on almost the same days in the both papers.

The two dailies did not differ markedly in their treatment of the national political leader. But the high degree of uniformity between the two newspapers should not be surprising. All Japanese dailies are nearly identical in their coverage of events, selection of news, makeup, and formats because they use the same newsgathering methods, rely on a limited number of information sources, and conform to various informal customs. Consequently, there is a great deal of uniformity among all Japanese newspapers in the amount of emphasis they give to a particular news item (Feldman, 1993d). Since editorial cartoons reflect the political stories and editorials appearing in national dailies, they naturally tend to illustrate identical issues from very similar perspectives, thus contributing to the "harmony" of the Japanese media.

Significantly, there was a clear tendency to feature the prime minister in the context of domestic issues more frequently than in relation to foreign affairs. In 462 cartoons (70.3%), the different prime ministers appeared in issues related to political parties, party factions, and the government bureaucracy; in 195 cartoons (29.7%) the prime ministers appeared in the context of international matters such as relations with the United States or Europe, U.N.-related activities, or defense issues. Of the total of 462 cartoons focused on domestic issues, 229 (49.6%) were in the Yomiuri and 233 (50.4%) were in the Asahi. Of cartoons illustrating subject matter related to foreign affairs, the Yomiuri ran 106 cartoons (54.4%) and the Asahi ran 89 (45.6%).

Although there are many similarities between the two dailies, there was one conspicuous difference: As time passed in each examination period, an increasing proportion of the Yomiuri's cartoons were devoted to domestic issues (while the proportion of foreign affairs–related cartoons decreased).

Figure 10.1
Number and Proportion of Editorial Cartoons Illustrating Domestic Issues by the National Dailies

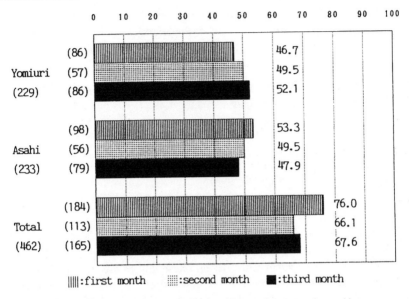

Note: Figures in parentheses indicate the number of editorial cartoons devoted by a newspaper
 (or by both newspapers) to domestic issues.

The *Asahi* showed the opposite tendency—that is, the proportion of domestic-theme cartoons decreased, while international-theme cartoons increased. This pattern is presented in Figure 10.1.

Portraying the National Leader

How did the editorial cartoons treat and evaluate the national leader over time? The breakdown of the number and percentages of cartoons illustrating the eight prime ministers during their first three months in office is presented in Table 10.2.

The table reveals, first, a gradual increase in the total number of cartoons showing successive prime ministers. Prime Minister Suzuki was featured in 34 editorial cartoons during his first three months in office, whereas the four most recent prime ministers (Miyazawa, Hosokawa, Murayama, and Hashimoto) were shown in at least three times as many. This trend is related to the fact that in recent years the prime minister has become an increasingly important source of news and object of media attention.

Table 10.2 also shows that the number of cartoons showing a prime minister varied from month to month; there was no constant rate of increase in the number during the period examined. Combining all the prime ministers, there were 242 cartoons in the first month, 171 in the second,

Table 10.2
Number and Proportion of Editorial Cartoons Illustrating the Eight Prime
Ministers by Month in Office

Prime Minister	First Month	Second Month	Third Month	Total
Zenko Suzuki	12 (35.3)	7 (20.6)	15 (44.1)	34
Yasuhiro Nakasone	19 (38.8)	14 (28.6)	16 (32.6)	49
Noboru Takeshita	26 (31.0)	22 (26.2)	36 (42.8)	84
Toshiki Kaifu	24 (33.8)	20 (28.2)	27 (38.0)	71
Kiichi Miyazawa	39 (34.5)	29 (25.7)	45 (39.8)	113
Morihiro Hosokawa	40 (40.0)	21 (21.0)	39 (39.0)	100
Tomiichi Murayama	47 (42.7)	31 (28.2)	32 (29.1)	110
Ryutaro Hashimoto	35 (36.5)	27 (28.1)	34 (35.4)	96
Total	242 (36.8)	171 (26.0)	244 (37.1)	657

Note: Figures in parentheses indicate the percentage of editorial cartoons illustrating a certain
prime minister relative to this prime minister's total number of cartoons.

and 244 in the third. The number of cartoons depicting each prime minister
decreased in the second month compared to the first month, then increased
in the third month compared to the second, for every prime minister without exception. For each prime minister, 30 to 44 percent of the total number of cartoons appeared during the first and third months; while 20 to 28
percent appeared in the second month.

This tendency is of great importance and deserves special attention. It is
related to a function of the press, particularly to the nature of coverage the
newspapers give a new administration and its prime minister. Examination
of the newspapers' editorials revealed that during the second month after
the inauguration of a new administration, there was a considerable decrease
in the number of pieces that referred to the prime minister. This trend
started about a month after each administration was formed (Feldman,
1993a). During the first three weeks from the day the prime minister took
office, there were many stories and editorials about the selection of the
prime minister. Stories and editorials featured leading politicians involved
in the process, initial talks that the new prime minister conducted with
opposition leaders and heads of economic organizations, and, particularly,
the views the prime minister held on various issues: his plans, ideas, and
promises regarding new policies.

Typically, an unusually large portion of political coverage during this
period was related to foreign/international affairs. This is because the prime
minister usually travels abroad during his first month in office to meet with
leaders of other nations, primarily the U.S. president and leaders of other

G-7 nations, to introduce himself and discuss mutual concerns. Editorials and political stories focus on these talks and the relationships that are established. This coverage gives the impression that the prime minister is an international figure who can talk with world leaders on equal terms and will represent Japan abroad with honor. Coupled with the prime minister's pledges on new policies, this type of coverage attracts much public attention and strengthens public confidence that change will come with the new administration. Overall, such coverage creates an optimistic atmosphere, inspires hope for better, more effective, and pragmatic leadership, and generates support for the new administration.

After the first three weeks, however, there is a sudden shift in political coverage, reflected in a decrease in the number of stories related to the prime minister and the new administration. The prime minister suddenly "disappears" from newspaper headlines. There are fewer reports on the national political leader's activities and on the government's activities. Instead, the political pages contain many feature stories and theses written by opinion leaders and scholars about how the government should react to issues such as the economic situation and world affairs. Newspapers give detailed reports on the results of their own public opinion polls regarding support for the new administration. During this period, there are many interviews with and profiles of government leaders and top bureaucrats.

The tendency to run fewer stories on the prime minister's performance and work begins to change at the beginning of the third month. Once the administration has more or less settled in and begun tackling controversial and/or pressing problems, more press attention is paid to such issues as implementing new taxes, revising the education system, and environmental protection. As discussed later, this results in the expression of more negative views toward the prime minister.

Further analysis disclosed that the Japanese prime minister seldom appeared alone in the editorial cartoons. Among the 657 cartoons, prime ministers were drawn alone in only 82 cases (12.5%). In 573 cartoons (87.5%), he appeared with other people. Among these people were world leaders such as the presidents of the United States and France, the prime ministers of Britain and Italy, or leaders of other G-7 nations (122 cartoons); leaders of their own political party, especially leaders of Liberal Democratic Party (LDP) factions (152); leaders of opposition parties (132); ministers (84); and "regular Japanese" such as farmers, housewives, or children (96).

It is worth noting that many of the cartoons that included "regular Japanese" depicted them as generally disinterested in the political process, confused by politicians' actions, unable to make decisions, or expressing apathy or cynicism toward the political process. For example, they were drawn as bored observers at a baseball game, separated from a table where

Table 10.3

Number and Proportion of Editorial Cartoons Illustrating the Eight Prime Ministers According to the Role They Played

Prime Minister	Main Role	Secondary Role	Total
Zenko Suzuki	25 (86.2)	4 (13.8)	29
Yasuhiro Nakasone	32 (84.2)	6 (15.8)	38
Noboru Takeshita	61 (88.4)	8 (11.6)	69
Toshiki Kaifu	53 (84.1)	10 (15.9)	63
Kiichi Miyazawa	87 (87.9)	12 (12.1)	99
Morihiro Hosokawa	85 (89.5)	10 (10.5)	95
Tomiichi Murayama	83 (93.3)	6 (6.7)	89
Ryutaro Hashimoto	79 (86.8)	12 (13.2)	91

Note: Figures in parentheses indicate the percentage of editorial cartoons illustrating a certain prime minister relative to this prime minister's total number of cartoons. The table refers only to the editorial cartoons in which the prime ministers were illustrated with other people. Excluded are 84 cartoons in which the prime ministers were illustrated alone.

politicians made decisions, or running after a bus that failed to stop and trying in vain to climb aboard.

The fact that the prime ministers usually appeared with other people enabled comparison of their relative role and size in the cartoons, as well as their relative power, sincerity, warmth, problem-solving ability and attitudes toward colleagues and the general public. When appearing with other figures, the prime minister played a secondary role in 65 cartoons (out of 573, 11.3%) and was the main figure in 508 cartoons (88.7%). He was bigger than the other figures in the same cartoon in 140 cases (24.4%), smaller in 154 cases (26.9%), and about the same size in 279 (48.7%).

As the main figure in one cartoon, a prime minister was depicted as the driver of a truck (symbolizing the force behind the country's political affairs). He tries to brake, but the truck is running away down a steep slope, out of his control. In another he was a baseball player who reached home base just as the game (symbolizing recent elections) was ending. He was shown as a patient suffering from a headache (decreased public support) while a leading figure in his party was arrested on bribery-related charges.

Table 10.3 reveals that all the prime ministers appeared as the main figure in at least 84 percent of the cartoons in which they were drawn.

The prime minister was also portrayed in a variety of forms and fashions. He was often drawn as a "regular" person (327 cases, 49.8%); as a sportsman (mainly a sumo wrestler or baseball player) in 84 cases (12.8%); and as a driver (of truck, bus or train), captain (of ship or airplane), cook, fireman, doctor, or sick person in 29 cases (4.4%). In 18 cases (2.7%), the prime minister appeared as an animal (fox, bird) or inanimate object such as a safe or a statue.

Evaluating the National Leader

By using various forms, the cartoons were able to convey messages that evoke and stimulate certain emotions. Like political anecdotes, they could channel readers' attention and affect their attitudes, creating or shaping specific impressions or images. How, then, was the prime minister perceived in these editorials? Figure 10.2 reveals how the different prime ministers appeared in the cartoons.

The analysis clearly reveals that the prime ministers were shown in a negative light during their first month of work. In their second month, without exception, the prime ministers were illustrated in an even more negative way than in the first month in office. As time passed and the administrations got under way, especially by the third month, the prime minister was attacked more harshly with the weapon of ridicule. He was shown as a weak, relatively unwise and indecisive person, one who lacks leadership abilities and does not work for the benefit of the general public.

The mean average in Figure 10.2 (in which a higher score indicates a more negative image) suggests that the prime minister was portrayed as less bright than others, less diligent, easily manipulated, unhealthy-looking and lacking in energy, conservative in his thinking and not benevolent toward the public. The typical illustration of a prime minister after two months in office was of a passive man who is cold-hearted and relatively unsociable and unhealthy. The image of the prime minister was the same in both national newspapers. He was often depicted with a distorted face, tired eyes, a wrinkled face, and as a person who tries to slip away from hard work. Compared to other figures in the same cartoon, the prime minister was shorter, slimmer, had weaker, shakier legs, and looked more fearful and less confident. He did not enjoy good luck, was always worried and defeated, and looked so miserable that he inspired sympathy.

Some Examples

In one cartoon (*Asahi*, December 5, 1987; see Figure 10.3), Prime Minister Takeshita appeared sitting on the floor uttering something in agreement after being beaten by a huge hammer (symbolizing the General Agreement on Tariffs and Trade). The caption says, "Tendency to say nothing and postpone difficult problems unless beaten over the head." This refers to Japan's prolonged, stubborn refusal to import rice and other products. Eventually, Japan became more flexible, realized its difficult situation vis-à-vis other countries, and finally agreed to open its rice market.

In a cartoon (*Yomiuri*, December 19, 1991; see Figure 10.4) that appeared after a sharp decline in the approval rating of Prime Minister Mi-

Figure 10.2
Means and SD Evaluations of the Eight Prime Ministers for Each of Ten Items

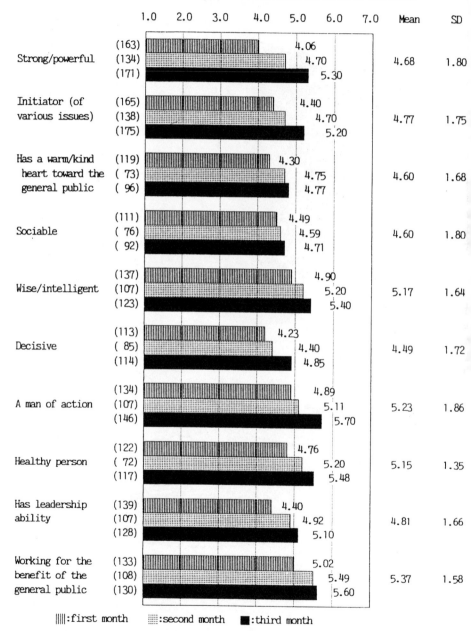

Notes: The range of the evaluation is from 1 = "apply very much" (to the prime minister) to 7 = "doe not apply at all."

Figures in parentheses indicates the number of editorial cartoons in which a particular item appears.

Figure 10.3
Shin Yamada, *Asahi Shimbun*, December 5, 1987

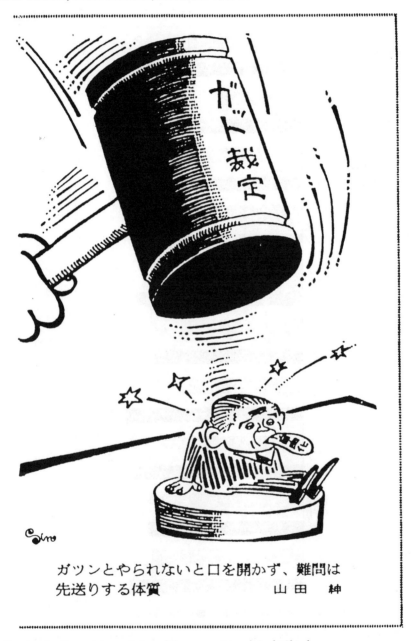

Figure 10.4
Saburo Yutenji, *Yomiuri Shimbun*, December 19, 1991

こっちも助けてーッ　　　　祐天寺　三郎

yazawa's administration (which plummeted to 44.0% in December 1991 from 55.7% a month earlier), Miyazawa was shown on a cliff hanging over a river, with U.S. President George Bush standing in a boat (symbolizing public support) below. Bush grabs Miyazawa's hand and pleads for help as his boat is sinking. Miyazawa looks surprised and frightened, as he himself is in danger of falling into the water (lack of public support).

In another cartoon (*Asahi*, September 4, 1994; see Figure 10.5), Prime Minister Murayama is shown lying in a hospital bed while a doctor shows an X-ray to a nurse. The doctor remarks that Murayama is severely ill due to a terrible tangle in his digestive organs, symbolizing the confusing and perplexing new policies and ideas adopted at his recent party convention.

The last example (*Yomiuri*, January 25, 1996; see Figure 10.6) shows Prime Minister Hashimoto as a street performer struggling with all his might to balance a globe and airplane on one foot (representing the importance that must be accorded to the Japan–United States Security Pact) along with a stack of small objects on a rod in his mouth (representing shrinkage of U.S. military bases in Okinawa Prefecture in response to protests from local residents). From a balcony in the background, the Governor of Okinawa—a leading figure in the drive to reduce the presence of American forces—observes the prime minister's performance.

CONCLUSIONS

Editorial cartoons present politicized contexts whose satire, irony, and/ or parody can play a significant role in educating the public about the political process. By stimulating thought about issues, questions about ideologies, and laughter at the foibles of political leaders and candidates, cartoons can inspire changes in sensibility and, like other forms of political media, can set political agendas through the cartoonist's choice of what to depict. At the same time, editorial cartoons also portray and reflect political reality in relation to the roles political leaders play and the different styles of political leadership that exist in a particular country.

This is especially true in the case of Japan, where, as illustrated in the cartoons, the prime minister does in fact have less power than his counterparts in Western countries. He does not have political authority to guide the state, govern the people, or politically dominate the institutions of government. He cannot decide national priorities or issues that he perceives to be important (Hayao, 1993). Frequently, his appearance in cartoons as weak, confused, and lacking confidence hints at the fact that rather than being a charismatic leader out to mobilize the masses, the prime minister is more like a Japanese business manager: He attaches much importance to group dynamics and achieving a consensus of opinion from all members of the group, and he "leads" by steering clear of ideological conflicts. Like the cartoons that portray him, the Japanese prime minister is much con-

Figure 10.5
Ko Kojima, *Asahi Shimbun,* **September 4, 1994**

ひどい腸ねん転だ　重体だよ
　　　　　小島　功

Figure 10.6
Saburo Yutenji, *Yomiuri Shimbun*, January 25, 1996

cerned with behind-the-scenes politics involving secret negotiations among various political groups. He invests much of his energy in deal-making behind closed doors in order to maintain harmonious relations with other individuals and groups.

In this sense, political cartoons serve as clear reflections of Japanese political culture, political leaders, and their roles and are a form of commentary that combines the power of visual and verbal images. But, even more important, political cartoons play an important role in shaping images of the political process. A cartoon's satiric "bite" can influence perceptions about specific issues or a prime minister's qualities and working style. It can also shape deep-seated attitudes toward the political system as a whole.

Although the Japanese prime minister's work resembles that of a manager and he may not be able to politically dominate the organs of government, he is still the person out front, the symbol of political authority for the news media—and for cartoonists. If something does not go well, it is his fault. If there is growing evidence of money influencing politics and corruption in government, he is the one to be blamed. If bureaucrats express dissatisfaction with a policy, he is the target of attack.

Apparently the prime minister has been, for a long time, the most readily available target for the press. When introduced in a cartoon with other world leaders, he cannot talk much. Instead, his message is contained in a suitcase full of yen, representing foreign aid, which he carries with him wherever he travels. He is the one wearing a military uniform in front of the U.N. Secretary-General before leaving on an overseas peace-keeping mission; the one whose head aches from the pressure of Japanese farmers' opposition to opening the rice market. He is the one who climbs steep mountains, traverses the desert in blazing summer, crosses the street in a typhoon with an umbrella full of holes. In the editorial cartoons of the Japanese dailies, he is sick, old, ugly, feeble, the one who makes fatal errors, the perennial loser. These cartoons serve as rich representations of the ideas and attitudes that formed and continue to shape Japanese culture and politics.

NOTE

This chapter draws on Feldman (1995).

1. There is a need to distinguish between humor and the "Japanese smile." Japanese often laugh nervously or smile at times that seem inappropriate to non-Japanese. Apparently, they smile to conceal anguish, to spare others sympathetic pain, and to cover embarrassment or discomfort. Their smiles may cover up sorrow, anger, or inconvenience, or they may serve as a polite signal to stop discussing a certain topic or to stop a particular action.

REFERENCES

Beniger, J. R., & Westney, D. E. (1981). Japanese and U.S. Media: Graphics as a Reflection of Newspapers' Social Role. *Journal of Communication*, 31, 14–27.

Berlyne, D. E. (1969). Laughter, Humor, and Play. In G. Lindsey & E. Aronson (Eds.), *Handbook of Social Psychology*, vol. 3 (pp. 795–852). Reading, MA: Addison-Wesley.

Bohrmann, E. G., Koester, J., & Bennett, J. (1978). Political Cartoons and Salient Rhetorical Fantasies: An Empirical Analysis of the '76 Presidential Campaign. *Communication Monographs*, 45, 317–329.

Bryder, T. (1993). Stereotypes, Ethnic Prejudice and Catharsis in Political Jokes and Graffiti. Paper presented at the Annual Scientific Meeting of the International Society of Political Psychology, Cambridge, MA.

De Vos, G. A. (1992). *Social Cohesion and Alienation: Minorities in the United States and Japan*. Boulder, CO: Westview.

Edwards, J. L., & Winkler, C. K. (1997). Representative Form and the Visual Ideograph: The Iwo Jima Images in Editorial Cartoons. *Quarterly Journal of Speech*, 83, 289–310.

Feldman, O. (1993a). Political Caricature and the Japanese Sense of Humor. Paper presented at the Annual Scientific Meeting of the International Society of Political Psychology, Cambridge, MA.

Feldman, O. (1993b). Political Alienation and Cynicism in Contemporary Japan. *Tsukuba Journal of Sociology*, 18, 1–58.

Feldman, O. (1993c). Seijimanga ni miru "Nihon no shusho" [How the Japanese prime minister is illustrated in the editorial cartoons of the national dailies]. *Ushio*, 12, 120–127.

Feldman, O. (1993d). *Politics and the News Media in Japan*. Ann Arbor: University of Michigan Press.

Feldman, O. (1995). Political Reality and Editorial Cartoons in Japan: How the National Dailies Illustrate the Japanese Prime Minister. *Journalism and Mass Communication Quarterly*, 72, 571–580.

Feldman, O. (1997). Culture, Society, and the Individual: Cross-cultural Political Psychology in Japan. *Political Psychology*, 18, 327–353.

Freud, S. (1905/1960). *Jokes and Their Relation to the Unconsciousness*. New York: Norton.

Fukusaku, M. (1977). *Nihonjin no warai*. Tokyo: Tamagawa daigaku shippanbu.

Galnoor, I., & Lukes, S. (1985). *No Laughing Matter*. London: Routledge & Kegan Paul.

Gamson, W. A., & Stuart, D. (1992). Media Discourse as a Symbolic Contest: The Bomb in Political Cartoons. *Sociological Forum*, March, 55–86.

Gombrich, E. H. (1982). *The Image and the Eye*. Ithaca, NY: Cornell University Press.

Haga, Y. (1979). *Nihonjin no hyogen shinri*. Tokyo: Chuo Koronsha.

Hayao, K. (1993). *The Japanese Prime Minister and Public Policy*. Pittsburgh: University of Pittsburgh Press.

CHAPTER 11

g the Internet in Political Campaigns:
ampaign Evidence from Interactive
Interviews with Novice Users

MONTAGUE KERN, MARION JUST,
ANN CRIGLER, AND HONG (IRIS) XIE

96 American presidential election cycle was marked by the recog-
that a new medium, the Internet, was coming of age on the political
Research probing citizen use of the Internet in the electoral process
infancy. Voter use of the medium has not been deemed significant,
ere has been a question concerning the value which citizens ascribe
medium. Studies during the 1996 election cycle put the percentage
ericans using the Web between 10 and 20 percent, with political use
hat less than that, but rising. One survey conducted immediately
he 1996 election found that 23 percent of the respondents claimed
e engaged in some politically related Internet activity (Katz, Aspden,
d, 1997). Other surveys put campaign-related Internet use quite a bit
A panel study conducted by the Roper Center in the 1996 presiden-
ction, for example, found that a small but growing number of reg-
l voters had "visited a politically oriented Web site." Five percent of
ample of 503 registered voters visited a political Web site in February,
:ent in August, and 8 percent in November. (Dautrich and Hartley,
:oming). In another voter survey at the end of the 1996 election cam-
, only 7 percent reported using the Internet for campaign information.
six percent of the smaller number who did use the Internet felt that
date Web pages had been somewhat or very helpful, but less than half
e 1,235 survey respondents thought that free access to campaign in-
ation on the World Wide Web would be helpful to them in the future
ciding how to vote (Campaign Discourse and Civic Engagement Sur-
1996).
June 1998, however, according to a Pew Research Center poll, this
e had grown considerably, to 30 percent, with 20 percent of all adults

Inoue, H. (1984). *Warai no ningen kankei* [Laughter as]
    Kodansha.
Johnson, F. A. (1993). *Dependency and Japanese Socializ*
    Anthropological Investigations into Amae. New Yo
    Press.
Keith-Spiegel, P. (1972). Early Conceptions of Humor: Vai
    McGhee & J. H. Goldstein (Eds.), *Handbook of*
    York: Springer-Verlag.
Kodansha Encyclopedia of Japan. (1983). Tokyo: Kodansl
Kumon, S. (1988). Nationalism of Long Intestine. *Japan T*
Langeveld, W. (1981). Political Cartoons as a Medium of P
    International Journal of Political Education, 4, 343-
McGee, M. C. (1980). The "Ideograph": A Link between
    Quarterly Journal of Speech, 66, 1–16.
Paletz, D. R. (1990). Political Humor and Authority: From
    International Political Science Review, 11, 483–493.
Ryan, T. A., & Schwartz, C. B (1956). Speed of Perception
    of Representation. *American Journal of Psychology,*
Sakaiya, T. (1994). *Nihon towa nanika* [What is Japan?].
Schutz, C. E. (1977). *Political Humor.* Rutherford, N.J.: Fa
    versity Press.
Schutz, C. E. (1995). Cryptic Humor: The Subversive Mess
    Humor: International Journal of Humor Research, 8,
Sekine, M. (1967). *Kodan rakugoko* [A consideration of ral
    kyo: Yuzankaku.
Seymour-Ure, C. (1986). Drawn and Quartered: The Electi
    Crewe and M. Haroop (Eds.), *Political Communicatio*
    tion Campaign of 1983 (pp. 160–176). Cambridge: (
    Press.
Sheppard, A. (1977). Developmental Levels in Explanations o
    hood to Late Adolescence. In A. J. Chapman & H. (
    Funny Thing, Humour (pp. 225–228). New York: Per;
Sotoyama, S. (1976). *Nichijo no kotoba.* Tokyo: Mizuumi Sh
Spellman, M. (1997). *Senryu: Haiku Reflections of the Times.*
Tsuruki, M. (1982). Frame-imposing Function of the Mass N
    Japanese Press. *Keio Communication Review,* 3, 27–37
Ziv, A. (1988). *National Styles of Humor.* Westport, CT: Gre

Usir
C

The 1
nition
scene.
is in i
and t
to the
of An
some
after
to ha
& Re
lowe:
tial e
ister
their
6 pe
forth
paig
Fifty
canc
of tl
forn
in c
vey.
B
figu

going online to get news at least once a week (Pew Research Center on the Press and Politics, June 1998). Critics, however, continued to point out that expansion of citizens' use of the World Wide Web depends on whether the new medium becomes economically and technologically accessible, user-friendly, and interactive (Davis & Owen, 1998).

Until recently, users of the World Wide Web have not been typical of the population at large—and this certainly includes the small number of users who have been using the World Wide Web for political information. Indeed, they have been somewhat older, more white, educated, male, and economically upscale—indeed an "elite" audience. The size and composition of the audience has raised concern about whether the medium will contribute to an information gap, in a fashion that further disenfranchises women, persons of color, and those lower on the economic spectrum. Those who go online for news are disproportionately younger, better educated, and affluent (Pew Research Center on the Press and Politics, June 1998). Although serious *demographic* gaps persist, it appears that the Internet is moving toward critical mass as a commercial mass medium.

In the United States the World Wide Web will thus soon be a significant source of election information. Will such technological change, involving a mass audience, have a desirable or undesirable effect in terms of empowering citizens in the electoral process? To answer this question, it is instructive to study the lessons of the 1996 election. We will undertake this here, from a political science and mass communication perspective. We examine "talk aloud" protocols gathered as novice users, from all ends of the demographic spectrum, were introduced to World Wide Web sites to determine patterns of choice by novice users.

It is important to point out that the method we use here, a structured introduction to World Wide Web sites, is innovative. Its purpose is to examine what might happen if citizens gain significant access to computers. In the 1996 election cycle, not only were most users novices, such as those in our study; but presidential candidates had for the first time seriously developed Web sites designed to persuade. Uniquely, these included sites not only by the major party candidates, Republican Bob Dole and Democrat Bill Clinton, but also for minor party candidates such as the Reform Party's Ross Perot, the Green Party's Ralph Nader, and the Libertarian Party's John Hagelin. News media sites were also on line, including those not only of individual newspapers such as the *New York Times* and the *Los Angeles Times* but also of combined newspaper/television sites, such as *Allpolitics* (*Time* and CNN), and magazines as well, including alternative news magazines such as *Mother Jones*. In addition, non-partisan groups, interested in voter education, set up Web sites. The *Project Vote-Smart*, for example, offered citizens comparative information about a broad range of candidate issue positions. Voters could access such information by clicking the name of their state in a box and then selecting from a menu of candidates.

Web sites were also set up by both the major and independent political parties, as well as a variety of political organizations, such as the Christian Coalition and the Green Party. These offered voter information, along with community and solidarity-building encouragement. All of this clearly opened a broader range of persuasive and solidarity-building messages to citizens, in comparison with those that could be found on the traditional mass media.

We included such Web sites on a home page for citizen use that we installed in our university computers, for citizen use at our structured introduction to the Web. How helpful would various sites be to citizens, from the perspective of the three communication functions that the Internet has the capability of performing—information, persuasion, and solidarity-building. Based on the talk-aloud protocols, can we identify different Web site search strategies used by different types of voters? Can we identify common problems for different types of voters in using political Web sites?

Here, we address such questions, based on in-depth analysis of the "talk-aloud" protocols at one site, New Jersey, using cases which further illuminate the broad conclusions of the full study.

METHODS

The current research is part of a study of the 1996 election campaign that involves multiple research methods, including survey and experimental designs, content analysis, focus groups, and in-depth interviews. This 1996 study of voter use of World Wide Web sites during a presidential campaign draws from the focus group and interview data sets.

Six focus groups were conducted in Los Angeles and New Jersey on October 22 and 23, 1996. The focus groups examined how partisans and independents assessed different campaign message formats including candidate statements during free TV air time, political advertising, debates, and televised interview programming. The focus group participants consisted of a purposive sample of registered voters from Northern New Jersey and Southern California. Professional marketing firms in each location recruited the focus group participants with the goal of varying age, gender, ethnicity, employment status, political ideology, and interest. The focus group participants were also asked if they would be available for a second research evening. Twenty-eight Los Angeles citizens and 27 New Jersey residents completed the focus groups, including a pretest questionnaire, the protocol, and a post-test questionnaire. Twenty-one of the Los Angeles participants and 20 of the New Jersey participants were recruited at random for the second evening when the Internet study was conducted. Subjects did not know ahead of time that they would be using a computer or accessing the Internet. In fact, most had never previously used the Internet.

For the Internet study, each participant was paired with a student interviewer so that the students could help them with any computer questions and closely monitor each subject's use of the Internet. The interviewers greeted each subject and escorted them to a computer displaying the study's home page. The home page listed campaign-relevant sites that subjects could "click on" to visit. The sites included news media, presidential candidates, non-partisan organizations, political parties and organizations, and parodies and political cartoons. Subjects were free to visit any site, including ones that were not on the home page.

After showing subjects how to access the Web, the interviewers tape recorded the subject's comments while they used the computer, using a "talk-aloud" methodology. At the end of an hour, the interviewers stopped the subjects and asked them a series of open-ended questions. These interviews were also taped, transcribed, and coded for the subjects' feelings about using the World Wide Web, their likes and dislikes about the Web, their favorite and least favorite Web sites, their comparisons of the World Wide Web to television and newspapers, and their learning about the presidential campaign and candidates from their hour on the Web. The interviews lasted approximately 15 minutes. In addition to the information gathered during the interview, the interviewers also retrieved from the computer a complete listing of the sites each subject visited. The list measured the number of sites visited as well as the number of pages visited per site (hits).

Repeated tests on demographic variables showed no statistical difference between the two geographic sites in terms of age, gender, education, partisanship, or computer use; therefore, for purposes of our quantitative analysis we aggregated the responses from the two research locations (New Jersey and California). The talk-aloud data report findings from the New Jersey site.

It is important to point out that this study was conducted during the final phase of an election, and one that the polls clearly indicated would not be a close election. In national polls, the Democratic presidential candidate, Bill Clinton, was ahead of the Republican candidate by over 10 points, and the Reform Party candidate, Ross Perot, was in the low single digits. Previous studies have shown that a competitive race generates greater interest and stimulates greater learning late in a campaign (Just et al., 1996).

HOW CITIZENS USE POLITICAL WEB SITES

Overall, our subjects liked the greater information choice that the Internet afforded them. Although some participants expressed concern about the currency of the information on the Web, most reported that they learned politically relevant information from the medium. Analysis of the debriefing interviews and questionnaires shows that the participants were engaged with the Internet as a political tool and appreciated the range and depth of information available (Just, Crigler, & Kern, 1997).

Engagement with Political Information

The results showed that the Web made it particularly easy for citizens to survey a range of media or other types of sites—far more broadly and conveniently than the average person could pursue in any other venue. When given the opportunity, people typically browsed several related sites on the Internet. Many made serendipitous discoveries while pursuing a surveillance or purposive approach to the information. Even participants who most enjoyed the solidary benefits of visiting sites that shared their identities, interests, or preferences became curious and visited competing Web sites as well. It is doubtful that the medium performed any strong persuasive function.

Access to Information

An advantage of the Internet is that users have access to information sources unavailable in traditional mass media. Of particular interest are access to news sources, including the alternative press, and minority political parties that are generally not covered by the mainstream media. This diversity of information sources is central to the medium's democratic relevance. A third of our participants pointed to the broad range of information available to them. They were pleased that they could access views or opinions on the Internet to which they would not ordinarily be exposed. For example, a California bookkeeper explained approvingly: "not many of us take more than one newspaper, very few of us watch more than one news station at a time, this gives a greater opportunity for more diversity. I can choose what I want to look at. I can choose the slant that I want to see." [Carrie] Jean, a medical assistant from California, specifically commented on his access to non-mainstream party organizations on the Web:

to be honest with you, as I said to you, I knew very little about any of the parties other than the Republican and Democratic parties, 'cause they're the most highly visible. They have access to the media most of all. . . . I learned some things about the parties I didn't know. I had no information at all about Perot's type of party. I didn't read much about it right now, but I could have. I had the access to it.

Our participants clearly appreciated the breadth of information and opinion available on the Web.

Clustered Browsing and the Joy of Discovery

Most users of the structured political Web page followed a "clustered browsing" strategy (Bates, 1989). Most participants visited more than one site in their first cluster and more than one site in their second cluster. For example, if they visited the Dole/Kemp web site, they were likely to visit the Clinton/Gore web site as well. There was cross-partisan monitoring. Strong partisans were not the only ones to visit a range of sites in a cluster; focused browsing was exhibited by independents who visited third party sites as well.

A finding in one cluster might lead to the pursuit of new clusters, as curiosity reinforced itself. Thus one woman reported how curiosity led her to access information on the Internet that she would not otherwise have had. "I didn't know about Harry Browne. I had no . . . I really. . . . The only ones I really knew about were Clinton/Gore, Dole/Kemp, Perot, Ralph Nader. I had no idea about anything else. . . . That's why I went into Harry Browne. . . . So at least it gave me some insight on that." She continued, "I went into *Mother Jones Magazine* because I didn't know what that was either" [Theresa].

Fredin (1997: 5) has suggested that the Web might stimulate browsing, "which can result in emotionally satisfying discoveries characterized as serendipitous." This appeared to be the case in our data.

Information over Solidarity Functions

Our findings made it clear that the primary function of Web sites was information gathering, or surveillance. Analysis of all sites visited clearly favored the news media. Fifty-nine percent of all sites visited were news media sites (compared with 17 percent candidate sites, 11 percent nonpartisan sites, 6 percent parties and organizations, and 7 percent humor/parodies).

This was not surprising, since one study suggests that a majority of those who used the Internet for political purposes in the 1996 election were also newspaper readers (Katz et al., 1997). Further, a study of the most popular sites in 1996, as measured by overall number of site visits, makes it clear that they were not strongly interactive, while arguing that interactivity is necessary to encourage the building of community, which is necessary for the development of feelings of solidarity (Barber, Mattson, & Peterson, 1997). As if to illuminate this point, a number of our participants complained that the candidate web sites, which should serve not only a persuasive but a solidarity purpose, even of those of such major party candidates as Robert Dole, were inadequate, not only in the area of interactivity but also in terms of providing up-to-date and timely information to visitors.

Although there is clear potential for the medium (Schwartz, 1996), it is not fulfilled. Still, some evidence from our study suggested that some people do use the Web in the same way that DeTocqueville described American newspapers: as a form of association at a distance. For example, different choices were made by participants with different characteristics such as gender or strength of partisanship. Men were more likely than women to visit the Republican National Committee Web site; women were far more likely than men to visit the League of Women Voters site; and independents and weak partisans were far more likely than strong partisans to visit the third-party sites.

Informational and Structural Problems

Finally, disappointment was expressed in virtually all of the extended comments our participants made about the Web, although males experienced the Internet more positively than females, and those who visited more sites (i.e., could "get around" the Internet) were more satisfied than those who had greater difficulty. The main cause of this disappointment was that there was not enough information that was current, reliable, or interesting.

PARTISAN, ISSUE-ORIENTED, AND UNCERTAIN INFORMATION SEEKERS

The talk-aloud protocols allow us to examine user strategies from a different perspective than the debriefing interviews, since the data were gathered during rather than after the experience with the Internet. The findings for the New Jersey talk-aloud interviews illuminate the statistical conclusions of the full study. In particular, the talk-aloud data help to identify three different Web site search strategies and offer clues about optimal political Web site design.

From the talk-aloud transcripts it is possible to identify three unique patterns of information seeking: the *partisan*, the *issue seeker*, and the *uncertain user*, who may still be forming impressions about the candidates and their positions on issues late in the campaign (see Table 11.1). We will describe each of these types of information seekers and some of the problems which they experienced at the computers.

Partisan Seekers

The talk-aloud data indicate that there is a *partisan* information seeker, whose search strategy is influenced by commitment to a political party. Such information seekers monitored information for party cues, which they used to evaluate candidates and interpret issue positions. They monitored information provided by a variety of sources, focusing heavily on news

Table 11.1
Three Patterns of Information Seeking

	Partisan	Issue Seeker	Uncertain User	
			Browser	Site Attractiveness
Site Selection Criteria	Political party	Issues of concern	Voting decision	Convenience Appearance Curiosity
Types of Site Selected	Polls News media Candidates' information	News sites Candidate sites	Candidate sites	Political parties and organizations Parodies and political cartoons News media Presidential candidates Non-partisan organizations
Seeking Strategies	Monitor	Search	Browse	Serendipity
Types of Information Sought	Polls of favored candidates Positive information related to favored candidates News outlets	Candidates' issues Media issues Issues of voters	Candidates' issues	Style Attractive content
Problems Encountered	Failed to find archive data (e.g., historical polling information)	Not satisfied with the organization of the sites (e.g., index, content, etc.) Not knowing how to search for issues	Not knowing how to search for issues	Not all sites recognize media's full interactive potential

media, poll, and candidate Web sites. They were not seriously interested in unearthing information about their own candidates. They were particularly interested, however, in finding out how their favored candidate was faring in the polls and in a variety of news media outlets.

For example, Emmanuel, a moderate Republican utility worker, had already made up his mind to support Bob Dole. Most of his attention was devoted to visiting political polling Web sites. He first visited the Gallup polling headquarters, then the Roper Center for Public Opinion Research, and then the Data and Program Library Home Service. He was quite concerned, indeed hopeful, that the polls might prove wrong. "Are the polls in fact ever wrong?" he asked, even while he reaffirmed the fact that his own candidate was lagging seriously behind. In monitoring the public opinion sites, he said he wanted to keep the pollsters "honest." He also hoped that the polls might fail to predict the vote. Although he visited a number of sites, he found only current polling information, however, with no links to related information addressing his burning issue—the possibility that the polls might be wrong! As a result, he encountered some frustration in the search process.

Like the other partisans in the study who had a favored candidate, he also monitored the news media. Here, though, he did not look for information about the candidates or their issue positions. At the PBS Web site he spotted a headline "Why America Hates the Media." The headline proved misleading, however. It turned out that he selected the site to find exactly what the headline implied—public opinion about the media. Instead, as he ruefully reported, he found "what *the press* thinks about the press," which was not of interest. He visited one candidate Web site, that of the Democratic presidential candidate, Bill Clinton. He did this to satisfy his curiosity concerning why "Clinton is so concerned about getting all the schools connected to the World Wide Web." Like most of our study participants, he was interested in finding some up-to-date information—in this case, about a "hot" topic, education and the Internet.

Justin, a union construction worker and a strongly partisan conservative Republican, utilized a similar search strategy. Instead of first turning to polls, however, he screened the output of a variety of news sources. He visited a number of sites because he was "curious to see what information is new or different, or what I might be able to receive through the Internet." His monitoring purpose included the hope that he would find positive information that he could interpret in a fashion that would advance his candidate's fortunes. He visited a variety of sites for this purpose.

Like most of the subjects in the study, he turned first to a familiar, valued, cable news source—because he was "interested in CNN and cable." He used this site to monitor other news sources. He then visited *Allpolitics*, a joint network television and national newspaper site. Subsequently, he visited the *Los Angeles Times*. He observed, "If I were to look up [only] the *Los Angeles Times* or [one] national news network. . . . I might only see certain key stories." Far from seeking information for the purpose of making his own voting choice, he monitored what others in the political environment were up to. Thus, at the CNN site, he commented that "hopefully, you know [I will find] no tricks."

A union construction worker, who fell on the conservative side of party politics, he was committed to conservative change. Thus Justin also visited *The Democracy Project/Amendments to the Constitution* site looking for "commentary on certain aspects of the Constitution" and whether the site could "serve as an educational tool." Nolan, a partisan information seeker from a higher rung of the social ladder—he was a financial manager—similarly monitored news programs and polls. He visited ABC News to examine its polls and raised a question concerning whether there was bias in the site's prediction that Democrats led Republicans 51–43 in the year's U.S. House of Representatives electoral contests. He found some consolation, however, from his visit to the interactive part of the Dole home page, but he was disappointed to find that its typeface was too small for him to read easily.

Issue Seekers

In contrast to partisans, there are *issue-oriented* information seekers who search around three types of issues: the candidates' issues, issues covered by the media, and issues of concern to other voters. One type of issue-seeker targeted a single issue such as abortion or school prayer, wherever it could be found. Another was more interested in adding to his or her store of knowledge about candidate issue positions.

For example, Mary Ann, a Democrat, and an employee of the State School system, sought information around her strong area of interest, women's issues. She went primarily to news media sites—the *Los Angeles Times*, the *New York Times*, MSNBC, PBS, *Mother Jones*, and *USA Today*—looking for news reports and commentary on women's issues. "I was wanting to find out what women's issues are in the election," she said.

She encountered two serious problems, however. The first was that she had an *index orientation* throughout. Thus, she asked, "Once you access a section, like *Mother Jones*, why isn't there a directory that you can go to . . . to point to . . . what you are looking for? Is there? Is it there, and I just don't know how to use it?"

The problem of categorization and relevance become particularly acute when Mary Ann, like a disproportionate number of women in the sample, visited the League of Women Voters Web site, which as we have noted, gave them little satisfaction. She remarked that she didn't know the context for the issue positions that she was seeing. If candidates said something, was it "ten years ago, five days ago, two days ago? I don't know what I'm seeing!"

Further, she was concerned about the fact that most of the sites assume that voters already know candidate issue positions. Thus she asked, how could she find "Dole's position, and what Clinton's position is? If I didn't know their position already, I'm not finding it very easily."

Her search led to a frequently expressed statement of frustration: "This is for people with a lot of time, I think. . . . Why does it take so long? Other people are on the line, or whatever?"

Andrew, a maintenance mechanic and an Independent, who voted for Ross Perot in the previous election, was similarly concerned about issues, although different ones. He believed school prayer should be reinstated, would like to see more life sentencing, and was worried that a growing number of immigrants will contribute to increasing job scarcity.

Like Mary Ann, he experienced a lot of frustration, as he did not know how to search for his issues. "If there is a search engine," he said, "I do not know how to use it." Like Mary Ann, he was also interested in finding something new. He visited the Clinton/Gore 96 Web site, and found an email message from Bill Clinton. The reason he selected the site, he said, was to see if he would learn anything new from it. He was disappointed.

For the issue seeker, issue concerns ran deep at this point in the election contest, deeper than any concern about a candidate. Such seekers, however, were frustrated because they didn't know how to find what they were looking for. Further, as Mary Ann said, "This is slow."

Uncertain Information Seekers

A final category of information seeking is made up of users who are less clear about what they want. While some of these participants had reached either a tentative or a firm decision about which candidate to support, others had not. In either case, they were not aggressive information seekers. Some were indeed passive. As previous research suggests, many voters are not active information seekers (Graber, 1984; Neuman, 1991). They did, however, express an interest in finding out about issues in order to help them make a more educated voting choice. We found, overall, two types of *uncertain information seekers*. One group we might categorize as *browsers*, and the other was a group for whom *site and attractiveness* came first.

The Browser

John N., an Independent and a designer for an engineering firm, had not decided whom he would vote for in November. Information about issues and the candidates was, he said, relevant to him as he moved toward a voting choice. He explained that he wanted to find out about the issue positions of each candidate because "that would, I think, help me make [a] more educated vote, when you can see them, when you can compare them." He visited Ross Perot's candidate site first, and then *Allpolitics (Time/CNN)*. At the latter he tapped into "It's the Issues, Stupid!" Unlike the issue seeker, however, he explained that he was "browsing, if anything. I would probably be just looking at economic issues." But, "I'm uninvolved in politics . . . that's why I'm browsing. . . . I'm just checking it out."

Site Convenience and Attractiveness First

Like John N., Susan, a merchandiser and a weak Democrat, did not express an opinion about the issues. For her, site attractiveness came first. She went to *Politicsnow* and really liked the graphics. Throughout her experience with the Web, she was more likely to pay attention to sites with good visuals.

She visited an independent candidate site, the Harry Browne site, and said that she had no interest because it took "too long to download information." She wanted things on the screen right away. She visited an independent party site, that of the Green party, and commented that she didn't like the picture of the woman vice presidential candidate.

At the League of Women Voters page, she didn't find much that was political that captured her attention—but she did like the blue and red color. She went to *Scampaign 396-Comedy* and visited and liked a variety of humor pages. She liked her favorite site, *USA Today*, because of color and the graphics. She was also interested in the speeches of the past presidents.

Her reason for her lack of interest in approaching more issue-oriented sites directly was oversaturation with the candidates. She said this was the reason she did not click on Dole and Clinton's sites.

At one candidate site, however, *Fairfield.com*, she encountered John Hagelin, an Independent candidate. The reason that she clicked on this site was that she had never heard of him before. She was driven by curiosity, and also by the attractiveness of the site. Issues were altogether unimportant—style and attractive content came first.

Interestingly, this type of participant raises broad questions that still need to be addressed. An analysis of past studies of the introduction of new media technologies, such as radio, have indicated that during the "massification" process, in the absence of literacy training, citizens have largely gravitated toward mediated messages that are more expensively and creatively produced, failing to recognize the medium's full interactive potential (Napoli, 1999). We are at just this stage in the process of movement in the use of Web sites for electoral purposes.

Clearly, the Web sites that were most attractive and timely were the major news media Web sites, which were most visited. And for users such as those for whom *site and attractiveness come first*—as well as timeliness—it is clear that production quality, which is still an expensive commodity, may be important. This of course gives an advantage not to the independent candidate site, which in our example didn't even seem to be

Table 11.2
Criteria for a Good Political Web Site

	Current Problems	Ideal Political Web Site
Site Selection Criteria	Very few good sites have both attractive appearance and high-quality content.	Balance appearance and content
Types of Site Selected	It is difficult to find sites that can satisfy different types of users' special needs.	Be clear about their target users Provide different access points Offer various types of information
Seeking Strategies	Current Web sites do not offer functions to guide them properly to apply users' search strategies (e.g., monitoring, searching, browsing, and clustered browsing).	Facilitate monitoring Facilitate issue search Facilitate browsing and clustered browsing
	Web sites do not fully support old search tools that novice users use for the traditional media.	Facilitate old search strategies (e.g., indexes)
Types of Information Sought	Voters were disappointed that they could not find new and unique information on the Internet that other media have not provided and will not provide.	Offer new information Offer unique information Offer interactive features

able to produce an attractive picture of its vice-presidential candidate, nor to media sites lacking in attractive visuals but, instead, to major party and news media sites. Table 11.2 lists the criteria for a good political Web site.

The two types of *uncertain users* join more intentional users as part of the mix that characterizes the contemporary political Web environment. Though not at all uninterested in candidates and their issues, other factors contribute to their strategy for using Web information.

Commonalties among Different Types of Users

The analysis of computer talk-aloud protocols presents three kinds of novice political search strategies: partisan, issue-oriented, and uncertain

Table 11.3
Common Patterns of Information Seeking

	Voters' Information Seeking
Site Selection Criteria	Trust
	Novelty
Types of Information Sought	New information
	Unique information
Seeking Strategies	Apply old seeking strategies to the Internet

users, employing either a browsing or a visual attraction strategy. In addition to some differences, however, there are also similarities (see Table 11.3).

First, although many of our participants wanted to find *new information*, they often employed *old strategies*. Several of our participants looked for information that they could not find in the one or two major media to which they normally attend. As one voter, Nolan, said, "I am looking for something either that's new, or . . . that I can [use to] gain a little insight into something that I already know about." They were disappointed when they could not find any new information. As one participant said: "I thought I'd learn something new, but it seems to be pretty much what I [already] know" (Josephine).

In spite of the search for novelty, however, most users tried to *apply old seeking strategies* to the Internet. They looked for indices, directories, and other things that were familiar to them. As Mary Ann said, "I thought there would be an index, like in a library, like on a topic you wanted. I was going to do women's issues." She continued, "I got whatever I got on my screen, I had no selection of what was going to come on my screen."

Second, most selection strategies were based upon two criteria: *trust and novelty*. John, for example, expressed the need for trust: "I like the way PBS does programming. It's not as slanted as the other stations, to me." But other participants were attracted by novelty, which is related to the dimension of *curiosity* and *serendipitous* discovery that our broad dataset also suggested the Internet makes possible. As John noted, in discussing a further choice, "This looks interesting—*Mother Jones Magazine*."

CONCLUSION

From this study it is possible to conclude that, in one country, the United States, where the political communication environment is in a process of rapid change, technology is creating greater opportunity for citizens to gain information about candidates and issues in presidential election campaigns.

This should contribute to more vibrant presidential election campaigns if Web sites represent a broad range of not only mainstream but also minority choices of political information.

Novice users who were introduced to a variety of political Web sites in the final phase of the 1996 presidential election valued the diversity of information available to them on the Internet. If citizens are going to make wide use of the Internet as a political tool, the problem of access will also have to be overcome. There are other obstacles as well. The first is related to access and involves the need for computer education so that users can have satisfactory experiences on line. Computer education must include an understanding of media interactivity, as well as technique. The second problem involves Web site design to make access, searching, and navigation less frustrating and relevant to the user's needs.

It is important to note that the experimental design used in this study, which illuminates the possibilities of Internet enhancement of civic engagement, included both marginal independent party and political organization sites as well as alternative media sites. This diversity was recognized and was an important part of the satisfaction that users experienced in concluding that they had increased access to diverse information. It is important that for this satisfaction to persist, future development of the Internet must not replicate that of current major broadcasting systems and news outlets, which largely ignore minority candidates and media. The Internet should not become a communication structure that ignores the diversity of political expression, however unindexed, that is currently available. Minority expression and recognition of the vibrant public interest in diversity of opinion are vital in the democratic process.

Future research should pay special attention to two further problems suggested by this analysis. One issue that was raised by our participants and has been explored by others is the lack of two-way communication on most Web sites. This lack of interactivity depresses the democratic potential of political Web sites (Barber, Mattson, & Peterson, 1997).

The second is the possibility that news media sites, which in this study have a clear advantage, may benefit not only from voter familiarity but also from a *funding advantage*, which contributes to the production of attractive, convenient, and "speedy" sites unavailable to minority voices. Such a funding advantage should also soon be available to major party political candidates.

Here it is important to point out the need to encourage space for minorities and interests that are not heavily funded, at all stages of the evolution of this medium. Given its popularity with novice users, the Web should be on its way to becoming a mass medium, heavily used in the U.S. electoral process.

REFERENCES

Annenberg Public Policy Center Report. (August 6, 1996). Directed by J. N. Cappella, J. Turow, & K. H. Jamieson. Call-in Talk Radio: Background, Content, Audiences, Portrayal in Mainstream Media. University of Pennsylvania.

Barber, Benjamin R., Kevin Mattson, & John Peterson (October 1997). The State of "Electronically Enhanced Democracy": A Survey of the Internet. Walt Whitman Center for the Culture and Politics of Democracy, Rutgers University.

Campaign Discourse and Civic Engagement Panel Survey. (1996). Sponsored by Pew Charitable Trust, directed by M. Just, Wellesley College, and conducted by the University of Michigan Survey Research Center.

CommerceNet/Nielsen Internet Demographics Survey. (1996). Available at: http://www.Commerce.new/work/pilot/nielsen_96.

Dautrich, K., & T. H. Hartley (1999). *How the News Media Fail American Voters: Causes, Consequences and Remedies.* New York: Columbia University Press.

Davis, R., & D. Owen (1998). *New Media and American Politics.* New York: Oxford University Press.

Fredin, E. S. (September 1997). *Rethinking the News Story for the Internet: Hyperstory Prototypes and a Model of the User,* Monograph 163. Association for Education in Journalism and Mass Communication.

Fredin, E. S., & David, P. (1997). The Hypermedia Interaction Cycle: A Study of Motivation and Goal Dynamics. Unpublished manuscript.

Graber, D. A. (1984). *Processing the News: How People Tame the Information Tide.* New York: Longman.

Gronbeck, B. (April 11, 1997). Politicking on the Information Superhighway. Paper presented at the Touchstone Symposium on Postmodern Culture, Global Capitalism and Democratic Action, University of Maryland.

Hacker, K. (1996). Virtual Democracy and Computer-Mediated Political Communication (CMPC): The Role of the Clinton White House in Facilitating Electronic Democratization and Political Interactivity. National Communication Association Conference paper.

Joslyn, R. (1984). *Mass Media and Elections.* Readings, MA: Addison-Wesley.

Just, M., Crigler, A., Alger, D., Cook, T., Kern, M., & West, D. (1996). *Crosstalk: Citizens, Candidates and the Media in a Presidential Campaign.* Chicago: University of Chicago Press.

Just, M., Crigler, A., & Kern M. (1997). Citizens and the Internet: Diversifying Information Sources in Cyberspace. Paper presented at the National Communication Association, Chicago, IL, November.

Just, M., Crigler A., & Wallach, L. (1990). Thirty Seconds or Thirty Minutes: What Viewers Learn from Spot Advertisements and Candidate Debates. *Journal of Communication,* 40, 120–133.

Katz, J. E., Aspden P., & Reid, W. (October 1997). Elections and Electrons: A National Opinion Survey on the Role of Cyberspace and Mass Media in Political Opinion Formation during the 1996 General Election. Telecommunications Policy Research Conference paper. Washington, DC.

Kern, M. (1989). *Thirty-Second Politics: Political Advertising in the 80s.* New York: Praeger.

Kern, M. (May 1997). Debates in the 1996 Presidential Election. International Communication Association Conference paper, Montreal, Canada.

McQuivey, J. (1996). Uses of the Web: How Users Frame the Web. American Association for Public Opinion Research Conference paper, Salt Lake City, Utah.

Napoli, P. N. (1999). The Internet and the Forces of Massification. *Electronic Journal of Communication.* Special Issue on "The Future of the Internet."

Neuman, W. R. (1991). *The Future of the Mass Audience.* Cambridge: Cambridge University Press.

Patterson, T. E. & McClure, R. D. (1976). *The Unseeing Eye: The Myth of Television Power in National Elections.* New York: G. P. Putnam's Sons.

Pew Research Center on the Press, Politics and Public Policy. (June 1998).

Pfau, M., Kendall, K. E., Reichert, T., Hellweg, S. A., Lee, W., Tusing, K. J., & Prosise, T. O., (1997). Communication during the 1996 Primary Campaign. National Communication Association Conference paper, Chicago, IL.

Schwartz, E. A. (1996). *Netactivism: How Citizens Use the Internet.* Sebastopol, CA: Songline Studios.

CHAPTER 12

Visions of a Tragedy: Symbolic Convergence in the Print Media Coverage of the Murrah Building Bombing in Oklahoma City

TRACEY L. MITCHELL

On April 19, 1995, the United States witnessed domestic terrorism on a scale unprecedented in that country. At 9:02 A.M., a truck bomb exploded in front of the Alfred P. Murrah Federal Building in Oklahoma City, Oklahoma. The explosion killed 168 people, wounded 500 others, and caused millions of dollars in damage. This act by a few individuals shattered the worldview of an entire nation, forcing them to re-evaluate deeply held convictions. Through the national news media, Americans everywhere saw the deadly results, listened to their government officials, and ultimately learned to fear a previously ignored segment of their own society.

This study examines the print media coverage of the Murrah Building bombing during the two weeks immediately following the incident. It is focused on communication: specifically, it looks at how media groups chose to report the facts and impact of the bombing in Oklahoma City to their readers. Bormann's (1972, 1980, 1982, 1985) symbolic convergence theory provides the framework for this rhetorical analysis. After summarizing the literature concerning news coverage of disasters and terrorism in the United States, symbolic convergence theory and its application here are briefly outlined. Finally, the results of the study are presented and conclusions made.

LITERATURE REVIEW

News as Melodrama

Terrorist attacks and disasters completely disrupt the order of reality for the affected groups. The group members immediately begin a search for a way to restore the order that has been suspended (Perry & Pugh, 1978;

Schneider, 1992; Wolfenstein, 1977). They accomplish this by communicating with each other, exchanging information, rumors, and narratives. The effect is not limited to face-to-face interaction: the mass media, including print, become important sources of information to the public in times of crisis (Dobkin, 1992; Nimmo & Combs, 1985; Perry & Pugh, 1978; Smith, 1992).

Media coverage of news events, such as the Murrah Building bombing, is generally narrative in structure (Dobkin, 1992; Dufour-Gompers, 1992; Nimmo & Combs, 1985; Rucinski, 1992; Smith, 1992). Journalists need to place the story in a compelling narrative form that draws upon the needs, values, and perceptions of their target audience, while simultaneously accommodating severe time and space constraints. This forces them to select certain facts, sources, and points of view while omitting others that might be equally valid.

Journalists often concentrate on the events while ignoring the larger story of causes and contexts, and on the individual actors rather than on institutions or social entities (Dobkin, 1992; Rucinski, 1992; Smith, 1992). There is a need for the media to find a symbol or image for every news event, which can cause misleading simplification or misdirected focus on certain aspects. News coverage will therefore tend to repeat certain images, stereotypes, myths, and narratives, which may or may not provide an accurate, complete reflection of the story.

Ultimately, the news media try to convert the world into a stage, and newsmaking events into the scenes of a melodrama (Dobkin, 1992; Dufour-Gompers, 1992; Nimmo & Combs, 1985; Rucinski, 1992).

News as melodrama possesses many easily recognized characteristics:

1. The individuals involved become the cast of characters, with the perceived hero(es) and villain(s) of the story receiving particular attention.

2. The conflict, which is established early in the story, centers on the action of the central characters, and the plot line is attributed to either the hero's quest or the villain's attempted conquest.

3. Every element of the story is presented in a dramatic manner, with every issue portrayed as a dichotomy (good versus evil) to eliminate any moral ambiguity.

4. The story is made to fit into the existing belief system of the dominant culture and to reinforce it, usually through "the ritualistic defeat of a perceived evil" (Dobkin, 1992: 56).

Terrorism seems especially to lend itself to the format of the melodrama. The terrorists become the central characters and perform the script, on a stage provided by the news media (Dowling, 1986; Dufour-Gompers, 1992; Weimann & Brosius, 1991). This gives the terrorists the very thing they most desire: a chance to communicate with a large audience.

While this may serve the terrorists' need, news coverage also tends to counteract terrorists' desire to win sympathy and credibility from the public. Dobkin's (1992) studies of how the American news media cover terrorism have shown that the terrorist is inevitably the villain, whose motivations are usually ignored. The terrorists become simply criminals, the evil villains, and their political message ignored. They lose legitimacy in the public mind. Hewitt (1992) and Dowling (1986) cite additional evidence that U.S. perceptions of terrorism are consistent with the interpretations of the news media. American culture has an ingrained image of the terrorist as an Arab, a Muslim, an outsider.

The news media's influence on public perceptions is increased in certain situations. The American public becomes more reliant on news coverage for information when a lack of familiarity (Entman, 1989; Hewitt, 1992), distance from the scene (Weimann, 1983), or a crisis state (Dobkin, 1992) are factors. Wright, Kunkel, Pinon, & Huston (1989) have noted the near impossibility of separating the effects of a publicized disaster from the effects of the news coverage. The news reports become part of the disaster in the minds of the audience.

Symbolic Convergence Theory

Bormann's (1972, 1980, 1985) symbolic convergence theory is based on the assumption that people view reality through a personal set of narratives, which represent "the truth" of how the world is. When the individual shares these personal narratives with a group, those narratives may be adopted and enlarged upon by the group. Once a group has accepted a shared set of narratives, it now also shares a symbol system and the views of its members have "converged" (Bormann, 1980).

Groups achieve symbolic convergence by sharing fantasy themes. A fantasy theme is a dramatic interpretation of an event that is set in either the past or the future, or in a different place, and that serves a psychological or rhetorical need for the group sharing it (Bormann, 1982, 1985). Related fantasy themes will at some point begin to weave together to form a rhetorical vision (Bormann, 1980, 1985). Not only does a rhetorical vision order the elements of fantasy themes into a single, complex narrative; the vision also serves to order and interpret reality.

Certain elements are present in all fantasy themes and rhetorical visions. These include the characters who act out the drama, including heroes, villains, and supporting actors, as well as the setting, plot line, and sanctioning agent (Bormann, 1980, 1985; Foss, Foss, & Trapp, 1991). By identifying these recurring elements in fantasy themes, the critic can then discover how the group sharing these themes perceives reality (Bormann, 1985). The mass media clearly play a role in symbolic convergence in American society. Bormann (1982) has noted that, in particular, newspaper reports of an event will contain clearly identifiable fantasy themes.

Application of Theory

In order to keep the data manageable, this study looks at a very narrow time span and only five sources from scores of possible news providers. The analysis examined 67 artifacts taken from four national news sources: *Time*, *Newsweek*, *U.S. News and World Report*, and the *New York Times*. For comparison, 59 artifacts were taken from the *Daily Oklahoman*, the only major newspaper in Oklahoma City, and the paper with the largest circulation rate in the state. The articles were limited to a time period of two weeks after the April 19 explosion. The entire editions of the weekly publications were examined, but for the two daily newspapers the artifacts were limited to front-page items. Editorials, cartoons, and stories only marginally related to the bombing were excluded. A total of 126 items, including news articles and photographs, were selected to be used as artifacts in the analysis. (See the References for a complete list of the artifacts.)

The ultimate objective of this study was to answer two research questions: (1) How were competing visions assimilated or rejected by the media groups? and (2) Why was one rhetorical vision chosen over another? To answer these questions, each artifact, whether visual or verbal, was examined for the possible fantasy themes contained within it. The process included recording each allusion to setting, character, and act. These allusions were then coded into the category to which they belonged. Fantasy themes that appeared often were identified as the major themes, while the others were eliminated. The major fantasy themes provided a basis to construct the rhetorical visions of the participating communities. Each vision was assigned to either the community comprised of the national print news source or the community of the local print news source.

Discussion and Comparison of National and Local Visions

Research Question 1

The first research question asked by this study concerns how the media groups assimilated the competing rhetorical visions. The two groups of concern in this case were the national media community, made up of four major print news sources, and the local media community, comprised of Oklahoma City's newspaper. It quickly became apparent that the national and local press had some differences in how each covered the bombing of the federal building in Oklahoma City.

During the earliest reports, the local and national sources were equally concerned with explaining the negative consequences of the blast. While the emphasis in the national sources did not change, the local press would turn its attention to the positive emotions and behavior engendered by the crisis. The two competing visions, for the most part, contained the same major themes. The difference would arise from the emphasis of positive messages as opposed to negative ones.

The analysis of the four national news sources revealed five major fantasy themes pervading their messages: the Heartland of America, innocence lost, good emerging from evil, the authorities in control, and the new face of terror. The local newspaper, the *Daily Oklahoman*, shared the first four of these fantasy themes with their national counterparts but did not use the fantasy of the new face of terror.

The Heartland of America

The fantasy theme of the Heartland is concerned with a setting: Oklahoma City. The theme begins with the simple myth: terrorism doesn't happen "here," meaning alternately the United States or Oklahoma. Reporters from national sources referred to Oklahoma as the "heartland" or "heart" of America 26 times ("A Blow," 1995; Duffy, 1995a; Johnston, 1995a; Kifner, 1995a; Manegold, 1995b; "Oklahoma City," 1995; Rainie, 1995; "The Terror," 1995; "This Doesn't," 1995; "This Is Not," 1995; Thomas, 1995a; Walsh & McGraw, 1995). The editors of the *Daily Oklahoman* used the word "heartland" within the paper's headings in every edition during the two-week period examined. The idea is that Oklahoma, as the heart of Middle America, possesses an innocence that separates it from the rest of the world and somehow keeps it safe from terrorism. The bombing of the federal building in downtown Oklahoma City shattered that belief. *Newsweek* expressed the changes it wrought: "The devastated building was deep in America's heartland, ending forever the illusion that here at home, we are safe" ("This Doesn't," 1995). In the *Daily Oklahoman*, Owen (1995a) explained how powerfully the blast had challenged Oklahoma's sense of security: "Oklahoma will never be the same. This is a place, after all, where terrorists don't venture. The heartland, people kept saying. Car bombs don't kill children here" (p. 1).

The new reality of the city's downtown said otherwise. News accounts tried to convey the horror of the evil wrought in Oklahoma City to the readers. One metaphor recurred often in all five sources: the comparison of downtown Oklahoma City to a war zone. References to bodies, body parts, and blood abounded. The demolished structure itself would become a dominant image.

Innocence Lost

The second major fantasy describes the lost innocence of a city and a nation. The victims and the villain portrayed in the media accounts of the bombing made this incident too compelling for any American to ignore. As one Oklahoma City woman wrote in her letter to the *Daily Oklahoman*, "I bid farewell to innocence. I will surely miss my old friend" (McReynolds, 1995: 15-A).

The victims. The injured, dead, and orphaned children would become the symbol of innocence lost. Over and over, the child victims and the second-floor daycare center appeared in the narratives of the news writers. Leland (1995a) wrote: "The random destruction of a government building shows a nation how vulnerable it is; the random destruction of innocent children shows how deep the pain can go" (p. 48). Reporters frequently referred to the image of the day-care children sitting down to breakfast just as the bomb exploded.

But it is another image, captured in a photograph, which would become the most memorable: firefighter Chris Fields cradling a dying child, one-year-old Baylee Almen. That image would reappear again and again, most notably on the magazine covers of *Newsweek* (LaRue, 1995) and *Time* (Hestoft & Porter, 1995), and on the front page of the April 20 edition of the *Daily Oklahoman* (Baldwin, 1995). McReynolds (1995) noted, "No words can say what is said by the now-famous photograph of 1-year-old Baylee Almon being carried from the building" (p. 15-A). The broken bodies of infants thus became symbols of the lost innocence of Americans. The unthinkable, that children could die in terrorist violence, had happened here. The innocence was lost forever.

The villain. In the national print media, there was an additional assault to the nation's innocence: the fact that the killers were alleged to be white, American males (Duffy, 1995a; Gibbs,1995; Johnston, 1995b; "This Is Not," 1995). People expressed a sense of betrayal: "For all the talk about the innocence of the heartland, some noted, the terrorists did not appear to be foreigners from some hard-to-pronounce sects, but young men bred, presumably, with the values of America" (Johnston, 1995b: B7). The arrest of a decorated American veteran of the Persian Gulf for this heinous deed meant that terrorism had come home.

Every fantasy must have at least one hero and one villain. The national press methodically and deliberately made Timothy McVeigh the central villain of this saga. Their reports painted a portrait of a violent, angry, remorseless executioner, obsessed with hatred of the federal government. The media and authorities closely observed McVeigh during his time in jail and during his court hearings, and his behavior was reported in generally negative terms by the national press. Photographs of McVeigh, taken during his transfer to federal custody, were shown in every source. For example, Duffy (1995b) quoted an official who said McVeigh's reaction to pictures of child victims of the bombing was "stone-cold" and that he showed "not a flicker of regret" (p. 31).

While reporters devoted some of their attention to the other suspects, Terry and James Nichols, they did not seem as interested in making the them into villains. The brothers appeared in the national news coverage as eccentric and paranoid, but as secondary figures to McVeigh. Essentially, McVeigh became an assassin, capable of murdering children without mercy or remorse, an inhuman and frightening figure. The villains personified the betrayal of the American people: one of their own had done this terrible crime. The innocence they had held to so long was gone, along with the 168 lives lost that morning.

Good Emerging from Evil

A third major fantasy theme was identified through the actions of the actors in Oklahoma City. This fantasy theme appeared in all five sources; however, its emphasis was much stronger in the local newspaper than in the national sources. Many of the actions from this fantasy theme centered on the bombed Murrah Building and the immediate area surrounding it. It also incorporated the vigil of missing victims' family and friends, the mourning of the entire state, and the altruistic behavior engendered by the bombing.

As terrible as the evil appeared, the national media sought and found good in the event as well. One photograph portrayed the coming together of the city in a single image. It appeared on the cover of *U.S. News and World Report* (Longstreath, 1995) and also within the coverage of *Newsweek* (Leland, 1995a: 51). In this photograph, an injured white woman holds a young black boy, who is also wounded, in her lap. A hand belonging to someone not shown rests comfortingly on the woman's shoulder. *Newsweek* captioned it, "The Comfort of Neighbors." Walsh (1995) insisted: "There was also a positive lesson to be learned, and it would be a shame if it were lost in the debate about the dark side of our culture. That lesson was clear to anyone in Oklahoma City last week: Everyday people have not lost their instinct for performing acts of goodness." The reports described these acts of goodness in detail. In the rubble of the bomb site, in hospitals and morgues, and in churches and homes where families and friends kept vigil, people demonstrated courage and determination in heroic proportions.

At first the *Daily Oklahoman* seemed preoccupied with coming to terms with the disaster, but soon the focus shifted to pride in how Oklahoma had united to respond to the crisis. The major turning point in this shift from a negative to a positive focus seemed to occur during the memorial service which was on held Sunday, April 23. Until that day, the newspaper used the header, "Terror in the Heartland." Then, on Monday, April 24, one day after the memorial service, the editors switched to "Together in the Heartland." The newspaper then focused on reporting behavior that evidenced a united populace in the time after the bombing.

The rescue workers, both volunteer and professional, quickly emerged as heroes of the disaster. Photographs portrayed them as dwarfed by the devastated scene, as they struggled valiantly to fight fires, clear away rubble, explore the building, and search for victims. Reporters in all the sources portrayed the job of rescue and recovery as difficult, dangerous, and emotionally draining.

The vigils of the waiting, grieving families also figured prominently in the news accounts. The families kept up their hope, as Leland (1995a) wrote, "in dogged determination, even as their odds dwindled" (p. 50). Since no survivors were found after that first Wednesday night, the vigil would ultimately prove to be a death watch for many. Goode (1995) described the fading optimism: "Hope was suddenly a luxury" (p. 33).

Meanwhile, the people of Oklahoma found important meaning in certain rituals and symbols as they coped with grief. These included memorials and religious observances, letters and signs, planting trees, and visiting the site of the crumpled building. Symbols, such as ribbons, teddy bears, angels, flowers, and flags, figured very prominently in the public grieving as well.

The *Daily Oklahoman* chose to focus on the positive response from the people in Oklahoma City. Through actions, symbols, religion, and rituals, Oklahoma residents drew "Together in the Heartland." The *Daily Oklahoman* chose to reflect a community that refused to be vanquished by a great tragedy. To the national print media, the people in Oklahoma City, whether they were residents, rescuers, volunteers, or family members of the victims, were heroes. Because of their actions in response to their crisis, good would arise out of the evil. United together, the city and nation could stand against the evil, but the national sources emphasized that they could not overcome the damage done.

The Authorities in Control

Authority figures, the representatives of American society, acted out their parts valiantly as well. Reporters following the investigation adopted a fantasy theme of reassurance and affirmation of American society: our authorities were in control, and they would catch and punish the bombers. This fourth major fantasy theme followed the actions of federal officials in Washington, DC, and investigators across the nation on the trail of suspects and evidence.

The actors from Washington, DC—namely, President Bill Clinton and Attorney General Janet Reno—appeared in the media to express their anger and sympathy, and to promise swift capture and punishment for the bombers. On the local scene, state and other local authorities, particularly state Governor Frank Keating and Assistant Fire Chief Jon Hansen, provided leadership, information, and promises of their own concerning the rescue-and-recovery efforts. This theme followed the manhunt, the search for evidence, and the eventual arrest of the suspects. The news media expressed little doubt that the bombers would be caught, convicted, and punished. The representatives of law and order would triumph over those who sought to destroy the established structure of American society.

The New Face of Terror

National reporters did not stop with the vilification of Timothy McVeigh. The extreme right, particularly the militia movement, also received a good deal of attention. Until the bombing of the Murrah Building, these groups had seemed of little concern to the average person. Now they were thrust into the national news. It is interesting to note that, during the period under examination, the local newspaper did not devote the same degree of attention to vilifying McVeigh or exploring the militia movement. This fantasy theme remained confined to the national print media.

The media created a new face for the terrorist: not an Arab Muslim from a distant land, but a clean-cut, American male from Middle America. *Time* expressed this theme on its May 1 cover with a close-up of Timothy McVeigh's face in profile, and the words "The Face of Terror" (Hestoft & Porter, 1995).

Turning the focus from international terrorism to a homegrown variety was not easy. Duffy (1995a) wrote, "From the very beginning there had been an unspoken assumption among some investigators: The bombing had to have been the work of Islamic extremists" (p. 36). Early speculation that such American groups might be the perpetrators was not taken seriously until the suspects were identified. Even after the arrests were made, the desire to find outsiders responsible for the crime still manifested itself.

In exploring the motivations of the alleged bombers, the national media began to report on the beliefs of militia groups and the others in the extreme right. Reporters treated the groups as belonging to a different world than ordinary Americans, one of darkness, paranoia, hate, and conspiracy. As reporters and their audience sought motives for that horrendous act, they became explorers in that world. Thomas (1995b) wrote:

It is a world where loners are never alone, where delusion and fantasy echo back as conspiracy and fact. It has its own language and code and demonology. It is a peculiarly American world, met in woods where grown men play with real guns, in greasy spoons where an angry farmer can buy a lonely serviceman a cup of coffee and earnestly discuss how best to resist the global Zionist plot. It reaches across the airwaves and through cyberspace, into a thousand darkened rooms where twisted souls reside. (p. 29)

Reporters held up the militia movement's wilder theories to encourage distrust and ridicule of the movement. Many mentioned the extremists' enshrinement of the site of the highly publicized, 51-day siege of a heavily armed cult group called Branch Davidians by federal law enforcement groups. Exactly two years before the Murrah Building bombing, that siege at Waco, Texas ended when the FBI tried to raid the compound and the building caught fire. Everyone inside, including some children, were killed, either by the fire or by self-inflicted gunshot wounds. Reporters carefully noted that many extreme right-wing groups used Waco as a rallying cry (Gleick, 1995a; Lacayo, 1995b; McFadden, 1995a, 1995b; Thomas, 1995a, 1995b), and they pointed to the additional significance of April 19 to the extreme right movements (Duffy, 1995a; Gleick, 1995a; McFadden, 1995a). According to Gleick (1995a), the date was "intricately bound . . . to the mythologies of homegrown zealots like McVeigh" (p. 46).

McVeigh and the Nichols brothers were reported to be sympathizers with the Davidians, and to have ties to right-wing militia groups, particularly the Michigan Militia (Duffy, 1995a, 1995b; Gleick, 1995a, 1995b; McFadden, 1995b; Purdum, 1995a; Thomas, 1995a, 1995b; Watson, 1995b; Weiner, 1995a). Although the Michigan Militia denied having any real association with McVeigh or the Nichols brothers, the national media exposed and condemned the Michigan group and other militia organizations as instigators of violence and a threat to the nation's order (Duffy, 1995a; Gleick, 1995a; Lacayo, 1995b; Thomas, 1995b). One member of the Michigan Militia was quoted, "I consider Tim McVeigh to be a good guy. If I were in a war I would want him by my side" (Thomas, 1995a: 35). Militia members also were reported to claim that the Murrah Building bombing was a government plot to discredit their movement and justify a crackdown on them (Gleick, 1995a; Thomas, 1995b). Some claimed that the Japanese were responsible for the bombing (Lacayo, 1995b).

These groups of heavily armed, ultra-right-wing Americans had existed long before 1995, but only after the Murrah Building bombing did they receive any real attention in the legitimate press. Now, their existence was acknowledged, and their political message heard. However, as these marginalized Americans were quick to note, they had little chance for a sympathetic hearing. Instead, they became the villains. According to the national media, these individuals moved about in a dark, sinister underworld of secret rooms and deep wilderness areas, preaching and enacting shadowy deeds of violence and evil. Their ideology was presented as paranoid, bizarre, and incomprehensible to the average, intelligent American; and this underworld, the media predicted, would be the source of future terrorist acts and villains.

Research Question 2

The second research question asked why each group chose one rhetorical vision over the other. Both the national and local media engaged in a search for meaning in the terrorist attack, as would be the expected behavior of people traumatized by a crisis. The differences in what each group ultimately decided was the central message of the blast is linked to their audience's proximity to and personal involvement in the disaster.

The national print news sources had to find ways to link readers in distant cities to the residents of Oklahoma City. The bombing did not directly affect the majority of Americans. While the blast certainly had significance for them, the pain of the event could only be experienced vicariously. To draw readers into the story, the national media used themes that expressed the devastation caused by the bombing, which emphasized the negative themes of death, loss, and terror. The national media also had to find some meaning in the blast for the country as a whole. The meaning they would choose again brought the national audience closer to the affected community: The bombing became a warning that no one in America was safe from the extremists in their own midst. What had happened to Oklahoma City could happen in any of the nation's cities. This rhetorical vision, with its emphasis on negative messages, drew sympathy for the victims and united a vast, diverse group.

However, Oklahomans, particularly residents of the affected city, did not need the media to show them how the bombing affected their lives. The effects were obvious to them. What the local community needed was to unite and tackle the massive problems with which they were faced. The warning message that seemed important to the national media was irrelevant to a populace already stricken by terrorism. The local media had to find a different message to help their audience deal with the crisis, one of rebirth.

The national and local print media all sought to find a message in the bombing that would provide their audiences with a sense of meaning. The local media source chose a distinct rhetorical vision from the national media because their audience needed a more positive vision. Meanwhile, the national media had to draw a diverse audience from distant parts of the country into the tale of the Murrah Building bombing and make it relevant to their lives. The negative messages of the national rhetorical vision emphasized a threat to all, achieving the unification the national print media were seeking. Thus, the major differences in the two visions occurred because of the choice of a positive or negative emphasis in reporting on the bombing.

CONCLUSIONS

This study showed that the reporters for print news sources did create and share fantasy themes about the bombing in Oklahoma City, with the intent to provide a sense of meaning and order to the frightening events for themselves and their readers. These fantasy themes would eventually intertwine to compose two distinct rhetorical visions, one for the national media and one for the local source. The local newspaper presented a vision of a community united to overcome and conquer those who sought to disrupt society. The four major national sources gave their audience a vision of a new threat to the peace and security of their nation.

This particular attack altered the pre-existing notions of terrorism held by the U.S. population. While it would prove difficult to destroy the rhetorical vision of the terrorist as a foreigner with incomprehensible ideologies, the new reality of domestic terrorism necessitated a new vision. The national print media provided this. The bombing in Oklahoma City was seen as an attack on the federal government and the people it represented. The terrorists intended a message not just for Oklahoma City, but for the nation as a whole. Through one sudden, violent act, the bombers gained the valuable media attention they needed to reach their target audience to create terror in people who previously had known little or nothing about the bombers' agenda. The United States learned about the new face of terror, and an entire nation felt fear. However, once the bomb had gone off, the terrorists lost control of the drama. The media would craft the script to fit their desired vision. The terrorists' message would not be heard.

The 1995 terrorist bombing of the federal building in Oklahoma City provided the political leaders of the nation an opportunity to strengthen relations with citizens and present the image of a caring government that still remained in control. For once, the nation's discourse as presented in the media lost its contentious nature; almost everyone agreed that this was a heinous act, without any justification. The United States was able to unify behind its leaders wholeheartedly, at least on this one issue.

The events of April 19, 1995 thoroughly altered the worldview of the United States. This study identified two distinct rhetorical visions in the print media. Probably many more could be found in other media sources. The power of these visions has yet to be determined. But there can be little doubt that these rhetorical visions have become part of the mythology of modern America.

REFERENCES

Bormann, E. G. (1972). Fantasy and Rhetorical Vision: The Rhetorical Criticism of Social Reality. *Quarterly Journal of Speech*, 58, 398–407.

Bormann, E. G. (1980). *Communication Theory*. New York: Holt, Rinehart and Winston.

Bormann, E. G. (May 1982). A Fantasy Theme Analysis of the Television Coverage of the Hostage Release and the Reagan Inaugural. *Quarterly Journal of Speech*, 68, 133–145.

Bormann, E. G. (1985). Symbolic Convergence Theory: A Communication Formulation. *Journal of Communication*, 35, 128–138.

Dobkin, B. A. (1992). *Tales of Terror: Television News and the Construction of the Terrorist Threat*. Westport, CT: Praeger.

Dowling, R. E. (1986). Terrorism and the Media: A Rhetorical Genre. *Journal of Communication*, 36:1, 12–24.

Dufour-Gompers, R. Y. (1992). Watching the Violence of Warfare in the "Theatre" of Operations. *International Social Science Journal*, 44, 247–265.

Entman, R. M. (1989). How the Media Affect What People Think: An Information Processing Approach. *Journal of Politics*, 51:2, 347–370.

Foss, S. K., Foss, K. A., & Trapp, R. (1991). *Contemporary Perspectives on Rhetoric*, 2nd ed. Prospect Heights, IL: Waveland Press.

Hewitt, C. (1992). Public's Perspectives. In D. L. Paletz & A. P. Schmid (Eds.), *Terrorism and the Media* (pp. 170–207). Newbury Park, CA: Sage.

Nimmo, D., & Combs, J. E. (1985). *Nightly Horrors: Crisis Coverage by Television Network News*. Knoxville: University of Tennessee.

Perry, J. B., & Pugh, M. (1978). *Collective Behavior: Response to Social Stress*. St. Paul, MN: West.

Rucinski, D. (1992). Personalized Bias in News: The Potency of the Particular? *Communication Research*, 19:1, 91–108.

Schneider, S. K. (1992). Governmental Response to Disasters: The Conflict between Bureaucratic Procedures and Emergent Norms. *Public Administration Review*, 52:5, 135–145.

Smith, C. (1992). *Media and Apocalypse: News Coverage of the Yellowstone Fires, Exxon Valdez Oil Spill, and Loma Prieta Earthquake*. Westport, CT: Greenwood.

Weimann, G., & Brosius, H. (1991). The Newsworthiness of Terrorism. *Communication Research*, 18:3, 333–354.

Wolfenstein, M. (1977). *Disaster: A Psychological Essay*. New York: Arno.

Wright, J. C., Kunkel, D., Pinon, M., & Huston, A. C. (1989). How Children Reacted to Televised Coverage of the Space Shuttle Disaster. *Journal of Communication*, 39:2, 27–45.

List of Artifacts

From *Newsweek*:

Beck, M. (1995, May 1). Get me out of here!, pp. 40–47.

Blasted hopes (1995, May 1), p. 54.

LaRue, L. (photographer). (1995, May 1), cover.

Leland, J. (1995a, May 1). Why the children?, pp. 48–53.

Leland, J. (1995b, May 8). I think about it all the time, p. 35.

This doesn't happen here (1995, May 1), pp. 24–27.

This is not a movie. It's a town. It's our home (1995, May 1), pp. 28–29.

Thomas, E. (1995a, May 1). Cleverness—and luck, pp. 30–35.

Thomas, E. (1995b, May 8). The plot, pp. 28–34.

Watson, R. (1995a, May 1). It's a scary world, p. 53.

Watson, R. (1995b, May 1). Three strange friends, p. 32.

From *Time*:

A blow to the heart (1995, May 1), pp. 36–43.

Carney, J. (1995, May 1). Measure of a president, pp. 65–66.

Death in Oklahoma (1995, May 1), p. 21.

Gibbs, N. (1995, May 1). The blood of innocents, pp. 57–64.

Gleick, E. (1995a, May 1). Who are they?, pp. 44–51.

Gleick, E. (1995b, May 8). Something big is going to happen, pp. 50–53.

Hestoft, R., & Porter, C. IV (photographers). (1995, May 1), cover.

Lacayo, R. (1995a, May 1). Rushing to bash outsiders, p. 70.

Lacayo, R. (1995b, May 8). A moment of silence, pp. 42–48.

Law woman of the week (1995, May 1), p. 21.

The search continues (1995, May 8), p. 35.

The suspects (1995a, May 1), p. 21.
The suspects (1995b, May 8), p. 35.
The terror from within (1995), pp. 42–43.

From *U.S. News and World Report*:

Duffy, B. (1995a, May 1). The end of innocence, pp. 34–50.
Duffy, B. (1995b, May 8). The manhunt: Twisting trail, pp. 30–36.
Goode, E. (1995, May 8). When hope is both luxury and necessity, pp. 32–33.
Longstreath, D. (photographer). (1995, May 1), cover.
Oklahoma City: April 19, 1995. (1995, May 1), pp. 28–33.
Rainie, H. (1995, May 1). The buried sounds of children crying, pp. 10–11.
Walsh, K. T. (1995, May 8). The soul and character of America, pp. 10–11.
Walsh, K. T., & McGraw, D. (1995, May 1). A strike at the very heart of America, pp. 51–54.

From the *New York Times*:

At least 31 are dead, scores are missing after car bomb attack in Oklahoma City wrecks 9-story federal office building (1995, April 20). Headline and photos, p. A1.
Belluck, P. (1995, April 21). Identifying injured loved ones by clues of hair and birthmarks, pp. A1, A23.
Bernstein, E. (1995, April 28). Evidence linking suspect to blast offered in court, pp. A1, A24.
Bragg, R. (1995a, April 20). In shock, loathing, denial: This doesn't happen here, pp. A1, B11.
Bragg, R. (1995b, April 23). Ordinary lives of victims, remembered in grief, pp. 1, 35.
Bragg, R. (1995c, May 1). Decision at bomb site: Don't risk lives of living to free the dead, pp. A1, B7.
Crews near center of explosion rubble (1995, April 25), p. 1.
Defending a pariah (1995, April 28), p. 1.
Gonzalez, D. (1995, April 21). In twisted remains of building, hope and expectation vs. death, pp. A1, A25.
Henneberger, M. (1995, April 30). A shaken city, ever devout, turns to God, pp. 1, 26.
Inquiry in Arizona (1995, April 29), p. 1.
Johnston, D. (1995a, April 20). Clues are lacking, pp. A1, B8.
Johnston, D. (1995b, April 24). The living offer heart and song to the dead, pp. A1, B7.
Johnston, D. (1995c, April 25). Oklahoma bombing plotted for months, officials say, pp. A1, A18.
Johnston, D. (1995d, April 26). Michigan farmer and brother tied to bomb suspect, pp. A1, A20.
Johnston, D. (1995e, May 2). F.B.I. issues alert for 2 more sought in bombing inquiry, pp. A1, A18.
Johnston, D. (1995f, May 3). 2 are detained in bombing case but are freed after questioning, pp. A1, B6.

Kifner, J. (1995a, April 20). 12 victims were children in 2d-floor day-care center, pp. A1, B9.

Kifner, J. (1995b, April 21). FBI seeks 2 suspects in Oklahoma blast; Search for survivors, and bodies, is slow, pp. A1, A22.

Kleinfield, N. R. (1995a, April 30). For bombing suspects, looks aren't everything, pp. 1, 28.

Kleinfield, N. R. (1995b, May 1). Death scene is now lure for the curious, pp. A1, B7.

Manegold, C. S. (1995a, April 22). A slow and gruesome search through unstable wreckage, pp. 1, 11.

Manegold, C. S. (1995b, April 25). Coping with shock of blast: Lingering fear and anguish, pp. A1, A21.

McFadden, R. D. (1995a, April 22). Links in blast: Armed militia and a key date, pp. 1, 8.

McFadden, R. D. (1995b, April 23). One man's complex path extremism, pp. 1, 33.

Precisely at 9:02 A.M. (1995, April 27), p. A1.

Purdum, T. S. (1995a, April 22). Bomb suspect is held, another identified; Toll hits 65 as hope for survivors fades, pp. 1, 8.

Purdum, T. S. (1995b, April 24). Clinton seeks broad powers in battle against terrorism; Oklahomans mourn their loss, pp. A1, B6.

Purdum, T. S. (1995c, April 27). Clinton seeks more anti-terrorism measures, pp. A1, A21.

Salvaging a symbol (1995, April 29), p. 1.

The survivors, in their own words (1995, April 23), p. 1.

Verhovek, S. H. (1995, April 26). Many theories about choice of the target, pp. A1, A20.

Weiner, T. (1995a, April 23). F.B.I. hunts 2d bombing suspect and seeks links to far right; Rain stalls search of rubble, pp. 1, 32.

Weiner, T. (1995b, April 29). F.B.I. struggling to find answers in bombing case, pp. 1, 10.

From the *Daily Oklahoman*:

Aiken, C., & Owen, P. (1995, May 1). Search teams giving up hope: Crews bringing in equipment to finish job, pp. 1, 2.

Arizona pair hunted for questioning; At site, who are we to say we won't have a miracle?(1995, May 2). Headline, p. 1.

Baldwin, D. (1995, April 20). Small children victims in day-care center, pp. 1, 2.

Brush with bomb suspects described; 113 bodies pulled from building; 73 still missing (1995, April 29). Headline, p. 1.

Casteel, C. (1995, April 24). Clinton joins Oklahomans in mourning, pp. 1, 2.

Chemical tests point to McVeigh; Losses may total $510 million, insurers say (1995, April 26). *Daily Oklahoman*, p. 1.

Clay, N., Baldwin, D., Parker, J., Trammell, R., Ellis, R., & McNutt, M. (1995, April 22). Bomb suspect charged: Man upset by '93 raid near Waco, pp. 1, 11.

Clinton to visit (1995, April 21), p. 1.

Cromley, A. (1995, May 1). Agencies try to reassemble lost records, pp. 1, 2.

DeFrange, A. (1995, April 24). Memorial soothes state's broken heart, pp. 1, 3.

Ellis, R., Trammell, R., Baldwin, D., & Clay, N. (1995a, April 27). Bomb suspect talked about "something big," pp. 1, 16.

Ellis, R., Trammell, R., Baldwin, D., & Clay, N. (1995b, April 29). Eyewitness pointed way for suspects, pp. 1, 2.

English, P. (1995, May 2). Veteran helps with a gift from the heart, pp. 1, 2.

FBI combs through leads in bomb case; City rescuers remove bodies: They were our people (1995, April 25). Headline, p. 1.

Friend puts McVeigh in city on Easter; Recovery work force doubled at blast site (1995, April 27). Headline, p. 1.

Hinton, M. (1995a, April 23). Clintons, Graham join Oklahomans at service today, pp. 1-A, 2-A.

Hinton, M. (1995b, May 1). Keating reaches out to crews: Governor lends ear to families, rescuers, pp. 1, 2.

Hochenauger, K. (1995, May 3). Young survivor of explosion leaves hospital, pp. 1, 2.

Hogan, G. (1995a, April 25). Giving spirit helps chamber leader regain optimism, pp. 1, 2.

Hogan, G. (1995b, April 29). Survivor thanks unknown rescuers, pp. 1, 2.

Jones, C. T. (1995, April 21). Victims' kin seek solace in sanctuary, pp. 1, 2.

Killackey, J., & Owen, P. (1995, April 28). Toll increases to 107 as work speeds up, pp. 1, 2.

Lackmeyer, S. (1995, April 27). 9:02 A.M.: Pause, tears mark recall of explosion, pp. 1, 2.

Lackmeyer, S., & Zizzo, D. (1995, April 20). Scores killed in bomb blast; State stunned, pp. 1, 3.

Martin, S. (1995a, April 26). Insured damage might top costs at trade center, pp. 1, 2.

Martin, S. (1995b, April 28). Explosion damage could top $1 billion: Estimates not firm, commissioner says, pp. 1, 2.

McReynolds, J. E. (1995, April 30). Rage, sorrow flow in letters, poems, pp. 1-A, 15-A.

Money, J. (1995, April 27). List of blast-damaged buildings passes 220, pp. 1, 2.

Morning of terror: City struggles with shock of deadly bombing (1995, April 20). Headline, photo, p. 1.

Owen, P. (1995a, April 20). Fresh day in city turns to new-found horror, pp. 1, 2.

Owen, P. (1995b, April 25). Firefighters lead disaster rescue effort, pp. 1, 2.

Owen, P. (1995c, April 28). Downtown adapting to disaster's routine, pp. 1, 8.

Owen, P. (1995d, April 30). Building's instability threatens recovery: 2nd suspect's ability to hide surprises chief, pp. 1-A, 2-A.

Painter, B. (1995, April 30). Little survivor ventures home from hospital, pp. 1-A, 2-A.

Parker, J. (1995, April 28). McVeigh ordered to trial in bombing: Magistrate cites "indelible trail of evidence"; FBI hopes to stop "another bombing," pp. 1, 2.

Parker, J., & Baldwin, D. (1995, April 21). FBI seeks 2 in terrorist blast: Investigators trace truck to body shop, pp. 1, 4.

Parker, J., Baldwin, D., & Trammell, R. (1995, April 25). Help sought from businesses in clue search, pp. 1, 2.

Parker, J., Clay, N., Trammell, R., Ellis, R., Baldwin, D., & Breiner, J. (1995, April 23). Army of agents seeks 2nd suspect: Jailed militant's political views called radical, pp. 1-A, 11-A.

Plumberg, D. (1995a, April 26). 7 days: Death count slowly mounts, pp. 1, 2.

Plumberg, D. (1995b, April 27). Rescuers nearing day-care center, pp. 1, 2.

Plumberg, D. (1995c, April 29). Slab slips; Workers delayed, pp. 1, 2.

Plumberg, D. (1995d, May 3). Backhoes, cranes go through rubble, pp. 1, 11.

Recuperating (1995, April 21), p. 1.

Ross, B., Jr. (1995a, April 21). Neighbor cares for boys when mom doesn't return, pp. 1, 2.

Ross, B., Jr. (1995b, April 22). Somber vigil taking toll on families, pp. 1, 2.

Ross, B., Jr. (1995c, May 1). Churches cope with tragedy, pp. 1, 2.

Ross, B., Jr., & Painter, B. (1995, April 26). It just makes you scared, pp. 1, 5.

A time to grieve; In California, FBI quizzes deserter about blast (1995, April 24). Headline, p. 1.

Tramel, B. (1995a, April 23). Landlord not moved by blast, pp. 1-A, 2-A.

Tramel, B. (1995b, April 24). Gutherie family's story moves nation to help, pp. 1, 2.

Trammell, R., Baldwin, D., Ellis, R., & Clay, N. (1995, May 2). FBI combs Vinita, issues new sketch of 2nd suspect, pp. 1, 2.

Trammell, R., Baldwin, D., Ellis, R., Clay, N., & Parker, J. (1995, April 24). Search continues for 2nd suspect; Man questioned, pp. 1, 2.

Trammell, R., Baldwin, D., & McNutt, M. (1995, May 3). U.S. authorities careful to shun word "suspect," pp. 1, 2.

Trammell, R., Clay, N., Baldwin, D., & Ellis, R. (1995, April 26). FBI theorizes "John Doe 2" may be dead, pp. 1, 2.

2 held as witnesses in bombing; search hours, crews cut in half at city's federal building (1995, May 3). Headline, p. 1.

Zizzo, D. (1995a, April 21). Rescue teams crawl through rubble: Volunteers driven by hope, pp. 1, 2.

Zizzo, D. (1995b, April 22). Rescuers entering gruesome stage: Explosion death toll reaches 65, pp. 1, 2.

Zizzo, D. (1995c, April 23). Downpours dampen spirits in grim downtown search, pp. 1-A, 2-A.

Zizzo, D. (1995d, May 2). Searchers clinging to hope as they near "no-go zone," pp. 1, 2.

CHAPTER 13

Symbolism and Social Movements: How U.S. Political Debates Are Shaped and Citizens' Attitudes Influenced by Symbolic Communiqués

FRAUKE SCHNELL, NADYA TERKILDSEN, AND KAREN CALLAGAN

At a political rally a candidate for U.S. Senate stands on the podium flanked by the American flag and the flag from the state he seeks to represent. Throughout his speech he invokes numerous references to the Constitution, democracy, and free enterprise. Across town a school child learns to recite the "Pledge of Allegiance" and how to salute the flag. Her teacher discusses U.S. involvement in World War II and uses the phrase "Remember Pearl Harbor." In the local newsroom a reporter readies her story on suburban crime with a photo montage of defendants; all the stills show black suspects.

Every day, in every situation—be it political, educational, or social—symbols are used as mechanisms for effective communication and, more often than not, exert an attitudinal influence on those who attune to the messages. Symbols are popular because they constitute the lowest common denominator for message transmission and provide a shared basis of communication, familiar to the vast majority of the public. In terms of cognitive processing, symbols are influential for two important reasons. First, symbols elicit strong emotions, which are rarely based on the tangible costs and benefits of the matters to which the symbol refers to but rather on some enduring predisposition toward the symbol (Sears, 1993). Second, symbols are likely to become chronically accessible constructs, which may make them impossible to counter or modify (Terkildsen & Schnell, 1997; Sears, 1993; Miller & Fredericks, 1990).

This chapter examines the nature, usage, and influence of symbols attached to political groups. We refer to these labels or group emblems that have come to summarize a group's beliefs and actions as meta-symbols. Using theory from both political science and social psychology, we present evidence from a content analysis of news coverage of the U.S. women's movement and a series of experiments to illustrate our points concerning media use of meta-symbols and the influence these labeling shortcuts exert on citizens' attitudes and participation in a democratic system.

THE NATURE OF SYMBOLS AND THEIR ROLE IN DEMOCRATIC DISCOURSE

Politics are often described as is one symbolic contest after another (Edelman, 1988). Visual cues such as the raising of the flag at Ivo Jima, as well as verbal allusions to God, patriotism, and folk heroes, are all common examples of political symbols. Symbols distill or synthesize a more complex social and political reality and evoke "an attitude, a set of impressions, or a pattern of events associated through time, through space, through logic, or through imagination with the symbol" (Edelman, 1964: 3).

As the currency of the communication process, symbols mediate between macro- and micro-level political behavior. That is, symbols are employed by political elites—that is, politicians, policy entrepreneurs, interest groups, and the media, "speak" to public constituencies in ways that are supportive of their project or goals (Elder & Cobb, 1983). This streamlining of complex political information into easily comprehensible symbols allows citizens to negotiate political meaning because symbols provide a common frame of reference and relieve the individual of the burden of an extensive information search. The information processing literature also indicates that symbolic communication between political elites and the mass public is likely to accentuate affective responses and to increase the processing speed of information (Krosnick, 1988; Bargh, 1984; Devine, 1989).

Most analyses use the rather broad term "symbol" to refer to any political emblem that represents—by reason of relationship, association, or convention—something other than its original primary meaning. Our units of analysis are *meta-symbols*, which may be thought of as somewhat analogous to condensational or condensing symbols (see Bennett, 1996; Edelman, 1988; 1964). Condensational symbols are defined as those labels that evoke broad categories of meaning and strong affect, that is, they are low in cognition and dominated by emotions. They could include everything from democracy, to liberal, to feminist, which, of course, has left the definition open to much criticism. We construe meta-symbols more narrowly in that they are the common language used to discuss and condense a social movement and a protest group's beliefs. In other words, they are the overarching labels used to describe or represent an organization and its cause in cursory terms. Meta-symbols are higher-order summations of knowledge, affect, other group symbols and slogans, and idiosyncratic as well as systematic representations and misrepresentations about a movement.

META-SYMBOLS AND SOCIAL MOVEMENTS

Social movements are dependent on the media to advertise their cause. African Americans, women, Latinos, gays, and lesbians all need(ed) the media to move their organizations and advocacies onto the public agenda. While many elements contribute to the success of any given social movement (e.g., established networks to elites, skill of organizers, economic resources, mass support, tactics utilized, degree of militancy), no factor is more critical than the ability of reform groups to gain media attention (Gamson & Wolfsfeld, 1993; Parenti, 1986; Gitlin, 1980; Altheida & Gilmore, 1972; Lipsky, 1968; Turner & Killian, 1957). However, as crucial as media attention may be, acknowledging a movement is only the first step toward political and societal legitimacy. In the end, *how* protest movements are portrayed matters even more.

Every social movement exists in a public sphere, a dimension we refer to as an issue space. An issue space can be thought of as all the available information about a group—true or otherwise, complex or simple, self-generated or externally identified. Issue spaces include the rhetoric, beliefs, and policy positions ascribed to a social movement by its activists, the media, or its opponents. At the genesis of a social movement, its accompanying issue space is largely blank or filled with minimal factual information. As a movement develops, however, specific factors and players impinge on a group's public sphere. This process includes new information or opinions about a social movement, the actions and discourse of its opponents, media characterizations, group-advocated solutions, and movement rhetoric.[1]

As with any learning process, an increased flow of information creates an abundance of details and facts about a movement. During the course of its public maturation, a movement's issue space becomes saturated with information, as well as intertwined with other policy debates. However, as the issue space fills, a social movement is boiled down or abbreviated. Thus, paradoxically, as greater details about a movement emerge, the full range of knowledge about the group is less likely to be discussed or reported by the media. Instead, what comes to define a social movement and is reflected in the public debate is a crude distillation of the movement, exhibited through what we call meta-symbols.

As the currency or language used to discuss a social movement, meta-symbols convey a loose, universally accepted meaning, both intellectually and emotively. Their general meanings are societally derived, shaped by the press as well as by activists on both side of the controversy, and communicated primarily through the media. Eventually, meta-symbols—like other types of heuristics—become an integral part of citizens' cognitive structures and, thus, virtually synonymous with the protest group itself.

For example, the gay rights movement is one rubric of a social movement

that advocates greater legal rights and social freedoms for gays and lesbians. "Queer rights" is another meta-symbol for the same movement,
though one that for some citizens may convey greater militancy. As a heu-
ristic or group emblem, gay rights evoke certain facts or demands (e.g., the
extension of employment benefits to same-sex partners, the belief that soldiers can both serve their country and be "out of the closet"), societally
derived affect—typically highly negative—group-related slogans (e.g.,
We're here. We're queer. Get used to it.), other symbols associated with
the group or the group's beliefs (e.g., queens, queers, Stonewall, the Gay
and Lesbian Alliance), and related organizations and policy concerns (e.g.,
AIDS, Act Up, Silence = Death).[2]

HOW META-SYMBOLS EVOLVE

Social Movement Contributions

To the extent that social movements depend on the media to publicize
their cause (Gamson & Wolfsfeld, 1993; Tarrow, 1989; Altheida & Gilmore, 1972; Schattschneider, 1960; Turner & Killian, 1957), the media
both constrain and define a social movement's issue space.[3] Given journalistic norms about what constitutes news—particularly the need for simplicity—and, considering the consistency with which reporters develop and
interpret stories as well as the time and space constraints under which they
labor (Gamson & Wolfsfeld, 1993; Gans, 1979; Tuchman, 1978), social
activists quickly realize that "packaging" is everything. In this setting, the
more social movements are able to assist the press in explaining and condensing themselves, the more coverage a movement is likely to receive
(Shiner, 1996; Gamson & Wolfsfeld, 1993; Aberbach & Walker, 1970).
Toward this end, social movements often use meta-symbols to define themselves.[4] Meta-symbols allow groups to reach a broader audience by providing a "shrink-wrapped" version of their beliefs and goals, which, in turn,
appeals to citizens' need for cognitive reduction (Simon, 1985; Taylor &
Crocker, 1981; Tversky & Kahneman, 1982, 1974). A trade-off exists, of
course. Increased publicity comes at the expense of message accuracy; meta-
symbols provide the media, the movement's opposition, and citizens with
greater opportunities to distort a group's message.

Media Contributions

As information providers, the media package social movements using
"selected labels, and other vocabulary" (Parenti, 1986), as well as other
classic source and message factors (see Petty & Cacioppo, 1981). Although
meta-symbols are not the sole means by which the media package public
debates (see Callaghan & Schnell, 1999), they eventually become one of
the central linguistic determinants used to explain a movement. Meta-

symbols afford a simple information shortcut that journalists can rely on to telegraph complex information to readers with minimal effort. To promote drama and create balanced coverage, a journalist may incorporate either a group's meta-symbol, previous media-generated emblems, or opposition terminology or create his or her own labels (Terkildsen, Schnell, & Ling, 1998; Gamson & Wolfsfeld, 1993; Gans, 1979; Tuchman, 1978). In addition, given rhetoric rules that emphasize linguistic variance as one element of good writing, reporters may find it desirable to employ a number of overarching emblems to describe the same group.

In this manner, the meta-symbols or linguistic cues associated with a social movement—be they the movement's own labels, media-generated ones, or those transmitted by opposition groups—come to approximate one another. After repeated coverage, these various emblems evoke, if anything, only subtle connotative differences. That is, eventually the "women's movement" is seen as equal to "feminist/ism," which is perceived as being equivalent to "women's rights," which comes to approximate "women's liberation" and "the battle of the sexes." Over time, a social movement becomes virtually indistinguishable from its meta-symbols, and a handful of group emblems comes to represent the scope of the entire debate.

Consequences of Emblematic Affect

When meta-symbols are used to define a group's issue space, they lock group-related beliefs into a narrow, fixed space that represents a mere caricature of the movement itself, rather than its full range of ideas. This constriction allows for the easy transmission of group-related affect (Lazarus, 1984; Zajonc, 1980, 1984). To the extent that the media convey affectively ladened messages about a social movement, a permanent emotional bond is established. The tone of these early emotional links creates a tether that easily adheres from the group to its meta-symbols. Given the centrality of affect to all types of impression-formation tasks (Lazarus, 1984; Zajonc, 1984, 1980; Asch, 1946), initial group-associated emotions should prove particularly difficult to overturn. Thus, the magnitude of any group's distortion (i.e., the extent to which a group is symbolized) will proportionately influence citizens' perceptions of and support for a movement's advocacies.

THEORETICAL SUMMATION AND METHODOLOGICAL PROCEDURE

Given the preceding, we argue that message condensation and the formation of meta-symbols are a function of two interrelated criteria: (1) media norms that stress simplification and summarization as the appropriate means to convey and structure messages, which coincides with a social movement's own strategic aims and its dependency on the media for mass communication and (2) the processing limits of citizens, which result in a drive for cognitive simplification, thereby invoking meta-symbolized evaluations and automatic affectively ladened responses. As such, meta-symbols promote a cognitive dependency on ambiguous, distorted information and societally driven emotional reactions.

We now apply these arguments to the women's movement. First, we document media trends involving the use of meta-symbols and the transmission of group affect through the major news weeklies. Then, reporting a set of experiments, we probe the impact of symbolized coverage on attitudes about feminism and related issue domains, specifically, the issue of wage discrimination.

We believe that results garnered from an analysis of the women's movement will parallel other social movements such as the civil rights movement, the gay rights movement, and the farm workers movement, among others. Three central suppositions drive our assumptions: the public's stereotypic beliefs about group membership, the strength of a social movement's opposition, and the tactics employed by a protest group. First, we expect that social movements largely comprised of individuals from one social, economic, racial, ethnic, religious, or gender group, particularly those groups for whom society possesses well-defined, a priori beliefs about group members (i.e., traits and behavioral expectations based on group membership), will be perceived by the public as highly cohesive. This illusion of cohesion will produce judgments about the group and about individual members based, at least in part, on the original group stereotypes (Fiske & Taylor, 1991; Ashmore & DelBoca, 1981; Snyder, 1988; Lippmann, 1922). Since group stereotypes about African Americans, gays, migrant workers, Latinos, and women are either almost exclusively negative or contain strong negative components, we anticipate that both the original affect associated with those social movements and, at the least, early societally transmitted affect about these protest groups will be generally negative (Peffley, Hurwitz, & Sniderman, 1997; Devine, 1989; Ashmore & DelBoca, 1981; Katz & Braly, 1965).[5]

Second, each of these movements has or had highly vocal and well-organized opposition to their reform movements and any extension of group rights. Also, all these reform groups utilized similar types of tactics (e.g., protests, consciousness-raising techniques, marches, and lobbying, as well as more radical maneuvers) designed both to trigger media attention and to coalesce policy makers and the public around their plight (Gamson & Wolfsfeld, 1993; Tarrow, 1989; Staggenborg, 1991). Thus, national media coverage, as well as general opposition strategies and rhetoric, should have been parallel in each case.

DOCUMENTING MEDIA EFFECTS

Hypotheses

1. We hypothesize that to the extent the media link social movements to their beliefs and advocacies using meta-symbols rather than explicit, more complex linkages, a movement's public issue space is distorted. For example, if an issue like the wage gap is contextualized using only group symbols such as "the women's movement" or "feminism," without any further explanations or explicit links, or is associated with other related issues that ad hoc groups of women called feminists are working to erad-icate, the presence of such meta-symbols will enhance the group's public distortion. Thus, rather than creating clearer cognitive attachments between a movement and its beliefs (e.g., who are feminists; what they stand for; why they are concerned about the wage gap; whether only they perceive wage inequities; what they are actually doing to reduce wage inequities), meta-symbols simplify and misrepresent protest groups. We expect this as-sertion to be reflected through a greater number of articles that exclusively use meta-symbols to define the women's movement, compared to articles that make explicit links between feminist activity and social change. A greater reliance on meta-symbols should lead to greater distortions.

2. We further hypothesize that in the case of feminism, the media and opposition groups transmitted negative affect about the women's move-ment by connecting negative descriptors to the group's meta-symbols (though as noted in note 5, affect toward reform movements is not always expected to be uniformly negative).

Methods

All articles at the height of the women's movement—on the movement and related concerns—published in each of the three major news weeklies between 1970 and 1979 were collected and analyzed.[6] Coders were in-structed to make an initial judgment as to whether or not a meta-symbol was present in the article. If a meta-symbol was present (e.g., women's rights, feminist, feminism, radicals, radical feminists, battle of the sexes), coders were instructed to tally a count of the number of times each symbol appeared and the source of the meta-symbol (e.g., direct media usage, at-tributed to the opposition, or used by a spokesperson for the women's movement). Then, after thoroughly reading the article, coders were asked to determine whether a more complex or thorough discussion of feminism had been included by the reporter (i.e., any discussion of the movement's aims and beliefs or an attempt to more clearly define the group or a splinter organization or to create causation). Inter-coder reliability for tasks related to meta-symbols was very high, at .91 (Pearson's r).

Table 13.1
Average Number of Meta-Symbols Included in Coverage of the Women's
Movement, 1970–1979

	Media-Transmitted Meta-Symbols	Movement-Transmitted Meta-Symbols	Opponent-Transmitted Meta-Symbols
Phase I: Pre-ERA Years, January 1970 to March 1972	10.1	.003	.005
Phase II: Primary ERA Battles, April 1972 to 1976	12.5	1.7	.200
Phase III: The Last Push, 1977–1979	15.2	0	1.1

Results

We found that in accordance with our first hypothesis, 54 percent of the articles published by the three major news weeklies—*Time, Newsweek, U.S. News & World Report*—only linked women's collective action to feminism and the women's movement through meta-symbols. Of the remaining coverage, 5 percent of the articles provided a more complex link between feminist beliefs and issue discussions, as well as incorporated meta-symbols, while 41 percent of all articles failed to make any connection between women's concerns and the women's movement (i.e., they neither mentioned nor alluded to the movement or to a specific feminist organization). We refer to this latter form of coverage as the "vacuum effect," undocumented political change that seems to have occurred as of its own accord.

Commonly cited meta-symbols included feminism, feminist, battle of the sexes, women's liberation, women's libbers, libbers, women's liberationists, women's liberation movement, radicals, militants, and women's rights movement. Another two dozen or so labels, typically linguistic variants on the preceding terms, were used less frequently (e.g., lib ladies, Amazons, the movement, women's rights organizations, revolutionary vaginas, new feminism/ist, feminist revolution, liberated women, black feminists). Over time, some of these labels declined in vogue, while the usage of other meta-symbols like feminism and feminist increased (see also Huddy, 1996).

The number of movement meta-symbols present in articles ranged from a low of three to a high of 47 (see Table 13.1). On average, 12.3 meta-symbols were attached to articles published by the news weeklies during this decade. Over time, the usage of meta-symbols by the media consistently increased. An average of 10.1 meta-symbols per article were used in the early 1970s, the years preceding the campaign for the Equal Rights

Amendment (ERA). By the late 1970s, the last push to ratify the ERA, journalists incorporated 15.2 meta-symbols per article, up from 12.5 during the mid-decade ratification battles. Further, comparing across columns in Table 13.1, it is clear that the media, not story sources, were the primary promoters of meta-symbols. Ninety-two percent of all meta-symbols originated from the media, that is, from the journalist writing the story rather than from a movement source (7% of all meta-symbols) or an opposition source (1% of group symbols) that she or he quoted. Opposition use of group emblems increased as the battle for ratification intensified, while, conversely, movement use of meta-symbols declined.[7]

Some examples of how meta-symbols were utilized: A 1975 *U.S. News and World Report* story on women and wealth, the writer, under the subheading "Effect of '*lib*,' " made the following observation: "Some women, it is true, have acquired affluence on their own, but despite advances in '*women's liberation*' the record is a negative one." In a lengthy 1976 article on "the year of the woman," a *Time* reporter described an attempt to organize a formal day of protest as "The *National Organization for Women* designated October 29 as 'Alice Doesn't' Day and called on women to stage a non-work strike; it was a spectacular failure."

Finally, what about direct attempts by the media to depict the movement in an affectively charged manner? The media attached descriptors to movement meta-symbols 26 percent of the time.[8] These direct descriptors almost always conveyed negative information and/or affect.[9] Adjectives typically characterized the movement and its supporters as either extremist (e.g., militant, radical, crusaders, extreme, pushy, menacing, revolutionary, steamrollers), emotionally unstable (e.g., neurotic, unreasonable, oddball, screamers, too emotional, enraged, angry, demonic), or bent on violating cherished societal values (e.g., men-haters, lesbians, marriage wreckers, female dominators). The use of negative descriptors declined over time; in the early 1970s, 45 percent of all meta-symbols incorporated by journalists were associated with adverse adjectives, while by the end of the decade only 20 percent of group emblems vilified the women's movement in such an obvious manner. We speculate that this decline in negative descriptors may reflect one or more of the following explanations: the front-loading of affect by the press; a more dramatic contrast between early movement demands and traditional gender roles, which lessened as new roles for women became more accepted; increased self-monitoring on the part of journalists as feminism grew in strength or was more widely embraced by society; or the hiring of greater numbers of women—specifically, those sensitive to feminism—by news organizations after a series of prominent sex-discrimination lawsuits directed toward the press in the early 1970s were resolved.

Having established the parameters of media coverage, we now turn our attention to the question of how the use of meta-symbols influences atti-tudes toward women's rights and related issues.

THE ATTITUDINAL EFFECT OF SYMBOLIC COVERAGE

The Impact of Symbolic versus Non-symbolic Coverage

Does the presence of meta-symbols influence citizen's perceptions about and willingness to support the women's movement's agenda? Experimental results reported by Terkildsen and Schnell (1997) suggest that the answer to this question is yes—meta-symbolized coverage negatively influenced global assessments about the women's movement, levels of affect, and judg-ments about a feminist leader (i.e., Gloria Steinem, a feminist closely as-sociated with women's concerns during the 1970s), as well as willingness to donate money to feminist causes.[10] The presence of meta-symbols such as "the women's movement" or "feminism" did not only affect those with-out much interest in politics or sympathy for feminism. Instead, there were no substantive or statistically significant interactions with subject gender, feminism, partisanship, ideology, media usage, or political interest.

In sum, the presence of meta-symbols produced a pronounced and uni-form negative influence on support for women's rights and related con-cerns.[11] While these results substantiate much of our earlier theorizing on the attitudinal impact of meta-symbolized coverage, we sought additional evidence. One could argue that it is unclear as to whether respondents were reacting to the quantity of meta-symbols presented in the stimulus materials or to one meta-symbol in particular. Also, the extent to which citizens were able to distinguish between different movement emblems remains uncertain, as our initial design could not adequately address that issue.

The Influence of Individual Meta-Symbols

Our content analysis of media coverage of the women's movement showed that the media packaged the movement using selected labels or meta-symbols. We argue that these linguistic cues—be they the movement's own labels or generated by the media or by opposition groups—come to approximate one another and will evoke only subtle connotative differ-ences. In other words, information about the movement becomes detached from its original issue space, and negative affect, at least partially media transmitted, comes to be associated with feminism.

An experimental test (Terkildsen & Schnell, 1997) confirmed these as-sumptions. The experimental procedure involved the random assignment of participants ($N = 93$) to four different conditions. The stimulus mate-rials, promoted to participants as an excerpt from a national news maga-zine, discussed a fictional class-action suit alleging wage discrimination in the banking industry. The litigants, a group of female executives, were either described as (1) women, (2) women concerned about gender equality, (3) feminists, or (4) radical feminists, where the noun "women" was used to act as a control.[12] After reading the piece, subjects were asked to provide their reactions to the upcoming court case.

The three unique meta-symbols (i.e., women concerned about gender equality, feminists, radical feminists) produced identical evaluations across a variety of measures—global support and affect for the executives bringing suit, the legitimacy of the complaint, and assessments about a feminist leader.[13] All three meta-symbols had a negative impact, ranging from a 15 percent to a 40 percent decrease in support for each question on attitudes when compared to the control condition. For example, support for the litigants dropped by 30 percent when the women were described as either feminists, radical feminists, or women concerned about gender equality, as opposed to simply women. As with the first experiment reported earlier, tests for interactions with a variety of subject differences (e.g., gender, feminism, ideology, partisanship, knowledge, political interest, and media usage) proved to be statistically insignificant.

We take these patterns as evidence of two points. First subjects were not able to distinguish intellectually between these meta-symbols. Respondents associated women concerned about equality, feminists, and radical feminists with the same core set of beliefs.[14] This implies that knowledge about social movements is indeed simplistic and condensed, because of the media's role, the type of information processing the media promote, or citizens' levels of interest and processing strategies, or some combination of these factors. Second, while citizens are able to make minor differentiations between movement emblems, levels of affect are generally uniform from one meta-symbol to another. That is, affect represents an emotive approximation toward a social movement that remains constant, regardless of how the emblem changes.

DISCUSSION

Centuries ago, Machiavelli (1997) noted that "men are moved more by appearances than by the reality of things." Meta-symbols, abbreviated emblems applied to complex social movements, are the rhetorical versions of cosmetics, soft lighting, and airbrushing techniques. Meta-symbols create a false reality that moves public opinion by establishing ambiguity and distortions and promoting simplified information. Aristotle and Plato understood this. Lee Atwater and Tony Schwartz refined it. The symbolization of a protest group encourages citizens to cease thinking about a movement in anything other than simplistic terms. Therefore, meta-symbols not only become the appearance of reality but eventually define it as well.

And, let's face it, on an immediate level, the average citizen is more concerned about how heavy the traffic will be during the commute home from work or about who will win the NBA playoffs than about the complex ramifications of feminism or a thorough understanding of how the women's movement worked to equalize the wage gap. The media, driven by profit motives and fairly uniform reporting guidelines, understand this. Perhaps better than anyone they know what the public wants. Citizens don't want to know it "all," but neither do they wish to appear ignorant. Therefore, a variety of political forces combine to "give the people what they want," the appearance of knowledge and a vague version of reality packaged in an easy-to-digest encapsulated format. And, voilà! The reality about a social movement becomes the truth according to meta-symbols. Or, as Orwell (1946) noted, just as "thought corrupts language, language can also corrupt thought."

This research shows that meta-symbols do matter. In the setting we examined, they dominated national media coverage of the women's movement and had a pronounced negative impact on citizens' evaluations about the movement and related issues, an impact not moderated by respondents' personal beliefs or knowledge. Feminists were just as susceptible to the effects of meta-symbols as were non-feminists, the politically knowledgeable as influenced as the unknowledgeable, and partisans as vulnerable as non-partisans. Meta-symbols cross-cut a number of seemingly stable, long-term cognitions. In this light their power becomes even more impressive.

In terms of influencing levels of support for the women's movement, more than half of all print coverage used meta-symbols to characterize feminism. To the extent that citizens were exposed to such messages and attuned to them, negative affect toward gender equality likely increased and tangible support decreased. These figures are doubly important since meta-symbols transmit only a simplified summary of a group. Thus, the details they provide are more open to distortion, be it by the media and other players or citizens themselves, than are other forms of information.

Finally, what do our results say about the democratic process? "Symbols are the basic units of most human communication" (Bennett, 1996: 86) and are frequently used by political elites to convey more complex messages. "Packaging" is everything. Social movements condense their central ideas into symbols and meta-symbols to inspire and mobilize support for their policy campaigns and to assist the media in defining the movement's goals and strategies. Journalists and editors do not limit themselves to merely transmitting the symbols generated by interest groups or their opposition but also create their own symbolic language to delineate the public discourse. In turn, the condensation of complicated meaning into symbols fulfills citizens' need for cognitive reduction (Simon, 1985; Calvert, 1985; Tversky & Kahneman, 1982) and relieves them of the burdens of the search for information and deliberative decision making.

While symbols and meta-symbols are an essential component of the communication process between elites and the mass public, the condensation of political meaning can also represent a dilemma to democratic discourse. The exchange of information and ideas through a free press, as well as free and open public debate, is a crucial element of mass participation and a requirement for democratic responsiveness to public preferences (Sartori, 1987). Yet, this research has demonstrated that symbolic language has the potential to simplify and distort the democratic process. In particular, the effective manipulation of symbols can inhibit or enhance a social movement's ability to make itself heard effectively through the media and muster public support. In the case of the women's movement, we have shown that the simplification inherent in symbolic language contributed to negative affect and decreased support for the movement's agenda. Due to well-defined, a priori stereotypic beliefs about a group's members, we expect that the effect of symbolic communication will be parallel for other protest movements (e.g., the civil rights movement or the gay rights movement).

Ideally, we would like to see our hypotheses tested using other social movements, both those that we believe are typical of the women's movement (e.g., civil rights movement, farm workers and gay rights movements) and those we surmise to be atypical (e.g., Mothers Against Drunk Driving, Farm Aid, or other relief-based movements). We urge others to follow suit in this fertile intellectual ground with additional methodological tests and theoretical revisions. For if politics is about talk, then meta-symbols and "symbols are the currency of this communication process" (Elder & Cobb, 1983) and must be systematically and rigorously explored.

NOTES

1. Issues associated with a movement's public space may spin off into their own unique domains while still comprising a subcomponent of the group's doctrine. For example, abortion both overlaps with feminism and yet maintains its own independent issue space. Likewise, affirmative action is an unique issue in and of itself but encroaches into the issue space of the civil rights and women's movements as well.

2. Other examples of powerful group emblems that are meant to empower supporters of a cause by evoking a broad set of values are labels such as "pro-life," "pro-choice," "black power," "gray panthers," or "jihad" (i.e., holy war).

3. While our focus for this chapter concerns the relationship between the media and social movements, we do not wish to imply that opposition groups and other political players (e.g., elected officials, policy entrepreneurs) do not impinge on a social movement's issue space or influence its meta-symbols and rhetoric. They do. See Terkildsen, Schnell, & Ling (1998) for a general discussion of the role these actors play in the formation of policy debates.

4. We are not arguing that by participating in the packaging process, social movements guarantee that their meta-symbols will be used by the press. The press

may opt to ignore their emblems or to ignore the movement itself. We are arguing, that as a method to increase exposure, self-labeling is a strategically relevant behavior in which social movements may elect to engage. For instance, individuals who favored the liberalization of state laws banning abortion began to define themselves as "pro-choice" rather than pro-abortion as a means to empower their supporters and gain the moral high ground. In a similar vein, opponents of abortion reform took to referring to themselves as "pro-lifers" (Yale, 1993).

5. We do not wish to imply that societally transmitted affect toward social movements will always be negative. Rather, we expect the degree of negative affect to be directly related to social stereotypes about group members, perceptions about the radical nature of a group's reforms (i.e., the number and centrality of societal values they seek to overthrow or displace), and the strength of their opposition. That is, groups either with no opposition or weak opposition or those that advocate status quo reforms (e.g., Mothers Against Drunk Driving) will be anchored to largely positive or more neutral emotions. In contrast, more radical or revolutionary groups with strong political and societal opposition, such as the Black Panthers or the Red Army Brigade, will be associated, by at least a majority of a society, with highly negative affect.

6. The three news weeklies were selected as representative of daily print coverage on major policy issues, as well as for their broad national circulation, readership accessibility, and the ideological range of their editorial positions. Together *Time, Newsweek*, and *U.S. News and World Report* cover 9.5 million readers and are the only print media capable of competing with television news in reaching a comparable mass audience while providing coverage trends similar to the major dailies (Willings, 1993; Hunt & Rubin, 1993; Gamson & Modigliani, 1987).

7. We would speculate that this decline in the number of feminist sources employing meta-symbols and the increase in their usage among opposition forces likely reflects these players' knowledge about the cumulative, affective nature of those fully evolved emblems. That is, in an effort to solidify support for the ERA, feminists backed away from the use of group labels, while anti-feminists highlighted feminist meta-symbols as a strategy to link the ERA directly to radicals, lesbians, and militants. For example, from a 1977 *Newsweek* article on the National Women's Conference, where delegates passed a resolution urging ratification of the ERA, Phyllis Schlafly, head of the Eagle Forum and an avid anti-feminist spokesperson, was quoted as remarking, "Houston will finish off the women's movement. It will show them off for the radical, anti-family, pro-lesbian people they are."

8. We operationalized this test very narrowly. Coders were instructed to note only adjectives associated with the group's meta-symbols. A broader definition of affective associations, one that includes context as well, yields much stronger results. Negative affect generated by the media escalates dramatically; see for example the two articles cited in the text.

9. Some positive images of the movement did exist; however, this affect was contextually derived and therefore more subtle in its tone, rather than being directly cued through positive adjectives or descriptors. In addition, not all women associated with feminism were portrayed in a negative manner. Journalists distinguished between movement leaders who chose traditional avenues of political participation, such as office holding, and feminist leaders who opted to participate in more traditional protest activities. The former were typically described in neutral to positive

terms, while the latter were classified in a largely negative light. Thus, media coverage clearly created and conveyed to the public the false dichotomy of "good" and "bad" feminists.

10. These results are based on a single factorial experiment in which participants ($N = 113$) were randomly assigned to read about women rights in which past changes and present concerns were either (1) linked to the women's movement via meta-symbols, (2) were vaguely linked to women's collective action without any mention of the movement or feminism, or (3) a control condition in which respondents answered questions about feminism and the movement without reading any stimulus material. The stimulus materials were a blend of ideas culled from actual coverage presented during the late 1970s and were carefully edited to describe women's efforts at collective actions as either linked to the women's movement through meta-symbols or without mentioning formal women's organizations or feminism. Otherwise the two fictional articles were linguistically parallel (see Terkildsen & Schnell, 1997).

11. The experimental results also indicate that participants who were exposed to meta-symbols were less accurate in their ability to recall previously presented information and attached more affect to their judgment than subjects who were exposed to identical information minus the group emblems (see Terkildsen & Schnell, 1997). This suggests that meta-symbols inhibit the acquisition of new information.

12. We elected to test these meta-symbols for two reasons: First, after about 1980, as the frequency of many meta-symbols once used to describe the women's movement declined (e.g., women's movement, liberation, libbers, etc.), the label feminist was more likely to be used (Huddy, 1996). Second, our choice of meta-symbols reflects our interest in providing a stronger test of how linguistic subtleties may influence group assessments. In this manner, adding the descriptor radical to feminist could potentially evoke stronger evaluations than the term feminist in isolation. Likewise, the term gender equality could be perceived as more inclusive and less threatening than either the emblem feminist or radical feminist.

13. Scale construction and reliability coefficients are reported in Terkildsen & Schnell (1997).

14. However, there were some slight differences in the content of the three meta-symbols. Radical feminists were more likely to be associated with highly irrational beliefs (e.g, gender conspiracy theories, hatred of men) and with extreme tactics and actions than were feminists or women concerned about equality.

REFERENCES

Aberbach, J., & Walker, J. (1970). The Meanings of Black Power: A Comparison of White and Black Interpretations of a Political Slogan. *American Political Science Review, 64,* 367–388.

Altheida, D., & Gilmore, R. (1972). The Credibility of Protest. *American Sociological Review, 37,* 99–108.

Asch, S. E. (1946). Forming Impressions of Personality. *Journal of Abnormal and Social Psychology, 41,* 258–290.

Ashmore, R., & DelBoca, F. (1981). Sex Stereotypes and Implicit Personality Theory. In D. Hamilton (Ed.), *Cognitive Processes in Stereotyping and Intergroup Behavior*. Hillsdale, NJ: Erlbaum.

Bargh, J. A. (1984). Automatic and Conscious Processing of Social Information. In R. S. Wyer & T. K. Srull (Eds.), *The Handbook of Social Cognition*, Vol. 2. Hillsdale, NJ: Erlbaum.

Bennett, W. L. (1996). *News: The Politics of Illusion*. New York: Longman.

Callaghan, K., & Schnell, F. (1999). Media Frames, Public Attitudes and Elite Response: An Analysis of the Gun Control Issue. *Public Integrity Annual*, 1: 4, 47–72.

Calvert, R. (1985). The Value of Biased Information: A Rational Choice Model of Political Advice. *Journal of Politics*, 47, 530–555.

Devine, P. G. (1989). Stereotypes and Prejudice: Their Automatic and Controlled Components. *Journal of Personality and Social Psychology*, 56, 5–18.

Downs, A. (1957). *An Economic Theory of Democracy*. New York: Harper and Row.

Edelman, M. (1964). *The Symbolic Uses of Politics*. Urbana: University of Illinois Press.

Edelman, M. (1988). *Constructing the Political Spectacle*. Chicago: University of Chicago Press.

Elder, C., & Cobb, R. (1983). *The Political Uses of Symbols*. New York: Longman.

Fiske, S., & Pavelchak, M. (1986). Category-based versus Piece-Meal Affective Responses. In R. M. Sorrentino & E. Higgins (Eds.), *The Handbook of Motivation and Cognition: Foundations of Social Behavior*. New York: Guilford Press.

Fiske, S., & Taylor, S. (1991). *Social Cognition*. New York: Random House.

Gamson, W., & Modigliani A. (1987). The Changing Culture of Affirmative Action. *Research in Political Sociology*, 3, 137–177.

Gamson, W., & Wolfsfeld, G. (1993). Movements and the Media as Interacting Systems. *Annals of the American Academy of Political and Social Sciences*, 528, 114–125.

Gans, H. (1979). *Deciding What's News*. New York: Vintage Books.

Gitlin, T. (1980). *The Whole World Is Watching*. Berkeley: University of California Press.

Huddy, L. (1996). Feminist and Feminism in the News: Transforming Political Ideology into Everyday Words. In P. Norris (Ed.), *Women, Media and Politics* (pp. 183–204). New York: Oxford University Press.

Hunt, T., & Rubin, B. (1993). *Mass Communication*. New York: HarperCollins.

Katz, D., & Braly, K. W. (1965). Verbal Stereotypes and Racial Prejudice. In H. Proshansky & B. Seidenberg (Eds.), *Basic Studies in Social Psychology*. New York: Holt, Rinehart & Winston.

Krosnick, J. (1988). The Role of Attitude Importance in Social Evaluations: A Study of Policy Preferences, Presidential Candidate Evaluations, and Voting Behavior. *Journal of Personality and Social Psychology*, 55, 196–210.

Lazarus, R. (1984). On the Primacy of Cognition. *American Psychologist*, 39, 124–129.

Lippmann, W. (1922). *Public Opinion*. New York: Free Press.

Lipsky, M. (1968). Protest as a Political Resource. *American Political Science Review*, 62, 1145–1158.

Machiavelli, N. (1997). *The Prince*. New Haven, CT: Yale University Press.

Miller, S. I., & Fredricks, M. (1990). Perceptions of the Crisis in American Public Education: The Relationship of Metaphors to Ideology. *Metaphor and Symbolic Activity*, 5, 67–81.

Orwell, G. (1946). Politics and the English Language. In *Shooting an Elephant and Other Essays*. New York: Harcourt Brace.

Parenti, M. (1986). *Inventing Reality: The Politics of the Mass Media*. New York: St. Martin's Press.

Peffley, M., Hurwitz, J., & Sniderman, P. (1997). Racial Stereotypes and Whites' Political Views of Blacks in the Context of Welfare and Crime. *American Journal of Political Science*, 41, 30–60.

Petty, R. E., & Cacioppo, J. T. (1981). *Attitudes and Persuasion: Classic and Contemporary Approaches*. Dubuque, IA: Wm. C. Brown Company.

Sartori, G. (1987). *The Theory of Democracy Revisited*. Chatham, NJ: Chatham House.

Schattschneider. E. E. 1960. *The Semi-Sovereign People: A Realist's View of Democracy in America*. New York: Holt, Rinehart, and Winston.

Sears, D. (1993). Symbolic Politics: A Socio-Psychological Theory. In S. Iyengar & W. McGuire (Eds.), *Explorations in Political Psychology*. Durham, NC: Duke University Press.

Shiner, J. (1996). Women, the Press, and the '96 Campaign. At the Joan Shorenstein Center on the Press, Politics and Public Policy Symposium on Women, Media, and Politics: Lessons for '96, Washington, DC, May 10.

Simon, H. (1985). *Models of Bounded Rationality*. Cambridge, MA: MIT Press.

Snyder, M. (1988). On the Self-Perpetuating Nature of Social Stereotypes. In T. Srull & R. Wyer (Eds.), *Advances in Social Cognition: A Dual Process Model of Impression Formation*, Vol. 1. Hillsdale, NJ: Erlbaum.

Staggenborg, S. (1991). *The Pro-Choice Movement: Organization and Activism in the Abortion Conflict*. New York: Oxford University Press.

Tarrow, S. G. (1989). *Democracy and Disorder: Protest and Politics in Italy 1965–1975*. New York: Oxford University Press.

Taylor, S., & Crocker, J. (1981). Schematic Bases of Social Information Processing. In E. Higgins, C. P. Herman, & M. Zanna (Eds.), *Social Cognition: The Ontario Symposium*. Hillsdale, NJ: Erlbaum.

Terkildsen, N., & Schnell, F. (1997). Meta-Symbols, Social Movements, and the Media: The Attitudinal Consequences of Condensing Complex Beliefs into Group Labels. Paper presented at the Annual Meeting of the International Society of Political Psychology, Krakow, Poland, July 21–24.

Terkildsen, N., Schnell, F., & Ling, C. (1998). Interest Groups, the Media, and Policy Debate Formation: An Analysis of Message Structure, Rhetoric, and Source Cues. *Political Communication*, 15:1, 45–61.

Tuchman, G. (1978). *Making News: A Study in the Construction of Reality*. New York: Free Press.

Turner, R., & Killian, L. (1957). *Collective Behavior*. New York: Prentice-Hall.

Tversky, A., & Kahneman, D. (1974). Judgment under Uncertainty: Heuristics and Biases. *Science*, 185, 1124–1131.

Tversky, A., & Kahneman, D. (1982). The Framing of Decisions and the Psychology of Choice. In R. Hogarth (Ed.), *Question Framing and Response Consistency*. San Francisco, CA: Jossey-Bass.

Willings Press Guide. (1993). *Alphabetical and Classified Index*, vol. 2. Great Britain: Reed Information Services Ltd.

Zajonc, R. (1980). Feeling and Thinking: Preferences Need No Inferences. *American Psychologist, 35*, 151–175.

Zajonc, R. (1984). On the Primacy of Affect. *American Psychologist, 39*, 117–123.

Yale, M. A. (1993). Abortion, Elections, and the Media. In M. L. Goggin (Ed.), *Understanding the New Politics of Abortion*. Newbury Park, CA: Sage.

PART IV

Conclusion

CHAPTER 14

Public Speech, Symbols, and Democratic Citizenship East and West

CHRIST'L DE LANDTSHEER

Let us start this concluding chapter with two questions. What are the secrets that lie beyond public speech and symbols? What do explorations in the rhetoric of politicians and the media reveal about its impact on democratic values (freedom, solidarity, and equal opportunity)? These are the questions that this volume and this conclusion address from an interdisciplinary, multi-method and multicultural perspective.

The chapters in *Beyond Public Speech and Symbols* represent different perspectives; among these are political science (Feldman, Ball), psychology (Suedfeld, Bull), sociology (Schnell, Terkildsen, & Callagan; Mitchell), mass communication (Kern, Just, Crigler & Hong Xie; Moshe & Lehman-Wilzig; Zhang), linguistics (Azuma), and international relations (De Landtsheer & van Oortmerssen).

All three parts of the volume include studies from different disciplinary origins, and methods. According to Azuma, his study is best characterized as a sociolinguistic study in the discipline of general linguistics. Most methods emphasize the important role of language, while they rely heavily on the research of sociologists, psychologists, and political scientists who study collective behavior. Essays are based on empirical materials collected in different cultures. Both the public discourse and its reception by the local audiences are the subject of inquiry.

This volume is a "globalized" study of political discourse. Scholars write chapters from different cultures. Local experts in political language studies report on various aspects of political discourse in their culture. Scholars in this volume show how culture affects their way of approaching political (public) discourse.

Question number 1 deals with the issue of "meaning." Answers may be hard to give; readers, however, know that of this book, especially Part II, throws some light on the crucial issue of meaning. Part II indeed can be seen as an illustration of the philosophical-linguistic perspective on political and speech communication.

Question number 2 investigates how the rhetoric of politicians and the mass media relates to democratic values such as freedom and equal opportunity. This book has addressed this question in regard to politicians in Part I and in regard to mass media in Part III. These sections respectively represent the political psychology and institutional views of political and speech communication.

This concluding chapter relates the chapters in this book to the main points of view in the field of speech communication and political communication. I agree with the French scholar Gerstlé (1992: 21), who wrote that the political communication field perfectly reflects the struggle between the main epistemological paradigms of the political and social sciences. Traditional political theory inspired both his differentiations between a systemic/strategic approach and a dialogic/behavioral one, and an interaction/constructivist approach (the influence of sociology). This approximately corresponds with my own categorization of these scientific approaches into three fields of research. These include the institutional approach with the traditional election paradigm and the critical media perspective ("systémique et stratégique," "systemic/strategic"), the critical-philosophical and linguistic approaches including modern-structuralistic and neo-Marxist views ("la construction sociale de la réalité," "the social construction of reality"), and the political psychology approach including propaganda and political language studies ("dialogique et comportement," "dialogic/behaviorial").

The structure of Beyond Public Speech and Symbols: Explorations in the Rhetoric of Politicians and the Media reflects these paradigms and views. Part I deals with the political psychology approaches (propaganda and political language studies); Part II details the critical-philosophical and linguistic (modern-structuralistic and neo-Marxist) views; Part III includes the institutional (the traditional election paradigm and the critical media perspective) approaches.

This concluding chapter discusses these approaches based on the book materials. It, however, also shows that Beyond Public Speech and Symbols goes one step further than Politically Speaking, the earlier volume edited by Feldman and De Landtsheer.

One difference between the current and the former volume lies in the conception of rhetoric and public speech. The current volume takes a broader perspective on language and politics; this volume also deals with symbols, with non-verbal speech acts and cultural utterances. Half of the contributions to Beyond Public Speech and Symbols deal with communication through symbols, images, cartoons, myth, or the Internet (Taran,

Mitchell, Zhang, Schnell, Terkildsen, and Callagan; Kern, Just, Crigler and Xie). This broad perspective on language is discussed in this chapter's first section, entitled "Public Speech, Rhetoric, and Symbols."

This volume can further be distinguished from the former volume because this volume centers on the citizen. The focus is on elements that contribute to resolving the basic question about the positive function of public speech in bridging "the gap" or "distance" between politicians and citizens. This chapter details this conception in its paragraphs on "The Rhetoric of Politicians and the Media."

The current book, finally, is based on a more extensive and wider collection of empirical data than the former, and it includes a wider variety of methods. These methods are detailed throughout the following paragraphs of this chapter. The essays collected in *Beyond Public Speech and Symbols* study, in a broad conception, rhetoric through its contents, meanings, and styles. Also studied are its senders (Part I), its institutions and strategies (Part II), and its effects on the audience (Part III). Epistemologically scholars did so both from an empirical-positivistic (e.g., Suedfeld; Terkildsen, Schnell, & Callagan) and from a theoretical-hermeneutic viewpoint (Montero; Moshe & Lehman-Wilzig; Mitchell), using methods ranging from theoretical-philosophical, qualitative, and descriptive (Bull, Azuma, Zhang) to quantitative-empirical, including empirical-analytical methods (De Landtsheer & van Oortmerssen), and experiments (Kern, Just, Crigler, & Xie) or a combination of methods (Taran, Feldman). Among applied methods are discourse analysis and the qualitative method of rhetorical criticism (of mass media), content analysis, experiments and effect studies (media effects, or citizen use and interpretation of messages). Tables, figures, cartoons, and photographs testify to the variety and wealth empirical data used in this book.

BEYOND PUBLIC SPEECH, RHETORIC, AND SYMBOLS

Part II of this book explores the rhetoric in national and multinational parliaments. It represents the critical-philosophical and political-linguistic views in the field of public speech and political communications, and it addresses the question concerned with the profound meaning of public speech, rhetoric, and symbols.

The meaning and the use of the terms speech, rhetoric, style, discourse, language, communication, and propaganda that are often used in connection with politics were clarified in the introductory chapter to *Politically Speaking*. "Introduction to the study of political discourse" demonstrated how these terms are used interchangeably, even though they stem from different traditions of study. The present volume confirms this conclusion. Bull, who works in the rhetorical tradition, details the "rhetoric" of Tony Blair, but Ball uses the method of rhetorical criticism and nevertheless writes about the "political language" of Lyndon B. Johnson. The term "discourse," which originates in the modern-structuralist tradition, is used by authors who follow this tradition (Moshe & Lehman-Wilzig; Azuma) and by others (Feldman; Montero). Most of the authors, however, define the concepts they are using.

The nice formulation by Emerson, that we are symbols and that we inhabit symbols fairly, suits our close-to-everyday-life conception of politics and public speech. Speech is the use of language by one person in a specific situation; it is an individual act. Public speech is the use of language by one person in a public situation. Public speech is always political speech, according to a broad conception of politics as used by cultural anthropologists and postmodern scholars. Symbols are those signs that people use to communicate one with another and as instruments of thought. Symbols in this volume always are interpreted according to their political function and or purpose. Rhetoric is the uniquely human ability to use symbols to communicate with one another. Communication, in this volume, is always interpreted according to its political function, regardless of its format or context (Ogden and Richards, 1938; de Saussure, 1955; Foss, Foss, & Trapp, 1991).

One can find public speech and political communication in the language of newspaper, television, Internet, film, and radio (including comments, interviews, debates, talk shows, news reporting, Web sites, films), in rhetoric and propaganda (including parliamentary debates, mass meetings, party meetings, election materials, and other political pamphlets), in administrative, judicial, and diplomatic language (including law texts, treaties, and international political negotiations), but also in tabloids, movies, soaps, billboards, graffiti, cartoons, theater, architecture, art, literature and music. One can, of course, find public speech and political communication in the human voice itself and in the image, appearance, clothes and non-verbal behavior of all human beings. In most countries, politicians and public personalities communicate with the vast majority of their constituents almost exclusively through the "public" channels such as television, radio, newspapers, and Web sites. In some countries like the United States, Japan, and Belgium, politicians still have much more personal contact with their voters.

The political science–oriented definition that limits political communication to communication in politics is widely shared among social scientists. Popular concepts that the audience, the political elite itself, and literary writers use tend to be restricted to politicians' communication. Yet some deploy a broader concept of political communication. The opinion of modern structuralists, traditional Marxists, anthropologists, and "critical" communication scientists is that almost every form or style of communication can be political. The editors of *Beyond Public Speech and Symbols* chose this broad concept, as they consider it more realistic, even though it may appear idealistic.

THE PHILOSOPHICAL-LINGUISTIC APPROACHES

We summarize the critical-philosophical and political-linguistic approaches into the philosophical-linguistic approaches. These approaches give us a better understanding of both motives and effects, that is, the functions and meanings of public speech. This section, which deals with that approach of language and philosophy, mainly helps to understand the underlying processes.

While these views relate to the critical communication studies approach, which I'll discuss in a following paragraph, their focus is on language, of which they often use a broad concept. Speech includes almost all human communications (rhetoric, symbols). All human communications are actions (e.g. "language use," "speech acts"). All human actions/communications ("symbols," "discourse") possess a "political" function. These philosophical-linguistic approaches include, besides the political-linguistic studies, a range of postmodernist and traditional Marxist conceptions (critical-philosophical studies).

While Chapters 5 and 6 represent the political-linguistic studies, Chapters 7 and 8 illustrate the critical philosophical studies of which both sides (postmodernist and traditional Marxist conceptions) produced "productive" as well as "non-productive" analyses. Postmodernism and Marxism emphasize the political function of language. They consider language to be a dominant power in the process of thinking. This is something of which citizens, journalists, and politicians ought to be constantly aware (Ulmann, 1975; Sapir, 1962). Rosenau (1992), who connected philosophical postmodernism to political attitudes, identified the most influential French philosophers Foucault, Derrida, Barthes, Lyotard, and Baudrillard as creating the "European skeptical form" of postmodernism. Comparable ideas in the United States and in other countries are seen as more active and positive. The predominantly Anglo–North American form "suggests" alternative political, social, and cultural projects. This "Anglo-Saxon form" that is called "affirmative postmodernism" results in political participation, new social movements, and non-traditional parties and deliberately invalidates voting. Negativism, ranging from nihilism and suicide to political terrorism, is "the darker side of postmodernism." This is mostly in the French philosophers domain. Shapiro's (1984; Shapiro & Der Derian, 1989) Anglo-Saxon "deconstructionism" reflects the thoughts of Marx and Foucault. It develops exciting notions of ideology and politics in relation to language, as a result of a critical compilation of various kind of philosophical thinking. In his "deconstruction" of sports he describes how both sports and politicians' use of sports metaphors prevents citizens (especially women) from full political participation. These are spectator-sports "rituals" that stimulate consensus and nationalism. Postmodern philosophers often consider themselves neo-Marxists. They are, nevertheless, criticized as being vague and conservative, because they neglect the historical dimension and the possibility for change (Schaff, 1978). Neo-Marxist modern structuralism (Shapiro, 1984) charges language and mass media as being "subjugating and dominating" while pretending to be "healing, nurturing, and caring." This awareness is one defense that citizens have.

Moshe and Lehman-Wilzig (Chapter 7) present a critical-philosophical analysis of innovations in the media landscape in Israel. The study belongs to (media) policy studies, and it is based on normative media theory. It uses a combination of qualitative and quantitative methodology. Even though it claims to be an empirical test of Habermas' theory, it is closely related to a modern-structuralist study. Chapter 7 should be seen as a combination of both the traditional Marxist and neo-Marxist or modern structuralist approaches, in which the "discourse project" is mostly seen as a positive one. The study investigates "national versus global public discourse in the era of multi-channelism."

"Discourse" is the key word behind modern structuralism. Foucault (1984) most clearly formulated this basic idea. All kinds of discourse are part of a power process. Things and people are, in several ways, excluded from the process, by limiting freedom of the press but also by giving them labels such as "mad," "unscientific," "trash," "fool," and "witch." Those who avoid content-oriented communication control this process.

Taran's study (Chapter 8) on mythical thinking, Aristotelian logic, and metaphors in the parliament of Ukraine is based on the principles of "philosophical semantics." The first part details theoretical concepts like myth, metaphor, and logic. The chapter also includes a quantitative-empirical content analysis. Taran quantitatively operationalizes philosophical concepts such as mythical thinking and Aristotelian logic analogical to the metaphorical model earlier developed by De Landtsheer (1994, 1998). His analysis contributes to an understanding of how politicians may manipulate the audience and create discourse where mythical thinking and metaphors prevail over logical reasoning.

Schaff, the theoretician of "philosophical semantics" (a school related to analytical philosophy), emphasized the symbolic function of language in fulfilling needs and providing personal benefits (1960, 1978, 1980). The work of this—basically—orthodox Marxist should not be confused with former Marxist-Leninist studies that analyzed the function of language in the construction of socialist societies (e.g., "propagandist and agitator" roles). Ludz properly described these studies in his "Mechanismen der Herrschaftssicherung" [Mechanisms of Ensuring Dominance](1980). These Marxist-Leninist scholars sometimes compared "constructive" Marxist-Leninist language to "capitalist" or "deceiving" prose (Schmidt, 1977). The

(Montero) to quantitative empirical methods such as the study of integrative complexity (Suedfeld).

Beyond Public Speech and Symbols examines the language of political elites and also discourses of minorities and social movements; the book deals with governmental discourse, parliamentary rhetoric, and mass media language including comics and strips as well as popular culture. The editors, accordingly, included in Part III approaches to mass media discourse, which mainly illustrate the critical media perspective within the institutional approach. Contributions to Part III were, again, written based on various empirical methods and extensive data collection. Methods range from the qualitative empirical including focus groups (Kern, Just, & Xie), and rhetorical criticism (Zhang; Mitchell) to the quantitative empirical including quantitative content (Schnell, Terkildsen, & Callagan) and semiotic analysis (Feldman).

The Rhetoric of the Media

This book makes a firm statement in the current public debate concerning a lack of "understanding" between citizen-electors and "their" politicians. This debate focuses on issues such as political cynicism and political participation. In accord with this view, journalists mainly seek to explain "the gap" or "the distance" between the citizens and their politicians, pointing to factors such as the electoral system, the secularization process, educational policy and political socialization, social stratification, and the present economic situation. Some social scientists, however, say there is no gap at all. They consider political participation to be at a sufficient level and that political cynicism exists at all times anyway. The (un)willingness of citizens to participate in politics may increase because of negative campaigning and commercializing of society, mass media, and politics. But politicians may be either not able or not motivated to stay in touch with their constituents' views. Any such gap between citizens and politics may really not exist, but some kind of a gap between citizens and politicians seems real. Blaming citizens ("political cynicism") or not blaming politicians ("there is no gap") are comfortable solutions for political elites. This elite consists of political journalists, politicians, and political scientists. It maintains its oligarchic decision making. *Beyond Public Speech and Symbols* shifts the laying of blame from the citizen to the political elites in light of their democratic responsibilities; the focus is on their responsibilities as communicators.

The Institutional Approach

The power of the media in general is a controversial item discussed from an institutional perspective as well as at theoretical, empirical, and applied levels. Part III of *Beyond Public Speech and Symbols* deals with the power of mass media and takes a critical media approach; the book starts from a problematic situation, the responsibility of political elites to improve democracy and political participation through skilful communication with the citizen. Contributors in this volume relate public speech type(s), which they examine for expectable as well as desirable and undesirable political function(s). They answer the question of how public or political speech in their country (or one or more countries they are examining) relates to democratic citizenship.

Several chapters in this volume analyze election communication (Bull; Suedfeld; Montero; Kern, Just, Crigler, & Xie), but these are not discussed within the traditional "election paradigm" approach. The authors who detailed the rhetoric of presidential candidates and political leaders or who investigated the use of new campaigning techniques focus on issues that are also playing and/ or are of equal importance outside election campaigns (rhetorical style, cognitive complexity, the effect of the image and appearance, political Web sites). Politicians may not neglect means of public communication outside election campaigns; neither may scholars.

A Critical Media Perspective

A current media critique deals with this general lack of political participation. Most critical media theories are based on public opinion research. This field is closely related to mass psychology and political psychology, of which several aspects are discussed later. These theories focused the attention of scholars on public opinion research. They emphasized the role of the family, groups, and political parties in opinion formation and on communications theory and mass media (Nimmo, 1978).

Three out of the four theoretical media schools consider the political power of mass media to be a negative influence. These include the mass society, critical (of the Frankfurt School), and the more current—often neo-Marxist—critical communication. This most modern school includes the political economy approach (e.g., the Birmingham and the Glasgow media group), the culturalist approach (e.g., Stuart Hall), and some other media theorists. The critical school emphasizes the manipulative (instead of the reflective) function of mass media, wherein the "power elite" has other interests than do citizens. The political economy approach concludes that this power elite imposes its "definition of reality" on society. The culturalists describe how bureaucratic news routines within media institutions combine with powerful interest groups. A series of "coding processes" construct our "social reality" theories. The discourse thus produced aims at maintaining a consensus and the status quo. Media institutions encourage journalistic and the audience's passive attitudes. Journalists constantly rely upon public bureaucrats, whose political and social authority allows them to produce "knowledge." Their "news" reports are "performance based," inexpensive and easy to collect. Journalists and politicians depend upon each other for information and for publicity respectively. These "bureaucratic news rituals" and "consensus mechanisms" allow journalists and politicians to feel less responsible for the construction of political events and news, which they do not consider as either self or group constructed. Public debate is fake, as it is entirely mass media manufactured. Members of the political elite are the only participants, that is, political actors, journalists, and the "attentive" part of the media audience (Fishman, 1982; Bennett, 1982; Curran, 1990; Witte, 1993; Price, 1992; McQuail, 1994). Their own autonomy is also false, since they depend entirely upon "institutional consensus" and "media routines."

Chapter 9 exemplifies critical media research that is closely related to propaganda research. Zhang performed a qualitative content analysis of the rhetoric by the political elite in China, the ruling Chinese Communist Party. She studied Chinese public speech as it appeared in the articles of the most important Party newspaper, the *People's Daily*. Zhang's propaganda analysis shows how newspaper articles on model intellectuals in the Chinese press served to raise the political and social status of Chinese intellectuals and to prescribe ideal behavior for Chinese citizens in the era of economic reform. She explains that intellectuals have always constituted a special social group in China. The Party had always attempted to reform and educate them rather than presenting them as part of the dependable working class, until the reform years. During the Chinese "Cultural Revolution," intellectuals were the subjects of scapegoating. In propaganda, the "enemy" party is reduced to one (kind of) person, who becomes a scapegoat. Scapegoating illustrates another propaganda technique, the "orchestration" of information. These practice and media concentrations are compatible. The stories of model intellectuals' lives complemented Party documents and Party newspaper editorials to promote new reform policies and encourage citizens to respect knowledge and pursue knowledge to modernize China. The official public speech in China served to promote the Party and the government's policies and official values such as altruism and self-sacrifice in the public interest.

Chapter 10 in *Beyond Public Speech and Symbols* is the chapter that most reflects a positive view of media. Feldman, who details political humor in editorial cartoons, satire, and attitudes toward authority, clearly shows how a free press can contribute to democracy and political participation. "Japanese-style democracy" makes it hard to criticize politicians and authorities through jokes and satire. Political cartoons in two widespread dailies nevertheless suggest that "the prime minister was portrayed as less bright than others, less diligent, easily manipulated, unhealthy-looking and lacking in energy, conservative in his thinking and not benevolent toward the public." Feldman's study therefore exemplifies the liberal-pluralistic school—the only school that conceives of mass media in a positive way. They are considered the fourth estate or a fourth factor in society, counterbalancing the power of governments and political parties. Also, since they provide for diversity in opinions and circulation of ideas, they support mediated democracy. Chapter 10 uses a combination of methods. The first part of the study is a hermeneutic qualitative analysis of the function of humor in Japanese society; the second part is a quantitative semiotic content analysis of different types of political cartoons.

The idealistic liberal theory is also represented in Chapter 11 of the volume. The study by Kern, Just, Crigler, & Xie deals with the question of what happens if equal access to the Web is given to all citizens during an election campaign. The experimental method used included the offering of a structured introduction to the World Wide Web to focus groups. These groups were selected in Northern New Jersey and Southern California by marketing firms. This study can be related to the "knowledge gap theory" by Tichenor, Donohue, and Olien (1972). This approach within the critical communication school argues that media are deepening the gap between higher and lower educated people. It seems less true for some "political subjects," however. In an earlier study, Neuman, Just, and Crigler (1992) proved that television and magazines have a democratizing function because they encourage attention to less popular subjects. The current study by Kern, Just, Crigler, and Xie shows that users bring old information seeking strategies to the new media. Using the Internet in political campaigns provides information to those information seekers who were interested anyhow, but attractiveness of the site influences uncertain seekers.

The liberal-pluralistic media theory was contradicted by many studies and by the facts. One fact is that Silvio Berlusconi is one media giant who gained political power from his control over the whole Italian information system. Mitchell's chapter in this volume argues that discourse in the United States has a competitive nature, with the most extreme voices on the opposing sides receiving the most attention. The less strident centralists and moderates are ignored and often despised. This thesis by Mitchell contradicts the influential "spiral of silence" theory of Noelle-Neumann (1980), yet another critical communication view. It was found that the (social-democratic) climate of opinion, which dominated German journalists in the early 1970s, affected public opinion. "Dissident" (conservative) opinions were no longer voiced in the media. Governmental dominance over media content in Germany resulted in both a *"Regierungsbonus"* and a *"Kanzlerbonus"* during elections (Semetko & Schoenbach, 1994). The liberal theory, however, states that diversity is guaranteed even in the case of concentration, because of conflicting interests between groups participating in the media system (owners, managers, editors, and journalists). Nine conflicting levels of interest from which influence is exerted on both the news selection process and the form and content of political messages have been described in one study (Dimmick & Coit, 1982). These include journalists' personal preferences, informal contacts between journalists and politicians, the organization of the media system, and the political and economic system. This analysis of the news process is based on White's gatekeeping theory (1950), which says that "gatekeepers" are holding back information in the news production process, on the micro-, meso-, and macro-level.

The Frankfurt School rightly countered liberal-pluralistic arguments with its adequately formulated critique of one "cultural industry" (e.g., Herbert Marcuse and Jürgen Habermas). Mass media create an ideological climate in which it is impossible to escape from the present situation. Media discourse is overwhelmingly concrete in offering images instead of concepts. Discussions are limited to questions about the best techniques to administer the present system. The audience is taught to think in "media terms," which makes "opposition thinking" problematical. Media are not considered to have a central place in the production of values. Liberal capitalism is responsible for changes in both media structures and media discourse (Bennett, 1982; McQuail, 1994).

By contrast, the oldest school preceded the Frankfurt School in its critical media approach. The mass society school criticized mass media and mass culture for entirely different reasons. Mass media are seen as a threat to elite culture and to democratic institutions. They transform society into a social mosaic and provide for citizen alienation. The cultural philosophers Ortega y Gasset and Friedrich Nietzsche, the political philosophers Alexis de Tocqueville and John Stuart Mill, the mass psychologists Wilhelm Reich and Hannah Arendt, and the sociologists Vilfredo Pareto and Gaetano Mosca (Bennett, 1982; McQuail, 1994) all were members of this influential school. Most representatives of the fourth school, the critical communication approach, operate under Frankfurt School influence.

Mitchell (Chapter 12) traces a phenomenon called "news as melodrama," the tendency of the news media to convert the world into a stage and events into the scenes of a melodrama. Her rhetorical analysis focuses on "narratives" in the print news media of the United States during a crisis situation caused by a terrorist act. During such crises, the function of the media is to provide information on the situation to the public, and in the process, provide a sense of meaning to a disruptive event. U.S. mass media tend to favor the sensational news stories over less dramatic ones, writes Mitchell. The characteristics of television may determine the type of political message that is successful on television. A political message can induce fear in an audience and be more successful on television or in the press. There is evidence that television enhances moderate political views and promotes materialistic attitudes. Materialistic attitudes are stimulated by threats to basic human needs. Every element of the story is presented in a dramatic manner, with any moral ambiguity eliminated. Dramatizing (reporting "crisis," "bad news," terrorism, and violence and an emphasis on competition) are all based on propaganda. There is a symbiotic relationship between terrorists and the mass media, each of which serves one another's interests for access to the public and to the political decision. *Dramatizing* of information is, besides personalizing, fragmenting, and actualizing, one of the symptoms of media commercialization (Inglehart, 1977; Gerbner et al., 1982; Reimer & Rosenberg, 1990; Farnen, 1990; Witte, 1993).

We can compare these commercial news techniques using traditional propaganda analysis. Simplicity and personalizing are two such basic techniques. Their use increases as the size of the audience grows. Media techniques and commercialization of mass media create favorable conditions for these "malicious" techniques. Often these propaganda techniques have as a goal the simple purpose "to convince and to subjugate" instead of "to educate" (Domenach, 1979: 8). Personalization means that the struggle between political ideas, political groups, and political parties is transformed into a personal and an individual battle. One's character, appearance, and private life are emphasized. Politics is depoliticized since ideas have been personalized. Non-political issues are politicized, for instance, using the tabloid approach. The competitive media climate produces no reflection, no profound information, and no help with informed opinion formation. Media provide us with many unrelated news fragments, so that one becomes "blind" in a blizzard of events. Politics becomes theater or a soap opera.

The study by Schnell, Terkildsen, and Callagan (Chapter 13) examines the impact of label-driven coverage on citizen attitudes toward social movements, specifically the U.S. women's movement. The first part details the concept of symbols, their use and impact. This chapter further offers a quantitative content analysis of news covering on the U.S. women's movement. It illustrates the newer versions of cultivation analysis, which is also related to the critical school. The critical school focuses on the processes that create media reality; cultivation analysis is concerned with the actual content of media reality and the effects this has on the audience. For women, people of color, and minorities, access to public discourse is often problematic. Political elites tend to exclude them from public speech either by stereotyping and negative labelling or by simple underrepresentation. Cultural, ethnic, and religious minorities engage, sometimes, in violent (terrorist) activities. They produce, sometimes, the accompanying violent discourse in order to receive their legitimate share of the public sphere, the media being "the terrorists' best friends." Although political values are not widely studied in cultivation analysis, there have been some such studies. The authors of Chapter 13 show how representation (including new technologies, political marketing) or symbolizing in rhetoric or mass media can affect public images of either public (political) personalities or (political) groups or movements. The authors concluded that the media were at least partly responsible for linking and transmitting negative affect through group emblems associated with the women's movement. This conclusion confirms the controversial "agenda-setting theory," which McCombs and Shaw (1972) developed. This theory emphasized the media power in politics. Mass media determine the political agendas and issues that voters actually think about (as well as, perhaps, how they think).

Modern institutional communication research mainly teaches us that the political elite (political journalists, politicians, and the "attentive" audience) (Price, 1992) forms an economic power elite as creators or masters. Journalists are less blamed for depoliticizing effects than are other "controlling factors" because their autonomy is recognized to be a fiction. Consequently, these economic giants are really responsible for citizens' political alienation.

We can conclude from Part III that in countries where the press is state controlled, mass media are deliberately used to change citizens' conceptions—about issues or fellow-citizens like intellectuals—according to party policy (Chapter 9). Traditional societies may have different conceptions of democracy than Western countries; free mass media nevertheless provide the citizen with a healthy critique of political leaders, for instance, through political cartoons (Chapter 10). Dramatization of information is, however, a technique that "democratic" mass media use for commercial purposes (Chapter 12). Also, mass media use of symbols, particularly in regard to women's and other social movements, often contributes to their negative image (Chapter 13). Free access for all citizens, nevertheless, to less current new media would be informative to all of them, especially during elections (Chapter 11).

The Electoral Paradigm

Both scientists and politicians pay lots of attention to communications during elections. Such communication involves opinion polls in the media, political debates, and election advertising on television and in the newspapers, propaganda materials, billboards, and political Web sites. Research on elections has dominated political communication studies for decades. This has been criticized over the years for being too narrow. Several American scholars were "pioneers" of this field. In the 1950s they began their "presidential communication studies." A conclusion to be drawn from recent parallel research is that the U.S. presidency has changed from a "statemanlike" into a "rhetorical" style of office. The 19th-century U.S. president was involved in determining the content of state policy. Since Franklin D. Roosevelt's time, it has become a "great communicator" and "popular leader" role (Meadow, 1980; Denton & Woodward, 1985; Tulis, 1987; Windt & Ingold, 1987; Nimmo & Swanson, 1990; Kendall, 1995).

Ball (Chapter 3) understates that President Lyndon B. Johnson was not such a successful communicator. Half of one's presidential term nowadays is dedicated to campaigning. Major advisors in the White House are former presidential campaign consultants. Political communication has largely become election communication, with scholars focusing on strategic communication problems and sometimes on political marketing. As for the politicians, they overwhelmingly desire the services of professionals in political marketing (Maarek, 1995; Thevissen, 1994).

Bull (Chapter 1) convincingly depicts Tony Blair's "rhetoric of modernization" as skilled communication. Winning an election is often based on small numerical differences in voters (This experience was shared by John Kennedy, Bill Clinton, and Jacques Chirac). Political argumentation is designed to attract the "floating" voters. In political marketing, content is depoliticized and adapted to the results of the opinion polls or to extreme populistic sentiments. The "neutralization" of political communication includes replacement of political arguments using formal and fundamental (moral) ones, with procedures, rituals, moral values, and ethics dominating political content. Bull shows that Blair's strategic use of the imprecise language of modernization can be regarded as a highly skilled form of political communication, a means not only of avoiding the risks of making face-damaging remarks but also of presenting the best possible face for himself and the party he represents, under the highly inclusive name of "New Labour."

Political marketers do not see political participation as their problem. They blame most European politicians who consider political marketing as an "emergency strategy for elections"; instead, they say that politicians should consider it as a modern media technique with which they have to be familiar all the time. Parties should order research on a regular basis. Politicians should permanently reflect on how to profit from marketing techniques and modern media techniques. This includes "teledemocracy," using computerized referenda for keeping in touch with citizen electors. After they saw a decline in political participation in Western democracies, scholars considered this trend to consulting professionals to be either a cause or a result of the decline. However, successful politicians may not neglect traditional means of political communication, such as local meetings, volunteers, and personal contacts with voters. These all encourage political participation (Huckfeldt and Sprague, 1995). The practice of "political clients" in Japan and Belgium, according to which politicians offer services to their voters (providing them with help for promotions, jobs, or inexpensive housing), is typical for a political culture with the habit of face-to-face contacts between citizens and politicians. One of the disadvantages of political marketing is the result of short-term thinking. It maximizes personalization of politics at the expense of developing concepts and content. To win elections, messages must be simple, formal, or banal (Maarek, 1995). Sound bites are stylistic means that simplify political communication. These political sentences by politicians often use alliteration, metaphors, and rhyme (e.g., "Read my lips," "the come-back kid"). They are frequently quoted and memorized (Anderson & Opfer, 1992). In traditional political communication, short and simple sentences with powerful content have powerful effects. They do not necessarily distort the contact between politicians and voters. Modern campaigning offers plenty of reason for concern but also gives reason for optimism by increasing the exposure to political information (Swanson & Mancini, 1996). Many authors emphasize the importance of restoring political parties and blame negative campaigning for decreasing political participation. Also, they argue that skillful campaigns are effective and that citizens learn from political information during elections (Ansolabehere and Iyengar, 1995; Crigler, 1996; Holbrook, 1996). Schoenbach's (1996) case study of the 1990 campaign in Germany suggests that Americanized, highly personalized election campaigns do not lead voters to fixate on candidates instead of issues.

Research on political psychology, political language, and propaganda illustrates another approach. As Part I of this book shows, these results provide politicians with "semantic strategies" for better electoral contacts.

The Rhetoric of Politicians

Part I teaches that the rhetoric of public personalities increasingly relies on marketing techniques. Metaphors and sound bites may be effective tools to keep in touch with citizen emotions. These linguistic devices have also prooved to be instruments for the preparation of war (Lyndon B. Johnson). Personality treats of political leaders are still important, especially in crisis situations. Rigid thinking and flexibility can be traced but may depend upon the situation or the domain. Appearance of politicians may grow more important in this television age, but citizens still prefer "symbolic leaders."

The Political Psychology Approach

Part I of *Beyond Public Speech and Symbols* represents the political psychology approach. Political psychology is a multidisciplinary approach, which studies the major relationships between political and psychological processes. Research topics range from the public effects of media, their ethical aspects, political language and image building, major dimensions of voting behavior and political socialization, political personality, and leadership styles. Its preference for empirical positivist methodology stems from its roots, which lie in propaganda analysis and political language research.

Leadership Styles

Chapter 1 and Chapter 2 of Part I ("The Rhetoric of Public Personalities") illustrate the leadership studies within political psychology. Bull (Chapter 1) demonstrates how Tony Blair's efficient leadership style suits the needs of most of British citizens. "Modernization" and "New Labour" are the sound bites that Blair produces as often as he can. What Bull concludes from his qualitative discourse analysis is highly relevant for practitioners in the field of political marketing. Suedfeld (Chapter 2) shows how most political leaders, except for Bill Clinton, vary their style according to the circumstances and the domain they have to deal with. Suedfeld details the principles of integrative complexity and methods to study personality traits based on archival materials. He further presents his elaborate study of domain-related variation in integrative complexity of several political (world) leaders.

From literature we can conclude that "symbolic" leadership enhances political participation. Nimmo (1978) made a useful distinction between "organization leaders" (who have no meaning outside certain organizations) and "symbolic leaders" (in whom people find meaning as persons). Revolutionary societies and societies in transition seem to be dependent upon "symbolic" leadership (Apter & Saich, 1994). Historically speaking, the brilliant journalism of the opposition newspapers ("Courrier de la Meuse" and "Courrier des Pays-bas") helped the Belgian revolution against Dutch rule in 1830. They served as the "symbolic" leaders of the revolution. "Institutional" leaders, however, founded an independent kingdom with captains of industry and the financial elite in charge (Kossmann & Kossmann, 1991). "In the initial stages of their involvement, people often respond with bewilderment since the nature of the candidate or cause is ambiguous," says Nimmo (1978: 356). This can be assumed for all kinds of political participation. Nimmo's own plausible explanation of differentiation during various electoral roles is as follows: electoral participation, identifying with a political party, registering to vote, voting in elections, taking part in campaigns, nonelectoral participation, keeping informed about politics, joining civic and political organizations, and contacting public officials (1978: 335–341). Promotion of symbolic, instead of institutional, leadership is a function that mass communication can fulfil to enhance political participation. Chapters 1 and 2 make us wonder where to place Bill Clinton, Michael Gorbachev, and Tony Blair on this scale, because all of them appear to be able to shift from one leadership style to another.

Political Language

Since the 1980s an increasing interest has emerged in political rhetoric, also within the discipline of "Presidential Studies." This area of study, practiced in the United States since the early 1960s can be characterized by the following terms: descriptive to journalistic, focused on recent events, and primarily critical in nature (Windt & Ingold, 1987). Chapter 3 in this volume exemplifies such a rhetorical approach to presidential language. It starts with a detailed account of the method of rhetorical criticism. It shows how linguistic devices can live their own lives, especially when packed in sound bites and metaphors. The use of sports, game, and boxing metaphors by President Lyndon B. Johnson and his environment in relation to war and their comparing of peace to fragile flowers all contributed to the semantic change of the "honorable peace" phrase formulated by former president Kennedy. Ball's chapter excels by far our expectations for this area of studies. Ball's excellently developed political analysis is most insightful for (non-U.S.) scholars, who are less familiar with post–World War II American political history. The well-written essay describes analyses and comments on the war rhetoric by Johnson. It seems to illustrate that dramatic communication strategies are the rituals of political crisis. This is what also can be concluded from the edited volume "The Modern Presidency and Crisis Rhetoric," by Amos Kiewe (1994), who wrote a chapter in *Politically Speaking.* While Kiewe's book provides a detailed account of American presidential crisis rhetoric since World War II, from Truman to Bush, Ball's chapter focuses on the speech by Lyndon B. Johnson and on his environment.

From antiquity, for instance in Greek rhetoric, until today, the importance of the subject of rhetoric has been recognized. But scientific development was somewhat hindered, as so many disciplines took an interest in it. In the 1930s, a controversial contribution to this field came from general semantics. This school of linguistic philosophers stated that language operated as a dominant factor in society, either causing neuroses and wars or helping prevent them (Korzybsky, 1933). Since the early 1920s American social science pioneers such as Lasswell and de Sola Pool studied key symbols, propaganda analysis, and international relations (Lasswell et al., 1949, 1952). The U.S. Defense Department financed much of their research. For the first time, these pioneers systematically studied the political functions of language. This field they named "quantitative semantics" or "political semantics." Totalitarianism itself uses highly standardized political language (Lasswell, 1949; de Sola Pool, 1956; Ludz, 1980; Gaus, 1981; Opp de Hipt, 1987, Rytlevsky, 1992; Apter & Saich, 1994). Dictators limit their vocabulary to the use of standard official phrases or words such as "right," "leader," "folk," "mass," and "destroy." They blanket their environment, the mass media, and the population as thoroughly they can with the same repetitive and standardized language. Whatever causative factors are involved (recession, war, totalitarianism, religion), severe tension in society increases the distance between daily life and language and elites' political language. It also influences daily language through a lack of spontaneity, many rules and regulations, and excessive hierarchies. During crisis periods metaphors and stereotypes dominate over content, while the content-oriented language of everyday life fits better with democratic leadership since it has less tension. It would be a mistake, however, to neglect the importance of culture. Some cultures are highly elaborate in their analogies, even during peacetime democracy in conjunction with periods of economic prosperity. Tradition, religion, and/or geography can restrict individual spontaneity, communication, and protest abilities, even resulting in high tension and suicide rates. Culture further manifests itself in frequency of use and content of stylistic means in a particular language (e.g., navigation metaphors in The Netherlands, culinary ones in France, poetic ones in China). Professional politicians incorporate all these factors in their public communications, but they can make mistakes. For example, Philip Jenninger, the president of the German Parliament, had to retire from office. His "Bundestag" speech on the "Reichskristallnacht" was completely misunderstood, which was a totally inappropriate reaction. The audience did not receive the honestly intended message as the speaker had expected they would (Ensink, 1992).

Image Components

Maritza Montero (Chapter 4) demonstrates how appearance can dominate over words, even though symbolic leadership seems to be preferred to a pretty face. Her "image" approach is based on a hermeneutic perspective, which she details quite well before elaborating step by step her qualitative analysis of the political campaign of Miss Universe during the 1998 presidential elections in Venezuela.

Speculative experiments such as Rosenberg's on "creating a political image and manipulating the vote" also illustrate the importance of appearance in politics. Similar experiments conducted in The Netherlands generated comparable results (Rosenberg & Kahn, 1987; De Landtsheer, Wolff, de Jonge, & Berkvens, 1999). The perception of qualities such as political competence, trustworthiness, and expertise is coupled with facial hair, hair style, makeup, clothes, verbal expression, and "body language" (Rosenberg & Kahn, 1987). During simulated U.S. elections, for example, in one study, Hollywood artists presented "candidates" in both a favorable and an unfavorable way. The "accurately" perceived candidates received 28 percent more of the vote, regardless of program type or party label. Female candidates increase their chances for election if they wear classic jewels, have short hair, use light colors, appear older, and wear a big smile.

Beside language, other image components (such as rhythm of speech and order of appearance) have been examined through experiments. The voices of French politicians as well as Hitler's voice have been oscillographically analyzed. One can distinguish between a quiet, soft, and fluent speech behavior ("ergothrophic") and a harsh, rude, and aggressive one ("trophothrophic"). Both behaviors evoke corresponding attitudes in the audience. Aggressive speech behaviour corresponds with the use of four-letter words, authoritarian leadership, and the firing of guns (Schnauber, 1972; *Mots*, 1980; Paletz & Harris, 1975). Circumstances influencing the preferences in the population for one rhythm of speech and use of a corresponding language type affect the type of politician that will be popularly successful. Popular values, preferences, and norms vary with changing conditions of life over the long run (Gaus, 1981). Such changes influence the proper interpretation of cognitive-psychological experiments regarding media and communication effects.

Political Socialization

Political psychology findings say that there are no omnivalent, omnipotent recipes for politicians to follow, but that the best contacts with the audience can be established if one has a positive appreciation of the audience's sentiments, which, of course, also depend upon many factors. Dekker and Portengen's survey on voting intentions for today's Dutch youth gives us a good understanding of the importance of many of these variables (Dekker & Portengen, 1994).

Chapters in *Beyond Public Speech and Symbols* do not focus on aspects of socialization. The impact of socialization factors for different cultures on the production, contents, and reception of public speech provides us with tempting issues for another project.

What is the impact of education, religion, unemployment, personality, gender, and age (generation) on the production, contents, and reception of public speech and symbols, of the rhetoric of politicians and the media? These factors have been widely studied in relation to determining a political career and for determining political preferences, values, and political attitudes that the audience and the voters have. The most important topics in studies on political personality, group phenomena and political socialization are ethnicity, nationalism, right-wing extremism, and xenophobia. The meanings and effects of extremist, right-wing, nationalistic discourse and actions still need more attention. Fear, stress, and anxiety, which are mental conditions at both the social and the individual level, are often identified as causes of xenophobia, racism, illiberal or ethnic nationalism, and extreme-right political movements (Gaus, 1981; Fritzsche, 1994; Kos, 1994). The buildup of fear among populations in the former Yugoslavia is assumed to be mainly responsible for the actual nationalism-based explosion in Bosnia. The acceleration of popular anxiety is a means used by mass media to increase the audience; politicians use this means to secure themselves in positions of power. The press may have accelerated the mass hysteria surrounding the death of Princess Diana for commercial purposes. The factors that contributed to public empathy with such public personalities are interesting for political psychologists; so are the political-psychological functions of gossip and popular mass media discourse (Hermes & Noordhuizen, 1999; van Zoonen, 1999a).

Scholars have proved the importance of gender questions for political communication studies of politicians and journalists as well as of audiences. Gender affects many aspects of communications, ranging from becoming a politician or a journalist to media portrayals, political arguments, and linguistic devices and to political attitudes such as xenophobia (Clarke, 1987; Becker, 1987; Watts, 1995; van Zoonen, 1994, 1999). Their estimation of one's chances prevents women from entering politics. This attitude becomes more justified as the positional or status level of a position that is desired becomes more important. Equal gender opportunities in politics could be facilitated if one's education were the responsibility of both parents, according to one Freudian explanation. Especially for the political sphere, parents' influence is still more important than that of teachers, peers, and mass media. Significant gender differences in political attitudes are still to be seen. Females are more progressive and altruistic than males. They are less xenophobic and feel less threatened. Foreigners are accepted and women less attracted by political xenophobia (e.g., throughout slogans, parties) (Belgium: De Landtsheer, 1988; The Netherlands: Hagendoorn & Janssen, 1984; Germany: Watts, 1995).

Youth's knowledge of war comes from their parents' values, but television coverage is also influential. Farnen (1988) has summarized television and television news effects on youth in several countries in a political socialization framework. Racial minorities are also more dependent on television for information. Violent television and film violence also influence aggressive behavior. Television also contributes to youth's short attention span, unrealistic expectations of high-status jobs, and the belief that life's serious problems can be solved in less than an hour. There are also many positive aspects of television viewing, which include broadened horizons for youth, the opportunity for parent-child and student-teacher interaction, and the use of television episodes as stimulus material for group discussions.

CONCLUSION AND DISCUSSION

This book is a good demonstration of the fact that, from East to West, public speech can function as a tool for citizens' emancipation. Public speech can be oppressive and subjugating; it may also generate liberation and educate people; it may even develop a warmly empathizing relationships between citizens and the political elite. Crisis situations provide opportunities for political leaders to show empathy and strengthen relations with citizens, particularly with those affected directly by tragedy.

What is the major political role that the media play? The institutional approach, reflected in Part III, deals with this problem. It mainly investigates electoral communications, political marketing, and public opinion. Furthermore, it discusses the power of media and some institutional factors that intervene in the communication process. Political psychology, represented in Part I, emphasizes the importance of a wide range of factors for political communication. It mostly prefers to place these within a broader context (relevant economic, social, cultural, political, and historical data). Political language, image components, personality factors, and political socialization (which seem to be of direct importance for political communication) are intensively investigated in the field of political psychology. This research gives us information on issues such as the way citizens want their politicians to behave toward them and the mistakes politicians and journalists make in their personal and public communications. These are problems also discussed in political marketing. Is it possible that mass media perform a positive role in bridging the gap between citizens and politicians?

The institutional approach presented in Part III provides us with descriptions of political communications (mainly during elections) and investigates its impact on the audience. Much recent literature discusses the power of mass media in a negative way. It teaches us that commercializing society and media depoliticizes politics and mass communication. The financial elite thus controls the political elite, which is itself alienated from the citizens. While critical communication theory emphasizes the dangers of commercial media ownership and "news rituals" for democracy, modern structuralism and modern Marxist philosophy encourage people's awareness of the manipulative power of language. Language and image are both forms of "discourse" that increase in importance as means of persuasive communication because of the commercialization of mass media techniques and political marketing.

The critical-philosophical and linguistic approach, reflected in Part II, considers this problematic situation in terms of a power discourse, in which language plays an essential role. While French postmodernists are sceptical about a solution, their American colleagues believe that "deconstruction" or "unmasking" of the "ideological" codes of language are useful political projects. Traditional Marxist philosophers "decode" personal gain through an investigation of "meaning." They leave the "collective propagandist project" of media and its Marxist-Leninist supporters to history.

While the institutional and the philosophical approach to political communications mainly describe and criticize, political psychology and political marketing, respectively, analyze and give practical advice without setting norms. Politicians are still often considered to be people with low self-confidence (Feldman, 1994). Nevertheless, they should not neglect opportunities for face-to-face contacts (often very effective), including listening to citizen-electors. This certainly provides them with useful feedback and encourages political participation. Also, they can profit from research and new technologies to improve their image and communication with their voters. It would be a mistake to limit this "learning attitude" just to election periods, according to political marketing experts. Politicians can affect people's voting behavior using modern mass media, especially television (radio and print media can be significant intervening variables). They must be constantly aware of this possibility, instead of just during elections.

Specifically, we hope the present volume contributes to the theme that political speech functions as a strategy in adjusting psychological distance between addressee (e.g., general public) and politicians. There remain

promising expectations and a hope that a true "public debate" will develop
on the topics discussed in this volume. As institutional power diminishes
and international communication is facilitated, useful political media content will influence voting behavior, and political leaders with authentic public personalities ("symbolic leaders") may become even more popular in the
future.

NOTE

This chapter draws on De Landtsheer (1995).

REFERENCES

Anderson, P. A., & Opfer, J. (1992). Explaining the Sound Bite: A Test of a Theory
    of Metaphor and Assonance. Paper presented at the Western Speech Communication Association Convention, Boise, ID.
Ansolabehere, S., & Iyengar, S. (1995). *Going Negative: How Political Advertisements Shrink and Polarize the Electorate.* New York: Free Press.
Apter, D. E., & Saich, T. (1994). *Revolutionary Discourse in Mao's Republic.* Cambridge, MA: Harvard University Press.
Awouters, H., & De Landtsheer, C. (1988). Maatschappelijk Engagement [Social
    engagement]. In M. Hellemans & K. De Clerck (Eds.), *Wegwijzer. Over de
    leerkracht als referentiefiguur* [Teachers as reference persons] (pp. 203–232).
    Ghent, Belgium: Ghent University Press.
Becker, C. (1987). Male Anxiety and the Fear of Female Authority. Paper presented
    at the Ninth Annual Scientific Meeting of the the International Society of
    Political Psychology, San Francisco.
Beer, F. A., & Kopstein, J. S. (1994). Between Maastricht and Sarajevo: European
    Identities, Narratives, Myths. Paper presented at the Seventeenth Annual Scientific Meeting of the International Society of Political Psychology, Santiago
    de Compostela, Spain.
Bennett, T. (1982). Theories of the Media, Theories of Society. In M. Gurevitch,
    T. Bennett, J. Curran, & J. Woollacot (Eds.), *Culture, Society and the Media*
    (pp. 30–55). London: Methuen.
Clarke, J. (1987). Woman and Political Leadership. Paper presented at the Ninth
    Annual Scientific Meeting of the the International Society of Political Psychology, San Francisco.
Crigler, A. N. (Ed.) (1996). *The Psychology of Political Communication.* Ann Arbor: University of Michigan Press.
Curran, J. (1990). Culturalist Perspectives of News Organisations. In M. Ferguson
    (Ed.), *Public Communication. The New Imperatives. Future Directions for
    Media Research* (pp. 114–134). London: Sage Publications.
De Landtsheer, C. (1988a). Geslachtsrolsocialisatie: School versus Media [Gender
    socialization: School and media]. In M. Hellemans & K. De Clerck (Eds.),
    Wegwijzer. Over de leerkracht als referentiefiguur [Teachers as reference figures] (pp. 75–92). Ghent, Belgium: Ghent University Press.

De Landtsheer, C. (1988b). Wat denken jongeren (dat hun leerkrachten denken)? [Adolescents' opinions about their teachers' opinions]. In M. Hellemans & K. De Clerck (Eds.), *Wegwijzer*. *Over de leerkracht als referentiefiguur* [Teachers as reference figures]. Ghent, Belgium: Ghent University Press.

De Landtsheer, C. (1994). The Language of Prosperity and Crisis. *Politics and the Individual*, 4, 63–85.

De Landtsheer, C. (1995). Political Communication. In C. De Landtsheer (Ed.), *Political Communication*. Special Issue of *Politics, Groups and the Individual*. *International Journal of Political Psychology and Political Socialization* (pp. 1–20). Norderstedt, Germany: APP Verlag.

De Landtsheer, C. (1998a). Introduction to the Study of Political Discourse. In O. Feldman & C. De Landtsheer (Eds.), *Politically Speaking: A Worldwide Examination of Language Used in the Public Sphere* (pp. 1–16). Westport, CT: Praeger.

De Landtsheer, C. (1998b). The Political Rhetoric of a Unified Europe. In O. Feldman & C. De Landtsheer (Eds.), *Politically Speaking: A Worldwide Examination of Language Used in the Public Sphere* (pp. 129–145). Westport, CT: Praeger.

De Landtsheer, C., & Feldman, O. (Eds.) (1998). *Politically Speaking: A Worldwide Examination of Language Used in the Public Sphere*. Westport, CT: Praeger.

De Landtsheer, C., Wolff, C., de Jonge, S., & Berkvens, S. (1999). Political Impression Management, A Dutch Case Study. Paper presented at the Twenty-Second Annual Scientific Meeting of the International Society for Political Psychology, Amsterdam, July 18–21.

De Saussure, F. (1855). *Cours de linguistique générale*. Paris: Payot.

De Sola Pool, I. (1956). Variety and Repetition in Political Language. In H. Eulau et al. (Eds), *Political Behavior: A Reader in Theory and Research* (pp. 217–231). Washington, DC: Library of Congress.

Dekker, H. (1991). Political Socialization Theory and Research. In H. Dekker & R. Meyenberg (Eds.), *Politics and the European Younger Generation* (pp. 16–58). Oldenburg, The Netherlands: Bis.

Dekker, H. (1994). Nationalism. Paper presented at the Eighth Annual Meeting of the Dutch Society for Political Psychology, Amsterdam, the Netherlands.

Dekker, H., & Portengen, R. (1994). Explaining Voting Intentions and Party Preferences for Dutch Youth. Paper presented at the Eighth Annual Meeting of the Dutch Society for Political Psychology, Amsterdam, the Netherlands.

Denton, R. E., & Woodward, G. C. (1985). *Political Communication in America*. New York: Praeger.

Dimmick, J., & Coit, P. (1982). Levels of Analysis in Mass Media Decision-Making. *Communication Research*, 9:1, 3–32.

Domenach, J. M. (1979). *La Propagande Politique* [Political propaganda]. Paris: Presses Universitaires de France.

Edelman, M. (1974). *The Symbolic Uses of Politics*. Urbana, IL: University of Chicago Press.

Ensink, T. (1992). *Jenninger: De ontvangst van een Duitse rede in Nederland. Een tekstwetenschappelijke en communicatiewetenschappelijke analyse, met een bijdrage van Ali Oussaid* [Jenninger: The reception of a German speech in the Netherlands. A text and communication analysis. With an introduction by Ali Oussaid]. Amsterdam, the Netherlands: Thesis Publishers.

Fagen, R. (1966). *Politics as Communication*. Boston: Little, Brown.

Farnen, R. (1988). Cross National Research on Television News Programming and Youth: Implications for Political Education. In B. Claussen & S. Kili (Eds.), *Changing Structures of Political Power, Socialisation and Political Education* (pp. 167–200). Frankfurt am Main: Verlag Peter Lang.

Farnen, R. (1990). Terrorism and the Mass Media: A Systemic Analysis of a Symbiotic Process. *Terrorism*, 13:2, 99–143.

Feldman, O. (1993). *Politics and the News Media in Japan*. Ann Arbor: University of Michigan Press.

Feldman, O. (1994). Personality and Politics in Japan. *Politics and the Individual*, 4:2, 27–46.

Fishman, M. (1982). News and Non-events: Making the Visible Invisible. In J. S. Ettema and D. C. Whitney (Eds.), *Individuals in Mass Organizations* (pp. 219–240). Beverly Hills, CA: Sage Publications.

Foss, S. W., Foss, K. A., & Trapp, R. (1991). *Contemporary Perspectives on Rhetoric*, 2nd ed. Prospect Heights, IL: Waveland Preaa.

Foucault, M. (1984). The Order of Discourse. In M. J. Shapiro (Ed.), *Language and Politics* (pp. 108–138). Oxford: Basil Blackwell.

Fritzsche, K. P. (1994). Social Stress: A New Approach to Explain Xenophobia. Paper presented at the Eighth Annual Meeting of the Dutch Society for Political Psychology, Amsterdam, the Netherlands.

Gaus, H. (1981). *Menselijk gedrag in perioden van langdurige economische recessie, een schets* [Human behavior during long-term economic recession]. Malle, Belgium: De Sikkel.

Gerbner, G., Gross, L., Morgan, M., & Signorielli, N. (1982). Charting the Mainstream: Television's Contribution to Political Orientations. *Journal of Communication*, 32:2, 100–127.

Gerstlé, J. (1992). *La communication politique* [Political communication]. Paris: Presses Universitaires de France.

Graber, D. (1976). *Verbal Behavior and Politics*. Chicago: University of Illinois Press.

Greenstein, F. (1969). *Personality and Politics: Problems of Evidence, Inference, and Conceptualization*. Chicago: Markheim.

Greenstein, F. (1970). *The American Party System and the American People*. New York: Prentice-Hall.

Hagendoorn, L., & Janssen, J. (1984). *Rechtsomkeer. Rechtsextreme opvattingen bij leerlingen van middelbare scholen* [Right-wing extremist opinions of high school students]. Baarn, the Netherlands: Ambo.

Hermes, J., & Noordhuizen, M. (1999). Blood on Their Hands: Reconstructing the Allocation of Blame for the Death of Princess Diana in the British and the Dutch Press. Paper presented at the Twenty-Second Annual Scientific Meeting of the International Society for Political Psychology, Amsterdam, July 18–21.

Hiebert, R. E. (Ed.) (1995). *Impact of Mass Media: Current Issues*. White Plains, NY: Longman.

Holbrook, T. (1996). *Do Campaigns Matter?* Thousand Oaks, CA: Sage Publications.

Huckfeldt, R., & Sprague, J. (1995). *Citizens, Politics, and Social Communication: Information and Influence in an Election Campaign.* Cambridge: Cambridge University Press.

Immelman, A. (1994a). A Million-Based Study of Political Personality: Nelson Mandela and F. W. de Klerk. Paper presented at the Seventeenth Annual Scientific Meeting of the International Society of Political Psychology, Santiago de Compostela, Spain.

Immelman, A. (1994b). South Africa in Transition: The Influence of the Political Personalities of Nelson Mandela and F. W. de Klerk. Paper presented at the Seventeenth Annual Scientific Meeting of the International Society of Political Psychology, Santiago de Compostela, Spain.

Immelman, A. (1995). The Political Personality of Bill Clinton: A Psychodiagnostic Meta-analysis. Paper presented at the Eighteenth Annual Scientific Meeting of the International Society of Political Psychology, Washington, DC.

Inglehart, R. (1977). *The Silent Revolution: Changing Values and Political Styles among Western Publics.* Princeton, NJ: Princeton University Press.

Kendall, K. (1995). *Presidential Campaign Discourse.* Albany, NY: State University of New York Press.

Kiewe, A. (Ed.) (1994). *The Modern Presidency and Crisis Rhetoric.* Westport, CT: Praeger.

Kocher, R. (1986). Bloodhounds and Missionaries. *European Journal of Communication,* 1:1, 43–64.

Korzybsky, A. (1933). *Science and Sanity: An Introduction to Non-Aristotelian Systems and General Semantics.* Lancaster, PA: International Non-Aristotelian Library.

Kos, I. (1994). Fearful Leadership: A Comparison of Communist and Postcommunist Leadership in the Former Yugoslavia. Paper presented at the Eighth Conference of the Dutch Society for Political Psychology, Amsterdam, the Netherlands.

Kossmann Putto, J. A., & Kossmann, E. H. (1991). *The Low Countries: History of the Northern and Southern Netherlands.* Rekkem, Belgium: Ons Erfdeel.

Lasswell, H. D. (1956). Power and Personality. In H. Eulau et al. (Eds.), *Political Behavior: A Reader in Theory and Research.* Washington, DC: Library of Congress.

Lasswell, H. D., Leites, N. et al. (Eds.) (1949). *Language of Politics: Studies in Quantitative Semantics.* New York: George W. Stewart.

Lasswell, H. D., Lerner, D., & de Sola Pool, I. (1952). *The Comparative Study of Symbols: An Introduction.* Stanford, CA: Hoover Institute on War, Revolution and Peace and Stanford University Press.

Lowery, S. A., & De Fleur, M. L. (1995). *Milestones in Mass Communication Research Media Effects.* White Plains, NY: Longman.

Ludz, P. C. (1980). *Mechanismen der Herrschaftssicherung. Eine sprachpolitische Analyze gesellschaftlichen wandels in der DDR* [Mechanisms of power. A linguistic analysis of social developments in the DDR]. Munich and Vienna: Carl Hanser Verlag.

Maarek, P. J. (1995). *Political Marketing and Communication*. London: John Libbey & Company.

McCombs, M. E., & Shaw, D. L. (1972). The Agenda-Setting Function of the Press. *Public Opinion Quarterly*, 36, 176–187.

McQuail, D. (1994). *Mass Communication Theory*. London: Sage Publications.

Meadow, R. (1980). *Politics as Communication*. Norwood, NJ: Ablex.

Mieder, W. (1997). *The Politics of Proverb: From Traditional Wisdom to Proverbial Stereotypes*. Madison: University of Wisconsin Press.

Montero, M. (1994). The Psychosocial Construction of a Political Myth. In C. De Landtsheer (Ed.), *Political Communication*. Special Issue of *Politics, Groups and the Individual*. *International Journal of Political Psychology and Political Socialisation*. Norderstedt, Germany: APP Verlag.

Mots/Ordinateurs, Textes/Sociétés. (1980). Paris: Presses de la Fondation Nationale des Sciences Politiques, Editions du CNRS.

Neuman, R., Just, R., & Crigler, A. (1992). *Common Knowledge: News and the Construction of Political Meaning*. Chicago: University of Chicago Press.

Nimmo, D. (1978). *Political Communication and Public Opinion in America*. Santa Monica, CA: Goodyear.

Nimmo, D., & Swanson, D. (Eds.) (1990). *New Directions in Political Communication*. Newbury Park, CA: Sage Publications.

Noelle-Neumann, E. (1980). *The Spiral of Silence*. Chicago: University of Chicago Press.

Ogden, C. W., & Richards, I. A. (1938). *The Meaning of Meaning: A Study of the Influence of Language upon Thought and the Science of Symbolism*. London: International Library of Psychology, Philosophy, and Scientific Method.

Opp de Hipt, M. (1987). *Denkbilder in der Politik. Der Staat in der Sprache von CDU und SPD* [Concepts in politics. The state in the language by German Christian Democrats and Social Democrats]. Opladen, Germany: Westdeutscher Verlag.

Paletz, D., & Harris, W. (1975). Four-letter Threats to Authority. *Journal of Politics*, 37, 955–979.

Post, J. M. (1993). Current Concepts of the Narcissistic Personality: Implications for Political Psychology. *Political Psychology*, 1, 99–121.

Price, V. (1992). *Public Opinion*. London: Sage Publications.

Reiner, B., & Rosengren, K. E. (1990). Cultivated Viewers and Readers. In N. Signorielli & M. Morgan (Eds.), *Cultivation Analysis* (pp. 181–206). Newbury Park, CA: Sage Publications.

Rosenau, P. M. (1992). *Post-modernism and the Social Sciences: Insights, Inroads, and Intrusions*. Princeton, NJ: Princeton University Press.

Rosenberg, S. W., & Kahn, S. (1987). Creating a Political Image and Manipulating the Vote: a Preliminary Report. Paper presented at the Ninth Annual Scientific Meeting of the International Society for Political Psychology, San Francisco.

Rytlevsky, R. (1992). Politische Kultur in der DDR vor und nach der Wende. In *Sprache im Umbruch. Politischer Sprachwandel im Zeichen von "Wende" und "Vereinigung."* Berlin: Walter de Gruyter.

Sanderson King, S., & Cushman, D. P. (Eds.) (1992). *Political Communication:*

Engineering Visions of Order in the Socialist World. Albany, NY: State University of New York Press.

Sapir, E. (1962). *Selected Writings in Language, Culture and Personality.* Berkeley, CA: Mandelbaum.

Schaff, A. (1960). *Introduction á la Sémantique.* Paris: Edition Anthropos.

Schaff, A. (1978). *Structuralism and Marxism.* Oxford: Pergamon Press.

Schaff, A. (1980). *Stereotypen und das Menschliche Handeln.* Vienna: Europaverlag.

Scheepers, P., Billiet J., & De Witte, H. (1994). Voters of Right-Wing Parties in Flanders, Belgium. Paper presented at the Eighth Annual Meeting of the Dutch Society for Political Psychology, Amsterdam, the Netherlands.

Schmidt, V. (1977). Zur Bildlichkeit ideologiegebundener Wörter und Wendungen [Images, ideologies, words and expressions]. *Zeitschrift für Phonetik, Sprachwissenschaft und Kommunikationsforschung* 30:1, 40–47.

Schnauber, C. (1972). *Wie Hitler Sprach und Schrieb. Zur Pzychologie und prosodik der Faschistischen Rhetorik.* Frankfurt am Main: Atheneum Verlag.

Schoenbach, K. (1996). The "Americanization" of German Election Campaigns: Any Impact on the Voters? In D. L. Swanson & P. Mancini (Eds.), *Politics, Media and Modern Democracy* (pp. 91–142). Westport, CT: Praeger.

Semetko, H. A., Blumler, J. G., Gurevitch, M., & Weaver, D. (1991). *The Formation of Campaign Agendas: A Comparative Analysis of Party and Media Roles in Recent American and British Elections.* Hillsdale, NJ: Erlbaum.

Semetko, H. A., & K. Schoenbach (1994). *Germany's Unity Election: Voters and the Media.* Cresskill, NJ: Hampton Press.

Shapiro, M. (Ed.). (1984). *Language and Politics.* Oxford: Basil Blackwell.

Shapiro, M., & Der Derian, J. (1989). *International/Intertextual Relations.* Lexington, MA: D. C. Heath and Company.

Suransky, L. (1994). Enhancing a Politician's Image by Applying the Varnish of Ethnicity: The Case of Buthelezi of Kwa-Zulu, South Africa. Paper presented at the Eighth Annual Meeting of the Dutch Society for Political Psychology, Amsterdam, the Netherlands.

Swanson, D. L., & Mancini, P. (1996). Patterns of Modern Electoral Campaigning and Their Consequences. In D. L. Swanson & P. Mancini (Eds.), *Politics, Media and Modern Democracy* (pp. 247–276). Westport, CT: Praeger.

Taylor, S. (1984). *Social Science and Revolutions.* New York: St. Martin's Press.

Thevissen, F. (1994). *Politieke Marketing* [Political marketing]. Brussels, Belgium: VUB Press.

Tichenor, P., Donohue, G., & Olien, C. (1970). Mass Media and the Differential Growth in Knowledge. *Public Opinion Quarterly,* 34, 158–170.

Toorn, M. C. van de. (1975). *Dietsch en Volksch. Een verkenning van het taalgebruik der nationaal-socialisten in Nederland* [Dutch and popular. An enquiry into the language of National-Socialists in the Netherlands]. Groningen, the Netherlands: Tjeenk Willink.

Trent, J. S., & Friedenberg, R. V. (1983). *Political Campaign Communication: Principles and Practices.* New York: Praeger.

Tulis, G. (1987). *The Rhetorical Presidency.* New York: Princeton University Press.

Ulmann, G. (1975). *Sprache und Wahrnehmung. Verfestigen und Aufbrechen von*

Anschauungen dürch Wörter [Language and perception. Consolidation and change of conceptions through words]. Frankfurt am Main: Campus Verlag.

Van Dijk, T. (1997). What Is Political Discourse Analysis? In J. Blommaert & C. Bulcaen (Eds.), *Political Linguistics*. Special Issue of the *Belgian Journal of Linguistics*, 11, 9–52.

Van Zoonen, L. (1994). *Feminist Media Studies*. London: Sage Publications.

Van Zoonen, L. (1999). The Personalization of Politics: Opportunities for Women? Paper presented at the Twenty-Second Annual Scientific Meeting of the International Society for Political Psychology, Amsterdam, July 18–21.

Van Zoonen, L., & Sreberny, A. (Eds.) (1999). *Women, Politics and Communication*. New York: Hampton Press.

Watts, M. (1995). Political Xenophobia in the Transition from Socialism: Threat, Racism and Ideology among East German Youth. Paper presented at the Eighteenth Annual Scientific Meeting of the International Society of Political Psychology, Washington, DC.

White, D. (1950). The Gate-keeper: A Case Study in the Selection of News. *Journalism Quarterly*, 27, 383–390.

Windt, T., & Ingold, B. (Eds.) (1987). *Essays in Presidential Rhetoric*. Dubuque, IA: Kendall/ Hunt Publishing Company.

Witte, E. (1993). *Media en Politiek. Een Inleiding tot de literatuur* [Media and politics. An introduction to the literature]. Brussels, Belgium: Free University/ VUB Press.

Index

About the Editors and Contributors

CHRIST'L DE LANDTSHEER is Associate Professor at the Amsterdam School of Communications Research of the University of Amsterdam (The Netherlands). She has over 100 publications and lectures on various topics in the area of the political psychology of language and communication, including a special issue on political communication that she edited for *Politics, Groups and the Individual* (1995). She is co-editor, with Ofer Feldman, of *Politically Speaking: A Worldwide Examination of Language Used in the Public Sphere* (Praeger, 1998).

OFER FELDMAN is Associate Professor at Naruto University of Education, Japan. He is the author of numerous journal articles, book chapters, and several books, including *Politics and the News Media in Japan* (1993). His present work centers on political personality and discourse in Japan. He is co-editor, with Christ'l De Landtsheer, of *Politically Speaking: A Worldwide Examination of Language Used in the Public Sphere* (Praeger, 1998).

SHOJI AZUMA is Associate Professor of Japanese at the University of Utah. He is the author of several books and articles including *Shakai Gengogaku Nyuumon* [An Introduction to Sociolinguistics] (1997), "Speech Accommodation and Japanese Emperor Hirohito" (*Discourse and Society* 1997) and "Lexical Categories and Code-Switching: A Study of Japanese/ English Code-Switching in Japan" (*Journal of the Association of Teachers of Japanese* 1997). His research interests include bilingualism, code-switching, and speech accommodation.

MOYA ANN BALL is Associate Professor of Speech Communication at Trinity University, San Antonio, Texas, where she teaches courses in political communication, small group communication, and rhetorical criticism. Her dissertation on Vietnam decision making received a national award from the Speech Communication Association in 1988. Her current research includes a long-term project on the communication surrounding the de-escalation of the Vietnam War.

PETER BULL is Senior Lecturer in the Department of Psychology at the University of York, United Kingdom. He has had a series of articles published on political communication, with particular respect to the analysis of discourse in televised political interviews in the United Kingdom. He has also written extensively on the topic of non-verbal communication, especially on the role of posture and gesture in social interaction. He is the author of *Body Movement and Interpersonal Communication, Posture and Gesture*, and co-editor, with Derek Roger, of *Conversation: An Interdisciplinary Perspective*.

KAREN CALLAGAN is Assistant Professor of Political Science at the University of Massachusetts at Boston. Her research interests are in the area of political psychology and behavior. Her work as been published in such outlets as the *Journal of Politics* and other edited volumes. She is currently collaborating on other communication-related projects, such as the framing of the U.S. gun control debate.

ANN CRIGLER is Associate Professor at the University of Southern California. She is co-editor of two books, including *The Psychology of Political Communication*, and numerous journal articles. Her research interests include citizens' interpretation of information.

MARION JUST is Professor of Political Science at Wellesley College, and co-author of *Crosstalk: Citizens, Candidates and the Media in a Presidential Campaign* (1996) and numerous journal articles. She is interested in public opinion and political media.

MONTAGUE KERN is Associate Professor at Rutgers School of Communication, Information and Library Science. She is the author or co-author of three books, including *Thirty-Second Politics: Political Advertising in the 80's* (Praeger, 1989) and numerous journal articles in the field of mass media and American politics.

SAM LEHMAN-WILZIG is Associate Professor in the Department of Political Studies, Bar-Ilan University, Israel, where he heads the Mass Communications program. He currently serves as Chairman of the Israel

Political Science Association (1997–1999); Founder and Editor-in-Chief of *PATUAKH*, an academic journal devoted to Israeli mass communications; author of several books and many articles on Israeli politics and the mass media; and academic advisor to the Ministry of Education and institutes of higher education regarding establishment of mass media programs.

TRACEY L. MITCHELL serves as an Adjunct Professor for West Texas A&M University. She also has taught for Clarendon Community College at Pampa. She teaches courses in public speaking, business and professional speaking, and interpersonal communication. Her publications include articles in the *Texas State Communication Journal* and the Educational Resources Information Center (ERIC). She was awarded the 1995–1996 Best Thesis Award for the Fine Arts and Humanities Area at West Texas A&M University.

MARITZA MONTERO is Professor at Universidad Central de Venezuela. She has written and edited several books and journal papers in Spanish, English, and French. Her research interests include social identity, alternative modes of political action, and discourse analysis.

MIRA MOSHE is Researcher and Lecturer in Mass Media at the Department of Political Studies at Bar-Ilan University. Her expertise lies in the field of institutional and cognitive aspects of multi-channel television.

FRAUKE SCHNELL is Associate Professor of Political Science at West Chester University in Pennsylvania. He has collaborated with Nayda Terkildsen on a number of media–public attitude studies involving the use and effects of framing, symbols, and source cues. They have recently edited a book on the micro and macro effects of framing, *Elite Discourse and the Dynamics of Public Opinion*.

PETER SUEDFELD is Professor of Psychology at the University of British Columbia, Canada. His research on adaptation and coping in challenging environments has led to some 200 journal articles and book chapters. He developed the procedure for scoring integrative complexity in archival materials, which has been used to study decision making among national and international leaders, as well as ordinary citizens.

SERGIY TARAN is the author of numerous publications on political issues, particularly on issues of political communication, and the editor of *Past and Present of Ukrainian Nationalism* (1993), which focuses on research on the history of the ideology of nationalism in Ukraine. He was a vice-president of the Institute of Mass Information (Ukraine-France), an international scientific institution that deals with the study of phenomena of transformation and transmittal of mass information in modern societies.

NAYDA TERKILDSEN is Assistant Professor of Political Science at the University of California, Davis. She publishes in the areas of political psychology, the media, and issues involving race and gender.

LISE VAN OORTMERSSEN received a master's degree in Communications at the University of Amsterdam in 1997 and works as a trainee at the European Parliament in Luxembourg.

HONG (IRIS) XIE is Assistant Professor of Information Science at the University of Wisconsin. Her research interest is citizen use of computer-based information.

MEI ZHANG received her Ph.D. from the Department of Communication at the University of Pittsburgh. She taught as a full-time faculty member in the School of Journalism at Fudan University in Shanghai, China, before coming to the United States to pursue her doctorate. Her areas of academic interest include Chinese rhetoric and communication, comparative rhetoric and intercultural communication, rhetorical criticism and theory, and rhetoric and mass media.

ISBN 0-275-96732-8

9 780275 967321

HARDCOVER BAR CODE